Kt Bla...

November 1985

THE NARCISSISTIC PURSUIT OF PERFECTION
Second Revised
Edition

THE NARCISSISTIC PURSUIT OF PERFECTION
Second Revised Edition

Arnold Rothstein, M.D.

INTERNATIONAL UNIVERSITIES PRESS, INC.

New York   New York

Library of Congress Cataloging in Publication Data

Rothstein, Arnold, 1936-

The narcissistic pursuit of perfection.

Bibliography: p.
Includes index.
1. Narcissism. 2. Personality, Disorders of.
I. Title.
RC553.N36R67 1984   616.85'82   84-25159
ISBN 0-8236-3494-9

Manufactured in the United States of America

to
ARDEN
and to
BARBARA, CHLOE, LISANNE, and MICHELLE

Contents

Acknowledgments

My most fundamental debt is to the Center for Psychoanalytic Training and Research of the College of Physicians and Surgeons of Columbia University for providing me with an ambience within which I could grow to be an analyst. It is from that experience that this book emerges.

A number of colleagues have read and commented on my papers and aspects of this manuscript. Their comments have helped me to develop, refine, and clarify my ideas. These colleagues, listed in alphabetical order, are Drs. Morton Aronson, Paul Bradlow, Stanley Coen, Gerald Fogel, Robert Michels, David Peretz, Melvin Scharfman, and John Weber. In addition, the critical comments of a number of program committee chairmen and editors have been helpful, particularly those of Drs. Harold Blum and Alberta Szalita.

The realistic support and encouragement of my wife, Dr. Arden Rothstein, has helped sustain me in my belief that I had something to contribute to an elucidation of the theory of narcissism. In addition, her consistent editorial assistance has influenced the development of my writing style.

The editorial staff of International Universities Press has been particularly helpful.

Finally, many thanks to Mrs. Selma Munz, Catharine Garcia, and Jeanette Guiliano, who typed the manuscript. Their skill, patience, and thoroughness made tedious aspects of this work sometimes seem pleasant.

Certain portions of this work are based on material that has appeared in other sources: "The Ego Attitude of Entitlement" in the *International Review of Psycho-Analysis*, 4(1977):409–417; "Oedipal Conflicts in Narcissistic Personality Disorders" in the *International Journal of Psycho-Analysis*, 60(1979):189–199; "An Exploration of the Diagnostic Term 'Narcissistic Personality Disorder' " in the *Journal of the American Psychoanalytic Association*, 27(1979):893–912; "The Implications of Early Psychopathology for the analyzability of Narcissistic Personality Disorders" in the *International Journal of Psycho-Analysis*, 63: (1982): 177-188; and "Fear of Humiliation" in the *Journal of the American Psychoanalytic Association*, 32(1984): 99-116. Grateful acknowledgment is made to these journals for their permission to use this material as well as to Little, Brown & Company and John Fowles for permission to quote from the following works: *The French Lieutenant's Woman*, copyright © 1969 by John Fowles; *The Ebony Tower*, copyright © 1974 by John R. Fowles Ltd.; and *The Magus: A Revised Version*, copyright © 1977 by John Fowles.

Preface to the Second Edition

I wrote *The Narcissistic Pursuit of Perfection* to clarify the theory of narcissism. Because the book was conceived while I was inexperienced as an analyst, the clinical material was supplemented by and resonated with "clinical material" from the creative writings of Leo Tolstoy and John Fowles.

The past six years since completing *The Narcissistic Pursuit of Perfection* have been spent gaining more analytic experience, which has influenced me to elaborate the book clinically. In particular, I have considered issues of analyzability in more depth as well as questions of the nature of the analytic process with patients considered narcissistic personality disorders. In a related vein, I have thought about countertransference in connection with the analysis and working through of narcissistic investments. Finally, I have pondered the relationship of narcissism to concepts of defensive identification, masochism, sadism, depression and negative therapeutic reaction.

Considerations of the relationship of narcissism to masochism can be found in chapter 6 of my book, *The Structural Hypothesis: An Evolutionary Perspective,* published in 1983. A related issue is that of humiliation: the fear of humiliation, the pursuit of humiliation, and pleasure in sadistically humiliating others are important clinical features of narcissistic personality disorders. These issues are explored in chapter 3 of this Revised Edition. In chapter 4, I present a schematic conception of the process of analysis of narcissistic investments as well as a description of countertransference experienced at its various phases. Chapter 5 the original chapter on analyzability of patients considered narcissistic personality disorders has been elaborated in order to explore the issue of clinical limits. This last theoretical consideration is illustrated by process from failed attempts at analysis of two patients considered narcissistic personality disorders with latent psychosis. These considerations are explored from a perspective that stresses interpretation of conflict as the primary mode of therapeutic action of psychoanalysis.

Preface to First Edition

Freud early defined narcissism's ubiquitous place in the human situation. Within an energic metaphor his concept of secondary narcissism stressed a dynamic defensive perspective. In response to ubiquitous disappointments in the object the toddler decathects object representations and invests the self-representation. Emotional alchemy transforms object libido into narcissistic libido.

Hartmann (1950b) has noted that: "Many analysts do not find it altogether easy to define the place which the concept of narcissism holds in present analytic theory. This, I think, is mainly due to the fact that this concept has not been explicitly redefined in terms of Freud's later structural psychology" (p. 83).

Hartmann and others—Andreas-Salomé, Wilhelm Reich, Jacobson, Annie Reich, Kohut, Kernberg, Sandler, Joffe, Pulver, Moore, and Stolorow—have contributed to this ongoing redefinition.

This book is written in that spirit. The first part presents theoretical considerations that are intended to serve as an organizing structure for the clinical material of Parts Two and Three.

Part One proposes a definition of the terms *narcissism* and *narcissistic personality disorder,* within a proposed classification of narcissism in the "character" of the ego. They are intended

xiii

to facilitate a dynamic perspective toward narcissistic phenomena, as well as to minimize a potential toward a pejorative orientation. The affective aspects of the narcissistically invested
experience and its relationship to conflict are stressed. These
conflicts are explored and their interminable nature highlighted.
The ubiquitous attraction, almost addiction, for illusions of narcissistic perfection is a fundamental tenet of this book. Man
grapples to reconcile wishes for self-involved and object-related
pleasures. Similarly he struggles with pursuits of narcissistic perfection for his self-representation and longings for a sense of
synchrony with his ego ideal, that structured repository of his
original sense of perfection. The inevitability of limits and of
imperfect choices confronts the ubiquitous longing for illusions
of perfection.

Part Two presents examples of a variety of expressions of
narcissism. These focus on the form, content, state of integration,
and dynamic relation to conflict of narcissistic investments in
character organization, highlighting the mobilization of narcissistically invested defenses in response to narcissistic injury.

Part Three explores the integration and defensive mobilization of narcissistic investments at various stages in the life cycle
and stresses conflicts typical of these developmental crossroads
and their relationship to narcissistically invested defensive solutions.

The clinical material of this book is drawn almost entirely
from the writings of Tolstoy and Fowles. The genius of these
authors for observation and description captures a spectrum of
human experiences with depth and clarity that clearly illustrate
the fundamental experience of narcissistic injury in the human
situation.

It should be emphasized that the literary material is employed
to facilitate the primary purpose of this book: the clarification of
narcissism. It is unusual, but not without precedent, to employ
literature as clinical material. In *Some Character-Types Met With
in Psycho-Analytic Work* (1916), Freud examined Lady Macbeth

and Ibsen's Rebecca West to illustrate "those wrecked by success." Of his use of Ibsen's tragic heroine, he stated: ". . . we have treated Rebecca West as if she were a living person and not a creation of Ibsen's imagination. . . ." (1916, p. 329). Such a character may often present more focused insight into a theoretical issue than could actual clinical material.

The material here has, of course, been chosen to complement and clarify the theoretical premises presented. However, since psychoanalytic theory is increasingly studied in universities, both as a primary field of interest and as a discipline that provides an additional perspective on other more traditional academic subjects, it is my hope that this book may find a second appeal and usefulness.

Part I

THEORETICAL CONSIDERATIONS

1

Narcissism

Three-quarters of a century after psychoanalytic theory adopted the term *narcissism* from Greek mythology, analysts still differ as to its meaning. The term has been used within several theoretical frameworks for a variety of purposes. As a concept, it has been elaborated from libidinal and ego-psychological perspectives. It has been employed both descriptively and to connote developmental phenomena. It has been considered as a defensive function, and it has been characterized both as normal and ubiquitous and as one or another form of pathology.

Much of this confusion can be seen to derive from the transitional nature of Freud's "war years" papers, in which he discussed structural development in terms inundated with metaphorical energic elaboration. The confusion between ego, self, and ego libido is still with us. In 1914, Freud defined narcissism as "the libidinal complement to the egoism of the instinct of self-preservation" (pp. 73–74).

Hartmann (1950b), attempting to distinguish between Freud's two meanings of ego, defined narcissism as the libidinal cathexis of the self-representation, but his attempt to meld energic and structural perspectives resulted in continued unclarity with regard to the term *narcissism.* Kohut's earlier writing defined narcissism as the libidinal cathexis of the self, but the term has disappeared from his more recent work to be replaced by the term *self.* Kernberg similarly equated ego development with the development of narcissism. For Kernberg pathologic narcissism is associated and seemingly synonymous with pathologic character development. For Sandler and Joffe, Pulver, and Stolorow narcissism is equated with self-esteem, the self, and the self-representation, respectively.

It is a premise of this book that narcissism is different from the ego, the self, and the self-representation. These terms refer to aspects of psychic structure—each with a characteristic development. I propose that the definition of the term *narcissism* be limited to *a felt quality of perfection.* This conscious or unconscious, affectively laden fantasy may be *invested* in a panoply of self- and/or object representations in a *spectrum of integrations.*

THE LITERATURE

It is characteristic of Freud's seminal papers that central terms and concepts have a variety of meanings. Freud (1914) defined narcissism as a quality of "perfection" (p. 94). In addition, he employed narcissism as a component of libido theory and used it metaphorically to describe aspects of human development from the perspective of libido development. In his prestructural metapsychological papers, Freud organized data within the libidinal concept of narcissism that would, subsequent to the introduction of the structural hypothesis, be discussed in terms of oral incorporative, defensive, identificatory responses of the ego. Thus

Freud used the term *narcissism* to describe a felt quality of perfection and as a prestructural concept to describe the development of psychic structure in response to ubiquitous narcissistic injuries. Confusion has resulted from these two very different developments of the meaning of the term and concept.

Most of Freud's views on narcissism were propounded within the context of theory focused on libido and the self-preservative instinct, prior to the introduction of the structural hypothesis and theory on aggression. The term was defined as the cathexis of the self with narcissistic or ego libido, as contrasted with object libido. It was considered as "a stage in the development of the libido which it passes through on the way from auto-erotism to object-love" (1911a, p. 60). In 1923, Freud extended this *developmental* perspective by describing narcissistic libido as a normal intermediate stage in the neutralization of libidinal energy (p. 30). In 1914, elaborating its ubiquitous nature and its "place in the regular course of human sexual development" (p. 73), he characterized narcissism as "the libidinal complement to the egoism of the instinct of self-preservation" (pp. 73–74). In energic language, Freud alluded to the role of narcissism in all character integrations and, anticipating the structural hypothesis, described the child's preservation of his primary narcissism within the ego ideal (p. 94). In describing parents' defenses against integrating the perception of their own limits and finiteness, he introduced the normal developmental concepts of narcissistic object choice, narcissistic injury, and, implicitly, narcissistic identification (pp. 90–91).

In addition to discussing the normal developmental vicissitudes of narcissism, Freud described some of its pathological elaborations. A footnote to *Three Essays on the Theory of Sexuality* (1905) pointed to narcissistic fixations and object choice in the genesis of homosexuality:

> ...the future inverts, in the earliest years of their childhood, pass through a phase of very intense but short-lived fixation to a woman (usually their mother), and, after leaving this behind, they identify themselves with a woman and take *themselves* as their sexual object. That is to say, they proceed from a narcissistic basis and look for a young man who resembles themselves and whom *they* may love as their mother loved *them* [p. 145n].

This ingenious note, written in 1910, clearly reflects a modern appreciation of the importance of preoedipal object relations in the genesis of this perversion. In structural terms, he (1915b) elaborated the genesis of melancholia as an alteration of the ego secondary to a narcissistic identification. In 1917, from a developmental perspective and in libidinal terms, he defined the genesis of the character trait defiance as "a narcissistic clinging to anal erotism" (p. 130). In 1918, he presented the Wolf Man's predisposition to neurosis as related, in part, to the "excessive strength of his narcissism" which left him vulnerable to narcissistic injury: "The precipitating cause of his neurosis" was "a *narcissistic* 'frustration'" (p. 118). He also commented on the limits of psychoanalytic treatment in such cases.[1]

---

[1] Blum (1974) has further elaborated the borderline and narcissistic features of the Wolf Man's character organization, commenting on his "feelings of entitlement and insatiable demanding" (p. 736): "This patient displayed narcissistic vulnerability and detachment, disturbed object relations and impulse control, apathy and affective impoverishment, and a tendency to severe regressive response" (p. 727).

Although the role of aggression—of anger in response to frustration, limits, and loss, as well as in relation to narcissistic phenomena—seems absent[2] from his considerations, there is much that is current and modern in Freud with reference to the theory of narcissism and its clinical elaborations. Freud was keenly aware of the relationship of narcissistic phenomena to a subject's experience of frustration, to his perception of limits of the self, and to real and imagined object loss. He employed the concept to describe oral incorporative identificatory processes of the ego in response to ubiquitous narcissistic injuries of development.

In *On Narcissism: An Introduction* (1914), Freud defined the development of the ego ideal as a response of the toddler to the perception of the limits of his differentiating self-representation, noting that the toddler "is not willing to forgo the narcissistic perfection of his childhood" (p. 94). In normal development, in response to the perception of these limits of the self-representation, the ego, via processes of internalization, creates its ego ideal: ". . . disturbed by the admonitions of others and by the awakening of his own critical judgement, so that he can no longer retain that perfection, he seeks to recover it in the new form of an ego ideal. What he projects before him as his ideal is the substitute for the lost narcissism of his childhood in which he was his own ideal" (p. 94).

In *The Ego and the Id* (1923), Freud alluded to the metamorphosis of the libidinal concept, secondary narcissism, into the structural concept, identification. He

[2] Moore (1975) states, "The relation between these concepts [narcissism and aggression] was never definitively discussed by Freud. Even in the *Outline* [reference deleted] he related narcissism to libido only." Nevertheless, Moore points to an implied relationship via "anlagen of the concept of undifferentiated drive energies developed by Jacobson" (p. 254).

described the development of the ego in the broadest sense—the development of "character" (p. 28)—as a response of the ego to the experience of narcissistic injury through perceptions of the inevitable limits of the object. These limits are experienced by the subject as equivalent to object losses, the pain of which motivates defensive internalizations that become the fabric of the ego. Freud noted: "We succeeded in explaining the painful disorder of melancholia by supposing that... an object which was lost has been set up again inside the ego—that is, that an object-cathexis has been replaced by an identification" (p. 28). In 1923, Freud deleted the qualification of that identification as "narcissistic." In 1915, the exposition of the identification in melancholia as a "narcissistic identification" had been a central premise and distinction of his explanation of the pathogenesis of that condition. In *The Ego and the Id*, he commented on this earlier hypothesis.

At that time, however, we did not appreciate the full significance of this process and did not know how common and how typical it is. Since then we have come to understand that this kind of substitution has a great share in determining the form taken by the ego and that it makes an essential contribution towards building up what is called its 'character.'
At the very beginning...object-cathexis and identification are no doubt indistinguishable.... It may be that this identification is the sole condition under which the id can give up its objects.... it [is] possible to suppose that the character of the ego is a precipitate of abandoned object-cathexes and that it contains the history of those object-choices [pp. 28–29].

Freud's (1911a, 1914) libidinal delineation of the ubiquitous nature of secondary narcissism was a metaphorical precursor of his later object-representation formulation of the genesis of the "character of the ego" (1923, p. 28). Freud (1911a) had defined primary narcissism as "a stage in the development of the libido which it passes through on the way from auto-erotism to object-love" (p. 60). In 1914 he stated:

> The libido that has been withdrawn from the external world has been directed to the ego and thus gives rise to an attitude which may be called narcissism. ... This leads us to look upon the narcissism which arises through the drawing in of object-cathexes as a secondary one, superimposed upon a primary narcissism that is obscured by a number of different influences [p. 75].

The withdrawal of libido from an object representation to the "self," associated with a transformation of object libido to ego or narcissistic libido, is another way of describing the process of identification with the disappointing or lost object. Prior to 1923, during the gestation of the structural hypothesis, the term *narcissism* was employed to refer to processes of internalization that contribute to ego, ego-ideal, and superego development. It seems clarifying to employ Freud's 1923 representational description of identificatory processes and to dispense with the libidinal concept of secondary narcissism as a tool for organizing these developmental events.

In 1921 Andreas-Salomé contributed an important paper, "The Dual Orientation of Narcissism." In libidinal terms, she made two points with current significance. Like Freud, she emphasized the ubiquitous place of narcissism as a component quality of human development: "Narcissism is not limited to a single phase of the libido, but is a part of our self-love which accompanies all phases. It is not merely a primitive point of departure of development but remains as a kind of fundamental continuity in all the subsequent object-cathexes of the libido" (p. 3). She also recognized the primal object's role in the development of narcissism. She described its genesis from internalizations of preindividuated self-object experiences. "It seems to me therefore to be dangerous not to emphasize the essential duality of the concept of narcissism, and to leave the problem unresolved by allowing narcissism to stand only for self-love. I should like to bring to the fore its other less obvious aspect; the persistent feeling of *identification with the totality*" (pp. 4–5; emphasis added).

With the introduction of the dual instinct theory and the structural hypothesis, the self-preservative instinct was subsumed under the ego organization and elaborated as part of "character." In 1933, Wilhelm Reich defined normal narcissism in structural terms and stated explicitly what Freud (1914, 1923) and Andreas-Salomé had implied: "that the character is essentially a narcissistic protection mechanism ... against dangers ... of the threatening outer world and the instinctual impulses which urged for expression" (p. 158).

In 1936, Waelder similarly defined character as the sum total of the ego's problem-solving modes in the service of "assimilation" (p. 48). Freud's (1923) descriptions of defensive internalization in response to frustration (in 1914 designated as secondary narcissism) define the ego's ubiquitous problem-solving mode in the service of assimilating the narcissistic injuries of development. When the subject's characteristic modes of problem solving work well, an illusion of narcissistic perfection may be transiently restored to the self-representation and contribute to the sense of well-being that is often associated with effective adaptation.

Hartmann (1950b) cast Freud's energic conception of narcissism in structural terms. In elaborating Freud's concept of the neutralization of drive energy, Hartmann noted that Freud used the term *self* to refer both to the subjectively felt self and to the system ego and its functions. To help clarify this confusion, he defined narcissism as the libidinal cathexis of the self-representation and suggested that the system ego was fueled by various forms of energy (both libidinal and aggressive drive energies) in various stages of neutralization (delibidinization, or sublimation, and deaggressivization).

Kohut (1966, 1971) similarly defined narcissism as the libidinal cathexis of the self, but he went on to describe a normal course of narcissistic libido development, independent from object libidinal investment and development. Kohut's concept of narcissistic libido represents more, however, than the development of a particular form of energy. In the course of development, narcissistic libido cathects various self- and object representations and becomes "idealizing libido" (1966, p. 247). Thus, the idealizing libido includes precipitates of the subject's representational world.

Kohut chose to elaborate the prestructural concept of secondary narcissism which Freud had relinquished in *The Ego and the Id* in deference to the ego-psychological concepts of identification, internalization, synthesis, and integration. In doing so Kohut blurred heuristic, meaningful distinctions that are possible when narcissism is employed within the structural hypothesis as a felt quality integrated by the ego in a variety of structures. As Kohut developed the concept of idealizing libido, he discussed aspects of ego, superego, and ego-ideal development within the prestructural rubric of libido theory. Thus the ego's development of such mature and sophisticated attributes as humor, creativity, empathy, wisdom, and the acceptance of one's finiteness were conceptualized by Kohut as mature transformations of narcissistic libido.

Kohut proposed a theory of the development of narcissistic libido that is strikingly similar to Freud's (1923) description of the genesis of the ego and "character" (pp. 28–29) in its focus on the response of the subject to inevitable developmental frustrations: "The balance of primary narcissism is disturbed by maturational pressures and painful psychic tensions which occur because the mother's ministrations are of necessity imperfect and traumatic delays cannot be prevented. The baby's psychic organization, however, attempts to deal with the disturbances by the building up of new systems of perfection" (Kohut, 1966, p. 246). Kohut noted that the toddler's maturing ego apparatus forces him to perceive the inevitable limits of the maternal object. As Freud had proposed the genesis of the ego ideal, so Kohut proposed that in response to the loss of felt perfection the toddler attempts to preserve the original perfection in two representational forms: "the grandiose self" (1968, p. 86) and the "idealized parent imago" (1966, p. 246). Kohut conceived of these new systems of perfection as representing "a maturational step . . . in the development of narcissistic libido" (p. 247).

Kohut's (1977) recent work was a departure from

an ego-psychological framework to a psychology of the self "in the broader sense" (p. xv). In his new paradigm, the terms *narcissism* and *narcissistic* are rarely used, but are replaced by the term *self* or *self-object*. It is a premise of this book that aspects of Kohut's earlier, pre-1977, contributions are of considerable heuristic value and do not require elaboration within the rubric of narcissistic or idealizing libido. His descriptions of narcissistic transferences and common transference responses to these phenomena are particularly helpful. His concept of an independent line of development of narcissistic libido may be a conceptual precursor of his later nonenergic formulations of a developing self, but it seems unnecessary and inconsistent with clinical data. His elaborations of narcissistic libido into more complex transformed states would be more clearly discussed in terms of structural development. His formulations of the grandiose self and the idealized parent imago, once divested of their earlier (1966, 1968) association with the concept of an independent line of narcissistic libido and their later (1977) association with the "bipolar self" concept (p. 171), can be viewed as *representational* precursors in the *development* of the ego ideal.

Kernberg (1975) placed significant emphasis on the distinction between normal and pathologic narcissism—a distinction which derives from Freud's prestructural, libidinal treatment of secondary narcissism as both ubiquitous *and* involved in a variety of pathological states. From the perspective of the structural hypothesis, Kernberg's descriptions of normal and pathologic narcissism can be more clearly explicated as normal and pathological integrations of psychic structure. Kernberg (1975) defined normal narcissism as "the libidinal investment of the self" (p. 315).

However, for Kernberg, normal narcissism implies differentiation and integration of energies (libido and aggression) and of structure (ego, superego, and ego ideal), as well as the attainment of some significant degree of individuation and object constancy (pp. 315–322), while pathologic narcissism is implicitly related to disordered differentiation and integration of these factors.

Like Freud (1923) and Kohut (1966), Kernberg (1970a) emphasized the importance of the maternal object in the genesis of particular aberrations of personality development. Stressing the importance of "extremely severe frustrations in relationships with significant early objects" (p. 55), he described a process of disturbed ego development that he considered a "pure culture of pathological development of narcissism" (p. 51), producing what he labeled "narcissistic personalities."

As Hartmann (1950b) noted, Freud did not redefine narcissism in his later structural psychology. In the past ten years a number of authors have attempted a redefinition in more limited ego-psychological terms. Sandler and Joffe (1967) deleted energic considerations in their proposed definition of narcissism. They suggested limiting narcissism to positive states of self-esteem: "an ideal state . . . which is fundamentally affective and which normally accompanies the harmonious and integrated functioning of all the biological and mental structures" (p. 63).

Pulver (1970) urged eliminating from the definition "certain phenomena currently called narcissistic . . . in which the concentration of psychological interest upon the self is only a minimal factor" (p. 338). He considered a "leading candidate for such revision the use of the term narcissism to describe a developmental stage and to describe immature object relationships" (p. 338). He would have the term limited to a "broad, nonspecific concept describing...some aspect of the self" and stressing "the dynamic and structural aspects of the phenomena" (p. 339). Stolorow (1975a) quoted Pulver's expression of dissatisfaction with the state of unclarity in regard to a theory of narcissism: "'A serious result of this vagueness is that the concept...has not received the elaboration in terms of ego psychology which...it so richly deserves'" (p. 179). In his own definition, Stolorow stressed function: "*Mental activity is narcissistic to the degree that its function is to maintain the structural cohesiveness, temporal stability and positive affective colouring of the self-representation*" (p. 179). For Stolorow any mental activity that contributes to the integration of the self-representation and which protects against its fragmentation or dedifferentiation is narcissistic. Thus, masochistic activity can have a "narcissistic function" by virtue of its contribution to the integration of the self-representation (1975b).

There are a variety of mechanisms that the ego employs to promote and maintain its representational integrity. As Freud (1923) described, the foremost among these integrative mechanisms are a variety of identificatory processes. These processes may be associated with both narcissistic and masochistic contents. The essential masochistic quality is that "satisfaction is conditional upon suffering physical or mental pain" (Freud, 1905, p. 158). Recently Blum (1976) has reiterated that the term refers to "pleasure associated with suffering" (p. 158). The point being emphasized is that *narcissism* and *masochism* refer to *felt qualities* of experience. These felt qualities can be elaborated by the ego in a variety of integrations. These integrations, rather than the felt qualities themselves, are better described in terms of functions of the ego. Stolorow's definition dilutes that distinction. Thus, what he refers to as the "narcissistic function" is more clearly understood as an integrative function of the ego.

Moore (1975) noted that "narcissism was the seed which germinated into ego psychology" (p. 243). In summarizing the development of the concept of narcissism within psychoanalytic theory from energic, structural and dynamic perspectives, he concluded that "*it is a nuclear concept which became for Freud an organizing matrix for the construction of psychoanalytic theory, hence an integral part of the whole*" (p. 272). He cautioned against attempts at limiting definitions: "Something is lost in such restrictions" (p. 272).

During the second decade of this century, Freud was experiencing the limits of the topographic theory. He grappled with these limits in many of the seminal papers of the war years, most notably in *Beyond the Pleasure Principle,* "Mourning and Melancholia," and *On Narcissism: An Introduction.* He was moving toward a radical revision of his psychoanalytic theory. In the process of that struggle, there was a transitional period when data were worked with from an ego-psychological perspective without the organizing tools of an explicit ego-psychological terminology. Many unclear issues and concepts were implicitly subsumed under the rubric of narcissism.

Forty years after the introduction of the structural theory, Arlow and Brenner wrote *Psychoanalytic Concepts and the Structural Theory* in order to demonstrate the incompatibility of the structural and topographic theories. Recently, however, Gedo and Goldberg (1973) proposed a theory of "theoretical complementarity." They stated:

The changeover from one set of concepts to another

need not indicate to us that one superseded the other. We believe that Freud did not intend to dispense with older concepts as he proposed newer ones; rather, he correctly assumed that a given set of data might be understood most clearly by utilizing one particular frame of reference or model of the mind, whereas another set of data demanded a different set of concepts for its clarification. The principle of several concurrent and valid avenues for organizing data of observation we shall call "theoretical complementarity" [p. 4].

Gedo and Goldberg employed a systems-theory approach to integrate the multiple perspectives offered by various theories. While their approach facilitates the acceptance of new theoretical formulations and has heuristic value, it may be employed to defend against accepting the loss of a "piece" of psychoanalytic theory. I differ with their view that Freud never intended to dispense with aspects of theory he no longer considered useful. He often noted that when such an aspect became obsolete it should be dismissed: "I shall be consistent enough [with my general rule] to drop this hypothesis if psycho-analytic work should itself produce some other, more serviceable hypothesis" (1914, p. 79).

A DEFINITION OF NARCISSISM

The term *narcissism* refers to a felt quality of perfection. The idea of perfection, or narcissistic perfection, should encompass the libidinal concept primary narcissism, the object-representational concept self-object duality, and Andreas-Salomé's (1921) "deep identification with the totality." The quality of perfection may be consciously perceived or may be an unconsciously active, affectively valent fantasy. It is a ubiquitous aspect of human experience that facilitates distortion of one's sense of reality, particularly as this relates to one's sense of vulnerability and finiteness. It differs from person to person in its elaboration and integration by the ego.

Perfection is originally perceived during the preindividuated era. In that era, prior to a more defined and firmly established representational world, the quality of narcissistic perfection is felt to be part of a self that includes within it qualities of an object narcissistically perceived as perfect. All adult experiences of narcissistic perfection are built on the core of these original experiences; later experiences that capture a similar state of being are remembered and hierarchically organized in ever more abstract content in relationship to the original preindividuated experiences. For a given individual, the pursuit of perfection might be invested, for example, in phallic activities derived primarily from oedipal issues and conflicts. However, whatever the narcissistic investment, it is *associatively linked* to preindividuated *fixation points* of perfection that remain unconscious and in a state of primary repression. These shape and influence all subsequent investments. A variety of affective signals may provoke ego elaboration, the result being a spectrum of possible integrations within a variety of psychic structures.

The content of narcissistic perfection, as experienced by an adult, usually has affective, physical, and cognitive components. The cognitive component is the conception of perfection, expressed in ideas of omniscience or omnipotence. A subject or object may be thought of as most knowing, most powerful, most beautiful, most successful, etc. What is common to all is a superlative designation, such as "most," and the absolute quality of this designation. Perfection is also associated with the number "one," and often with the wish to be "one and only."

A variety of affects are linked to these conceptions. When narcissistic perfection is felt to be part of the self-representation, the subject's positive self-esteem is experienced along a spectrum from well-being to elation. These feelings are often associated with a physical sense that the subject's body is functioning well. When narcissistic perfection is felt to be an attribute of the object, the subject may feel some degree of reverence or awe. By performing successfully for the narcissistically invested object, a subject feels a sense of positive self-esteem. A similar affective response is often associated with a subject's living up to the standards of his ego ideal or superego.

A discussion of the content of narcissistic perfection should be complemented by a description of its form and integration in self- and object representations, in ego functions and activities, and in such psychic structures as the ego ideal. The motives and affective signals that provoke the pursuit of perfection include a spectrum of real or imagined dangers, as well as painful and disappointing perceptions. Signal anxieties, and the often associated feelings of rage, disappointment, or sexual excitement, may motivate a subject to pursue one or another form of narcissistic perfection.

The term *narcissistic* can refer to an aspect of a number of experiences, processes, and situations. *Narcissistic gratification* refers to a subject's experience of perfection; *narcissistic injury*, to a subject's experience of the loss of perfection. The experience of any limit to the self-representation can be linked associatively to the original perception of limits and of lost narcissistic perfection. The rage associated with such an "injury" has been referred to as *narcissistic rage* (Kohut, 1972). Rage is also experienced when an object who has been narcissistically invested disappoints a subject who feels entitled to the presence of an idealized object.

The ego process of attributing narcissistic perfection to something is referred to as *narcissistic investment*. The choice of the word *investment* is intended to connote a process whereby a quality is added to something. When the investment is in the self-representation, it is accomplished by a process of *narcissistic identification*. When an object is perceived as narcissistically perfect, it is referred to as a *narcissistic object* (animate or inanimate). A regressive shift in the integration of a subject's narcissistic investments is designated a *narcissistic regression*.

The defensive investment of perfection in the analysand's self-representation in response to an analytic intervention or to the threat of progress in the analytic situation is referred to as *narcissistic resistance*. The two transference forms described by Kohut (1968), the mirror and the idealizing transferences (p. 88), which represent an attempt at recapitulation of an aspect of structural development in the analytic situation, are referred to as the *narcissistic transferences*. Kohut's valuable clinical descriptions refer, however, to more than narcissistic issues; his (1977) recent designation of these phenomena as "self-object transferences" (p. xiv) reflects his awareness of this fact. From the perspective of the structural hypothesis, the mirror transference can be viewed as an attempt by the analysand to recapture a sense of the original narcissistic perfection for the self-representation, but this transference reflects repetitions that derive from both preoedipal and oedipal conflicts. Preoedipal conflicts, often resulting in disturbed integration of primary identifications, are influenced by the nature of the subject's maturing character organization and by the relatedness of the primary object. It is important to note that these transference phenomena can be motivated in regressive defensive flight from intense oedipal conflicts. They may reflect wishes for a particular kind of paternal "mirroring," or responsiveness, that derives from both preoedipal and oedipal conflicts with the paternal object.

Similarly, the idealizing transference reflects the analysand's efforts to invest the object representation of the analyst with illusions of narcissistic perfection. Again, in contradiction to Kohut, these transference phenomena often are manifestations of much more than preoedipal developmental interferences. Frequently, they are an aspect of intense oedipal transference trends that reflect disorders of superego structuralization.

A more limited definition of narcissism need not result in loss; it may, rather, facilitate a number of distinctions that contribute to more precise communication. For example, the term *narcissism* is different from the terms *self* and *self-representation*. It is a perceived quality that *may* be experienced as part of the self-representation. In this sense, self-involvement is not equivalent to narcissistic involvement. The former may refer to any self-oriented activity in which the subject engages. The latter term refers to activity limited to the pursuit of illusions of narcissistic perfection in one or another form.

Exploring Annie Reich's (1953) term *narcissistic want* provides a final example of the increased precision gained from a more limited definition of narcissism. Reich used narcissistic want to describe a complex emotional state in women derived ultimately from an experience of preoedipal deprivation. She described a "narcissistic object choice" in these women that was intended to undo their sense of want, inner void, and defect. The men they chose were perceived as narcissistically perfect in the sense defined in this chapter, but the other aspects of this complex state of "want" could be more exactly described in terms of the representational worlds of these women and the integration of their psychic structures.

The definition being elaborated in this chapter is a unitary one. It views all narcissistic perfection as the same. Narcissistic perfection is a defensive distortion of reality—an affectively laden fantasy based on the original perfection of the self-object bliss of the symbiotic phase. Its loss is a ubiquitous developmental insult from which few, if any, human beings ever recover. Freud's (1923) formulations of ego development are based on the above perception: "It may be that this identification is the sole condition under which the id can give up its objects" (p. 29). Mahler (1972) similarly emphasized this point: "One could regard the entire life cycle as . . . an eternal longing for the actual or fantasied 'ideal state of self', with the latter standing for a symbiotic fusion with the 'all good' symbiotic mother, who was at one time part of the self in a blissful state of well-being" (p. 338).

Freud's quote can be elaborated, integrating the contribution of Kohut and Mahler to read: *Narcissistically invested* identification is the sole condition under which the id can give up its objects and is a fundamental concomitant of primary separation-individuation. The pursuit of narcissistic perfection in one form or another is a defensive distortion that is a ubiquitous characteristic of the ego. It is a goal of analysis to identify the nature of the analysand's narcissistic investments and to work through those aspects of the investments that contribute to suffering and maladaptation. It is questionable whether the total relinquishment of narcissistic perfection is possible or desirable.

The proposed definition is intended to facilitate a dynamic perspective. It should help an analyst accept his own and his analysand's narcissism as inevitable, more similar than different, and of potentially pleasurable and social value. This view of narcissism should facilitate a number of questions. What percepts and/or painful affects stimulate an analysand's pursuit of perfection? What painful memories do an analysand's continued pursuit of perfection protect him from remembering or re-experiencing? What fears and frightening perceptions (his own death, the death of a loved one, his own or the object's murderous rage, castration, loss of love, etc.) does the pursuit of perfection shield the analysand from?

Narcissism is neither healthy nor pathologic. Relatively healthy or pathologic egos integrate narcissism in healthy or pathologic manners. Such a perspective is of heuristic value for a number of reasons. First, it is based on an appreciation of the ubiquitous defensive nature of all narcissistic investment. Second, it is in greater harmony with the developing ego-psychological perspective of the structural theory proposed by Freud and elaborated by numerous others. Third, it mitigates against a common countertransference potential to respond pejoratively to a subject whose narcissism an analyst may consider pathological. This latter point will be elaborated in chapter 4.

In regard to the second point, I have suggested that Freud was moving in this direction and that it is implicit in his formulations, as it is explicit in the writings of Wilhelm Reich (1933), that all character is in part defensive and that illusions of narcissistic perfection are integrated within those structured defenses of the ego referred to as "character."

It is the ego that develops and not narcissism. An ego developing in a healthy manner facilitates a subject's experience of some significant degree of object love, of productive and humanistic work, and of satisfying self-involvement and play. Such an ego integrates its pursuit of narcissistic perfection in a manner that facilitates these pursuits. In addition, it is associated with an investment of narcissistic perfection in an ego ideal that finds some significant degree of harmony with the subject's self-representation and which contributes to a tone of positive self-esteem. Pathologic ego development is often associated with a more rigid, compulsive pursuit of narcissistic perfection—either for one's self-representation or in objects—in a form that is unattainable, isolating, and maladaptive and that, by virtue of these characteristics, is associated with fluctuations of mood. It is the ego, and not narcissism, that develops in a manner that permits a relatively more or less harmonious relationship with reality. The relatively healthy ego integrates its pursuits of narcissistic perfection in a manner that is in harmony with its endowments and the opportunities for identification and for gratification available in reality. The distortions of reality implicit in all narcissistic pursuits are integrated by such an ego in a manner that does not result in disharmony and maladaption. These intergrations often remain unchallenged or are only challenged when the subject faces death or some profound threat to his character integration.

Kernberg's (1970a) formulation of narcissistic personality has significant value. I differ with Kernberg, and others, over the concept of pathologic narcissism.

Such designations seem to ignore the defensive nature of so-called "normal" narcissism and encourage thinking of narcissism pejoratively. Kohut (1966) emphasized this problem:

> Although in theoretical discussions it will usually not be disputed that narcissism . . . is per se neither pathological nor obnoxious, there exists an understandable tendency to look at it with a negatively toned evaluation as soon as the field of theory is left. Where such a prejudice exists it is undoubtedly based on a comparison between narcissism and object love, and is justified by the assertion that it is the more primitive and the less adaptive of the two forms of libido distribution. I believe, however, that these views do not stem primarily from an objective assessment either of the developmental position or of the adaptive value of narcissism, but that they are due to the improper intrusion of the altruistic value system of Western civilization [pp. 243–244].

The distinction between pathologic and normal ego development is more consistent with the data and less vulnerable to pejorative elaboration. There has been a tendency to judge different forms of narcissistic pursuits more or less healthy. For example, the pursuit of narcissistic perfection for one's body has been considered less healthy than the pursuit of perfection for one's mind. Similarly, the pursuit of perfection in a humanitarian profession has been considered healthier than the pursuit of perfection in the performing arts. Such distinctions are clearly oversimplifications. What is required in assessing health and illness is a much more complex assessment of psychic structure — its adaptive or maladaptive relation to reality — as well as the subject's experience of his reality.

2

Narcissistic Personality Disorder

The present controversy concerning patients with narcissistic disturbances is reflected in the many descriptive and diagnostic labels used to refer to them: narcissistic character, phallic-narcissistic character, narcissistic character disorder, narcissistic personality, and narcissistic personality disorder. In addition the current controversy concerning diagnosis is influenced by the fact that while some analysts favor strictly defined diagnostic categories, others are less concerned with the question of classification. Different authors stress different *aspects* of the integration of narcissism, and various authors employ the same terms for different purposes without explicitly stating the distinctions. Thus, using different frames of reference, different authors refer to seemingly different groups of patients as, in some way, "narcissistic."

At the present time, analysts tend to think of narcissistic patients in terms of Kernberg's or Kohut's explications of these disorders. Many find aspects of their contributions valuable and creative, as well as confusing, and strive to integrate and preserve the contributions of both. Much of the unclarity derives from

Kernberg's and Kohut's failure to differentiate narcissism from ego, superego, and ego-ideal development. The limited definition of narcissism as a felt quality of perfection, presented in chapter 1, stresses the ubiquity of narcissistic investments and allows for an appreciation of the panoply of contents and integrations of narcissism in the "character" of the ego. It permits an ego-psychological definition of *narcissistic personality disorder*, as well as a classificatory schema of all narcissistic investments. A narcissistic personality disorder is defined by the predominant mode of investment of narcissism in the self-representation. This diagnostic designation, based on an appreciation of the predominant *mode* of investment, should be complemented by a consideration of its state of *integration* along a spectrum from psychotic to normal.

The definitions and classificatory schema proposed in this chapter derive from a hypothetical representational and structural perspective that is an ego-psychological synthesis of Freud's ideas on narcissism and on the genesis of "character" presented in his seminal works *On Narcissism: An Introduction* and *The Ego and the Id.*

THE LITERATURE

Freud's uses of the term (and concept) *narcissism* have been outlined in chapter 1. He employed the term sparingly with reference to diagnosis. In 1914, he used *narcissistic neurosis* to describe patients who today would be labeled schizophrenic. He explained such symptoms of that condition as megalomania and hypochondriasis as narcissistic aberrations of libidinal cathexes. However, it is probable that the analysands he described in 1916 in *Some Character-Types Met With in Psycho-Analytic Work* would be diagnosed as narcissistic personality disorders today.

In 1933, Wilhelm Reich presented the clinical category phallic-narcissistic character from descriptive, genetic, and dynamic points of view and elaborated a number of factors in its genesis:

> On the basis of a *phallic* mother-identification a phallic-narcissistic character usually develops, whose narcissism and sadism is directed especially toward women (vengeance on the strict mother). This attitude is the character defense against the deeply repressed original love of the mother which could not continue to exist in the face of her frustrating influence [pp. 152–153].

Reich identified the mobilization of rage in response to this frustration and its expression in sadistic and other sexual perversions and in the attitudes and behavior of these male patients toward women. With such patients, Reich noted a corresponding weakness or absence of the father (p. 203).

He added another important observation which has been greatly elaborated in Kohut's conceptualizations: "The infantile history regularly reveals serious disappointments in the object of the other sex, disappointments which occurred precisely at the time when attempts were made to win the object through phallic exhibition" (p. 203). Today we would broaden the spectrum of disorders in maternal relatedness that these patients might encounter.

Reich's rich clinical descriptions cover what is today considered a range of integrations of narcissistic character pathology—from a better integrated group who "in spite of their narcissistic preoccupation with their selves . . . often show strong attachments to people and things outside" (p. 201) to a more troubled group that includes "addicts, particularly alcoholics" (p. 205). The latter group of patients were described in energic terms and regarded as examples of oral regressions from phallic-oedipal and anal homosexual conflicts.

Reich's conceptualizations were limited by the theoretical emphasis on the central significance of the oedipal conflict which was prevalent in his day. While certain of these conditions might still be attributed to regression from oedipal issues, others would now be considered the result of very significant preoedipal fixations or developmental interferences.

Annie Reich wrote two important papers attempting to integrate Freud's energic conceptualizations with preoedipal and structural considerations, particularly those of Jacobson. These papers are rich in their appreciation of what she refers to as narcissistic issues, but I will select only those statements that deal with the question of diagnostic category.

Patients who suffer with "narcissistic disturbances" were considered to have a "narcissistic neurosis" (1960, p. 215). Reich modified Freud's term to exclude the psychoses and to include a much wider spectrum of conditions: "We now even question the usefulness of a too narrowly circumscribed nosology. We are much concerned with so-called borderline conditions, and we tend to look upon the boundary between psychosis and neurosis as somewhat fluid" (p. 216). Of these "borderline" patients, she wrote: "We know overlapping of phases [of development] to be ubiquitous. There is usually a partial regression to earlier ego and libidinal states mixed with later, more highly developed structures" (p. 215).

Reich (1953) described women who suffer from a state of "narcissistic want" (p. 24) due to "narcissistic injuries" of feeling "deserted and castrated" (p. 41). These fixations result in disorders of internalization and idealization of their "sexual ideal" and "ego ideal," which a "narcissistic object choice... is intended to undo" (p. 24). Men with "narcissistic disturbances" suffer similar problems of internalization and idealization related to similar genetics: "The primitive, crudely sexual quality of the ego ideals, conditioned by a fixation on the primitive levels where traumatization had occurred ...represents the quintessence of this pathology" (1960, p. 228).

Rather than considering a broad spectrum of patients with varying degrees of narcissistic problems, Kernberg (1970a) described as narcissistic personalities only a small group which he saw as "a pure culture of pathological development of narcissism" (p. 51). Like Annie Reich he reported that their "main problem appears to be the disturbance of their self-regard in connection with specific disturbances in their object relationships" (p. 51). He emphasized the importance of "oral rage" (p. 52) toward the maternal object. Like both Wilhelm and Annie Reich he stressed the importance in the defensive genesis of this personality organization of "extremely severe frustrations in relationships with significant early objects" (p. 55). He deepened the description of the mothers of these patients, characterizing them as "cold hostile" mothers who use their children narcissistically. Their behavior toward the child is characterized by "callousness, indifference, and nonverbalized spiteful aggression" (p. 59).

He extended the descriptions by Jacobson, Annie Reich, and Sandler and Rosenblatt to define a specific constellation of internal self- and object representations that are pathognomonic for this personality organization: "There is a fusion of ideal self, ideal object, and actual self images" (p. 55). This results in "stunted ego development" (p. 61) and a personality organization character-ized by "coldness and ruthlessness" (p. 52) and by defi-ciencies of "genuine feelings of sadness and mournful longing; their incapacity for experiencing depressive reactions is a basic feature of their personalities" (p. 53).

Kernberg (1970a) considered this narrow group of patients to have a poor prognosis but noted that "the prog-nosis improves with patients who preserve some capaci-ty for depression or mourning, especially when their de-pressions contain elements of guilt feelings" (p. 73). This latter group, he implies, may merge into another that has "less intensive overall character pathology" (p. 84) and is characterized by having "narcissistic defenses," (p. 84), rather than as a "narcissistic personality."

Since 1970, Kernberg has written a number of papers and a book elaborating his view of pathologic narcissism and the narcissistic personality. In attempt-ing a delineation of this diagnostic category, Kernberg's primary focus was the *state of integration* of the subject's narcissism. This integration is based on a description of drive and structural development, with particular emphasis on the elaboration of internalized object relations and defense organization.

In "A Psychoanalytic Classification of Character Pathology" (1970b), he described higher, intermediate, and lower organization levels of "character pathology" (pp. 802–803). The lower level, which corresponds to his (1967) borderline personality organization, is where "many narcissistic personalities are organized" (p. 809). According to Kernberg the lower level is delineated by the following characteristics: predominant pregenital aggression; lack of superego integration in varying degrees, accompanied by a predominance of sadistic superego forerunners; primitive dissociation, or split-ting, as the central mechanism of the defensive ego; im-paired synthetic function, and mechanisms of denial, concomitant with primitive forms of projection and omnipotence; and a lack of object constancy—no capacity for a total object relationship, one which tolerates and integrates good *and* bad aspects of both the object and the self (pp. 803–805).

In 1975, Kernberg added that the borderline personality organization is typified by: "non-specific manifestations of ego weakness"—characterized by "(a) *lack of anxiety tolerance,* (b) *lack of impulse control,* (c) *lack of sublimatory channels*" (p. 22). He also clarified the distinction between the narcissistic personality and the borderline personality organization by noting that although their egos' structural characteristics and defense organizations are "both strikingly similar," they are also "specifically different" (p. 331). The similarity resides in the predominance of "splitting" and "primitive types of projection and idealization, by omnipotent control, narcissistic withdrawal, and devaluation" (p. 332). In the narcissistic personality, however, "there is an integrated although highly pathological 'grandiose self'" (p. 332).

In 1975, Kernberg employed Kohut's (1968) term *grandiose self* but defined it differently. This distinction has not been clearly noted. Kohut's (1971) patients have "in essence attained a cohesive self" (p. 4). In 1975, Kernberg equated his fused representational definition of a narcissistic personality with Kohut's "grandiose self": "In my thinking, this grandiose self is a pathological condensation of rudiments of the real self, the ideal self, and the ideal objects of infancy and early childhood" (p. 332). A second source of confusion arises because Kernberg and Kohut employed the term *borderline* in different ways. Kernberg (1970b, p. 810) distinguished "borderline" from "psychotic" on the basis of the maintenance of reality testing in the former condition, but for Kohut

(1971), "borderline" refers to unanalyzable, "veiled or fended off" instances of "schizophrenic psychosis" (p. 18).

Kernberg (1975) divided narcissistic personalities into three groups derived from a description of their behavior. The third group functions "overtly on a borderline level" and presents "non-specific manifestations of ego weakness" (p. 334). The first group are "narcissistic personalities whose surface adaptation is more effective" (p. 332). Their talent allows them to adapt vocationally; however, they seek help because of "chronic difficulties in intimate relations with others" at "later stages of life" (p. 333). The second group represents "the majority of narcissistic personalities who come for treatment." These patients have severe "disturbances in object relations[,]. . . frequently present complicating neurotic symptoms and sexual difficulties, and are disturbed by the serious defects in their capacity for establishing lasting emotional and sexual relationships and by their chronic feelings of emptiness" (p. 333). Despite behavioral distinctions, all three levels are borderline and possess a pathologic grandiose self. Kernberg's 1975 view of prognosis was almost identical with his 1970 perspective—"guarded" (p. 248). He felt that "the prognostic considerations. . . illustrate the limitations and difficulties in the psychoanalytic treatment of patients with narcissistic personality structure" (p. 260). Because Kohut employs different diagnostic criteria, I suspect he would consider the first group to be larger, including within it patients that Kernberg might consider neurotic.

Kohut (1966, 1968, 1971), elaborating upon Freud's (1914) prestructural concept narcissistic libido, proposed a theory of narcissistic libidinal development. His concept of idealizing libido implicitly contains self-

and object representations within it, but blurs important heuristic distinctions that limiting the definition of narcissism can provide. Deriving from his developmental schema, outlined and commented upon in chapter 1, Kohut proposed that factors that interfere with the normal development of narcissistic libido result in aberrations of development that he calls "narcissistic personality disorders." The patients he discussed are not necessarily psychotic or borderline but cover a spectrum of "specific personality disturbance of lesser severity whose treatment constitutes a considerable part of present-day psychoanalytic practice" (1971, p. 1). He did not care to define this entity "according to the traditional medical model, that is, as disease entities or pathological syndromes which are to be diagnosed and differentiated on the basis of behavioral criteria" (pp. 2–3). As distinguished from psychosis and borderline states, the patients he described have "in essence attained a cohesive self and have constructed cohesive idealized archaic objects" (p. 4).

Kohut's perspective is developmental; his emphasis, on the *mode of investment* of narcissism. His main area of interest is the psychoanalytic situation; the state of integration of narcissistic investments is secondary. Kohut's two ubiquitous modes of narcissistic investment—the grandiose self and the idealized parent imago—are based on "cohesive, and more or less stable narcissistic configurations which belong to the *stage of narcissism* (i.e., to that step in psychological development which, according to Freud's formulation [1914], follows the stage of autoerotism)" (1971, pp. 31–32). Kohut (1971) described a "*stage of the cohesive self*" (p. 32) that is analogous to Freud's "stage of narcissism." For Kohut, the diagnosis of narcissistic personality disorder is "based not on the evaluation of presenting symptomatology or even life history, but on the nature of the spontaneously developing transference" (p. 23). These transferences derive from fixation at the archaically elaborated, narcissistically invested cohesive self- and object representations Kohut has referred to as the grandiose self and the idealized parent imago.

For Kohut, the psychoses and the borderline states are characterized, in part, by patients not becoming "available to the formation of [narcissistic] transferences." Instead they experience fragmentation "of the archaic grandiose self as well as...of the archaic idealized object." This is due to their fixation on a *stage of fragmented self* which "corresponds to the developmental phase to which Freud (1914) referred as the *stage of autoerotism*" (pp. 29–30).

It seems reasonable to conclude that, when considered from an object-representational perspective, Kernberg and Kohut discussed patients quite differently. In fact, they may be discussing different groups of patients. Kernberg's "pure culture" of narcissistic personalities suffer from a "fusion" of self- and object representations, while the group of patients Kohut described have more differentiated representations. Kohut's patients suffer "from specific disturbances in the realm of the self and of those archaic objects cathected with narcissistic libido (self-objects)" (p. 3). In summary of Kohut's pre-1977 conceptualizations, the diagnosis narcissistic personality disorder is based upon the elaboration of specific narcissistic transferences that depend on cohesive narcissistically invested self- and object representations and that are in and of themselves an indication of analyzability. These patients are considered nonpsychotic, nonborderline, and analyzable.

In *The Restoration of the Self* Kohut (1977) proposed a new paradigm, the psychology of the self "in the broader sense" (p. xv) of the term. In a manner characteristic of paradigm propagation, new terms replaced older ones without specific translation. In commenting on his earlier work, Kohut correctly pointed out: "I presented my findings concerning the psychology of the self mainly in the language of classical drive theory" (p. xiii). I am suggesting that had he presented his findings within the language of ego psychology he might not have found it necessary to propose a new psychoanalytic paradigm. What Kohut had previously termed a fixation or developmental interference in the development of narcissistic libido, he now referred to as the "primary defect of the self" (p. 50). This defect provokes the subject to respond with "defensive and compensatory structures" that are analogous to the grandiose self and the idealized parent imago, respectively. More explicitly, Kohut stated that the psychoses, the borderline states, and the schizoid and paranoid personalities "are in principle not analyzable" (p. 192) because they do not experience self-object transferences. He distinguished between two types of analyzable narcissistic personality disorders, the narcissistic personality disorder and the narcissistic behavior disorder (p. 193). The former is characterized by "autoplastic symptoms...,such as hypersensitivity to slights, hypochondria, or depression," as well as by a preference for sadistic "fantasies"; the latter, by "alloplastic symptoms...,such as perversion, delinquency, or addiction" and by a penchant for sadistic "behavior" (p. 193).

THE PRESENT UNCLARITY

The present unclarity with regard to diagnosis is related

to the fact that many analysts, feeling that the contributions of Kernberg and Kohut are significant and
creative, have attempted to integrate and preserve the
contributions of both authors. That each seems limited
in certain respects and that the two are often contradictory thus contributes to the present confusion. Kernberg's gift for description has resulted in an accurate
portrait of a sicker variety of narcissistic personality
disorder. His stress on their rage in response to
frustration and on their defensive denigration of objects is important, but his stress on a fused infra-
structure, and on an underlying unity to the psychopathology of all "narcissistic personalities" based on
that configuration, is not consistent with the data. It
seems a static conceptualization that is prone to pejorative elaboration.

Kernberg's conception seems to contribute to a
pessimistic view of these patients as hopelessly fixated
in their "refused" states. This view leads him to see
them as lacking in "capacity for empathic understanding of others" (1974, p. 215) and as "deficient in genuine
feelings of sadness and mournful longing; their incapacity for experiencing depressive reactions is a
basic feature of their personalities" (1970, p. 53). A
more optimistic view derives from the perception of
these patients as *defensive* rather than as *lacking, deficient,* and *incapable.*

It seems to be more clinically useful to understand
patients who correspond with Kernberg's behavioral
criteria as people with very rigid character defense
organizations. Two such patients I have seen had an intense need to control their animate and inanimate
worlds. Their behavior seemed to represent an organized, tenacious, and continual striving to maintain a
sense that their defined actual self-representation was

imbued with narcissistic perfection. These efforts reflected a perpetual struggle requiring very significant expenditures of emotional energy. Such character modes protected the subjects from feeling their survival threatened by dormant, archaically invested object representations structured as introjects within "self-as-place" (Schafer, 1968).[1] As long as they felt the self-representation was imbued with narcissistic perfection, they felt safe from the annihilating vivification of these ever-present object representations. When these character defenses failed, when a chink in the armor appeared, these patients were vulnerable to intense anxiety, rage, profound depression, dangerous acting-up and -out, and psychotic regressions. After a trial of analysis, I came to consider both these men as unanalyzable and, from an analytic diagnostic perspective, as narcissistic personality disorders with latent psychosis. Their narcissistic defenses were rigidly maintained to protect against psychosis. These men and their therapies are described in a discussion of unanalyzability (see pp. 40–41 and pp. 143–161).

I am suggesting, as Kohut has, that such patients have a defined actual self-representation. Conflict can threaten this representation with regressive dedifferentiation. In response to such a threat, these patients attempt to defend themselves by restoring illusions of perfection to their self-representations. More extreme examples of this diagnostic category rigidly pursue these defensive activities as a life style. They may perceive any frustration as a threat to the integrity of their self-representations and attempt to create the illusion that their actual self-representations are imbued with idealized qualities that will protect them from the

---

[1] Schafer's (1968) terms *self-as-agent, self-as-object,* and *self-as-place* are particularly valuable for organizing the feeling, or subjective, aspects of the self experience. In *Aspects of Internalization,* he states, "To deal with this ambiguity, it appears necessary to differentiate at least three kinds of subjective self: 'self-as-agent' (the 'I'), the 'self-as-object' (the 'me'), and the 'self-as-place' (for which no pronoun is specific)" (p. 80). Self-as-place is that part of the self system where object representations constituted as introjects exist.

experience of any frustration and against the imagined consequence of their rage in response to frustration.

Although Kohut's pre-1977 contributions are of considerable heuristic and clinical value, there is some difficulty in defining a group of patients by the form of their transference potential. This is particularly so when one considers that narcissistic transference potentials are perhaps ubiquitous and that elements of them may appear in analytic endeavors with patients whose narcissistic development is more neurotically integrated. Similarly, integrations of these transferences can be seen in psychotic form. For example, for Kohut (1971) the mirror transference represents the therapeutic reactivation of the grandiose self in the transference. He described three types of mirror transferences reflecting degrees of differentiation between the analysand-subject and analyst-object.

I have worked for six years in psychotherapy with a fifty-three-year-old man, Mr. Q, whose predominant integration corresponds to Kernberg's third and sicker group of narcissistic personality. At moments of intense conflict with his object world, moments when significant objects challenged his pursuit of narcissistic perfection for his self-representation, he became flagrantly paranoid or withdrew. At moments when the analyst's interventions challenged his integration of narcissistic perfection in his self-representation, his mirror transference was psychotically elaborated. At such moments the analyst became more than an extension of the patient's grandiose self—according to Kohut (1971) the ''merger'' form of the ''mirror transference'' (pp. 114–115). In paranoid response to interventions that he perceived as threats to his omnipotent control, he behaved as if he were the analyst. He slipped and referred to himself as the analyst and vehemently insisted upon hearing only his own associations and interpretations. Anything other than a mirroring response stimulated disorganizing affects that the patient struggled to defend against by paranoid grandiose attacks on the analyst and his object world and by withdrawal.

In this most recent work, Kohut (1977) referred to patients considered narcissistic personality disorders as suffering from a "primary defect of the self" (p. 50). The term *defect* connotes a static quality and is vulnerable to pejorative elaboration. These patients' self-representations are not defective. Rather they are imbued with distorted perceptions derived from childhood fixations associated with object representations that are preserved in the subject's representational world in a similarly misconstrued state. The subject's self-representation is intact and defined. However, the subject feels small and vulnerable in comparison to object representations perceived as large, invested with archaic qualities, and constituted as introjects in the "self-as-place." These frightening introjects threaten the subject with a spectrum of dangers (including castration and annihilation) that the subject may respond to with defensive attempts to restore illusions of narcissistic perfection to his self-representation. Kohut's concept of "defensive" narcissistic structures mobilized for the purpose of "covering over the primary defect in the self" presents the grandiose self as a structure designed for the "sole or predominant" purpose of undoing an early life (preoedipal, rapprochement) developmental interference (p. 3). It ignores the possibility of the defensive pursuit of illusions of perfection for the self-representation in regressive response to later (oedial and postoedipal) conflicts and/or traumatic experiences.

Kohut (1977) distinguished a narcissistic behavior disorder from a narcissistic personality disorder on the basis of the former's penchant for sadistic *behavior* rather than *fantasy*. For Kohut, patients with delinquent, perverse, or addictive tendencies are more difficult, but in principle are analyzable by virtue of their ability to establish stable "narcissistic" (1971; "self-object," 1977) transference configurations. Their more serious difficulties are related to their more serious superego pathology: Kohut's (1977) patient Mr. I was "lacking even the minimum goal setting structures" (p. 195).

Kohut's distinction between the two disorders—which may

have derived from his countertransference response to enactment and more direct and undisguised expressions of aggression, hate and sadism—carries with it a number of disadvantages. Foremost among them is the inference that narcissistic behavior disorders are sicker and more difficult to treat. A judgment of health or illness should derive from an assessment of a subject's *integration* of his defensive activity rather than from a distinction between a preference for defensive fantasy rather than defensive behavior. One often observes narcissistic personality disorders with both defensive behavior and defensive fantasy. Similarly, one may observe healthier patients (considered narcissistic personality disorders) whose narcissistically invested pursuits express themselves primarily in behavior. Conversely, sicker patients, particularly with schizoid characteristics, pursue illusions of perfection primarily in fantasy.

Rather than stressing a difference related to a description of behavior, I am emphasizing that these patients' behaviors always derive from an unconscious affectively laden fantasy often designed to restore illusions of narcissistic perfection to their self-representations. A threat to his integration of illusions of narcissistic perfection often provokes a narcissistic personality disorder to pursue activities that have an impulsive or compulsive quality and whose content may be sadistic. The analysis of these defensively motivated activities (both acting-up and acting-out) offers numerous challenges. As the analyses of these patients proceed, their knowledge inhibits their ability to enjoy narcissistically invested sadistic behavior. These ego (rather than superego) acquisitions are associated with a greater tendency toward fantasy over overt behavior, as well as with an increased capacity for depression. In addition, as defensive externalization of superego function is interpreted and worked through and as the often present intrasystemic superego conflict is analyzed, the ability of these patients to experience their own more realistic object-related values is potentiated. A more detailed description of this intrasystemic pathology of the superego and the penchant for regressive and defensive superego externalization is presented in chapters 3 and 4.

DIAGNOSTIC SCHEMA

There is heuristic value in maintaining the diagnostic designation narcissistic personality disorder, but it should be integrated with Freud's (1914) observation of man's ubiquitous defensive attempt to preserve illusions of his primary narcissism. Wilhelm Reich (1933) explicitly elaborated this proposition in his conception of character as "essentially a narcissistic protection mechanism." His diagnostic category of the phallic-narcissistic character (pp. 201–207) represents an exploration of a specific mode of investment of narcissism in various states of integration—a mode typically encountered in certain male patients.

The perspective presented in this chapter, which stresses that all people are narcissistic, is an extension of that proposed by Freud, Reich, and Kohut. What is required is a definition of the term *narcissistic personality disorder* and a complementary psychoanalytic classification of narcissism in the "character" (Freud, 1923) of the ego. Any classificatory schema must be limited and incomplete for it can only be a partial reflection of what are always more complex human phenomena. Nevertheless, an effort at clarifying the classifying rubrics employed to describe the panoply of expressions of narcissism in the human situation is of potential heuristic and clinical value. The classification presented here is based on an extension and elaboration of Kohut's construct of two different modes of narcissistic investment. This classification emphasizes the ubiquitous nature of narcissistic investment and attempts to consider both its predominant mode of investment and its state of integration.

A narcissistic personality disorder is defined by the predominant mode of investment of narcissism in the self-representation. Wilhelm Reich's phallic-narcissistic characters, as well as Kernberg's narcissistic personalities, would be considered narcissistic personality disorders in this classification. In contrast to Kohut's, this diagnostic designation is not based on transference phenomena. A secondary diagnostic statement that reflects a consideration of *the state of structural integration* of narcissism is necessary. Again in contrast to Kohut, it is proposed that the narcissistic personality disorder can be seen in psychotic, borderline, neurotic, and "normal" states of integration. Following the perspective of Arlow and Brenner, these categories are seen as representing a spectrum within which fluidity is possible. The diagnosis of a narcissistic personality disorder with latent psychosis has particularly important implications for analyzability. These are discussed on pp. 143–161.

A second possible mode of investment is in object representations. When the predominant mode of investment is in object representations and when the subject's ego has developed the degree of differentiation associated with well-integrated ego-ideal and superego structuralizations, the result is the traditional neurotic or normal character integration of narcissism. There are patients, however, whose psychic structures do not develop to that degree and whose predominant mode of investment is in object representations. As with the narcissistic personality disorder, this investment may be found along a spectrum of integrations from psychotic to normal. A predominant mode of investment in object representations is often associated with a suppliant, passive, or seductive attitude of the subject toward its narcissistically invested object. This suppliant attitude may be elaborated and complemented by masochistic content (in which the subject may feel the perfect sufferer) in order to gain the attention and approval of the idealized object. It is worth considering the term *suppliant personality disorder* to describe patients whose predominant mode of narcissistic investment is in object representations.

Narcissistic investment in object representations is implicit in the traditional diagnosis of neurosis in that neurotic and normal people delegate their lost narcissistic perfection to their ego ideals. Defensive pursuits of illusions of perfection are more easily denied when they are only implicit or when they are subsumed under such terms as "normal narcissism." The term *suppliant personality disorder* emphasizes the tenacious and ubiquitous nature of man's hunger for illusions of perfection. It emphasizes that all human beings pursue these illusions in one or another mode. What is different is the state of integration of these pursuits along a spectrum from psychotic to normal.

What has been called normal narcissism, in contrast to normal self-esteem or self-regard and despite its adaptive advantages, is a mechanism for self-aggrandizement and subtle self-delusion that man finds necessary to assuage the insult of his true being. This perspective emphasizes the irrational and interminable nature of man's pursuit of perfection.

In a broader context, Hartmann (1939a) emphasized the ubiquity of man's irrational nature. For Hartmann there is no "perfectly rational" man (p. 9). He noted that because "an analytic 'normal psychology' is still very largely nonexistent" (p. 14) health has been characterized by the absence of neurotic elements. He warned that the "contrast thus established with the neuroses can have no meaning so long as we fail to appreciate how much of these mechanisms, developmental stages, and modes of reaction is active in healthy individuals" (p. 14). Of man's ego he stated: "A system of regulation operating at the highest level of development is not sufficient to maintain a stable equilibrium; a more primitive system is needed to supplement it" (p. 13). Healthy individuals integrate their pursuits of perfection in adaptive manners. In this context, the diagnostic designations normal narcissistic and normal suppliant personality disorder emphasize and clarify an aspect of man's normal "primitive system."

These diagnostic considerations are intended to be no more than organizing rubrics to facilitate the categorization of data. They are intended to facilitate the correlation of the predominant mode of investment of narcissism with the state of the ego's integration of narcissism and to complement other diagnostic considerations that reflect non-narcissistic issues.

There are patients who show a consistent and distinct preference for one or another mode of investment. Similarly, many patients display a striking consistency and stability to their ego's integration of their investments. Some patients present mixed modes of investments with or without a potential for progressive and regressive shifts in the status of their ego organization. Finally, shifts in modes of investment and states of integration can occur during the vicissitudes of an analytic experience. For example, analysands may present for analysis with a character organization and adaptation that one appropriately judges to be neurotic. Regression in response to the intensity of the analytic situation and the analytic relationship may stimulate transference forms and defensive activity reflective of an underlying narcissistic personality disorder. I believe Freud (1916) was alluding to this, in part, when he wrote: "Peculiarities in him which he had seemed to possess only to ɛ modest degree are often brought to light in surprisingly increased intensity, or attitudes reveal themselves in him which had not been betrayed in other relations of life" (p. 311).

Because there is no classificatory schema for organizing narcissistic data within the "character" of the ego, various authors have described similar patients from different perspectives. Wilhelm Reich's phallic-narcissistic characters are men defined by descriptive criteria; genetic and dynamic factors are considered secondary. Kohut's narcissistic personality disorders are defined by the mobilization of specific narcissistic transferences. These depend upon the presence of defined archaic self- and object representations cathected with narcissistic libido. Annie Reich (1953) described women who, based on descriptive criteria, might be diagnosed as neurotic or borderline with hysteric and masochistic features. Her emphasis is on their incorporative identification with a male narcissistic object to undo their sense of narcissistic want. In Kohut's terms, the behavior of some of these women could be conceptualized as an enactment of an idealizing transference potential. Similarly, the men she described (1960) might be seen as attempting to gain a sense of synchrony between their self-representations and their grandiose selves in order to diminish a sense of imminent castration anxiety and more deeply repressed separation anxiety. The women described by Annie Reich (1953) who might have been diagnosed as hysteric or masochistic with borderline or neurotic integrations can be considered suppliant personality disorders, the healthier patients being considered neurotic and the sicker patients borderline. Most of the patients Kernberg considers borderline personality organizations could be considered suppliant personality disorders in this classification. His third group of narcissistic personalities would be considered narcissistic personality disorders with borderline integrations, while his first group would be considered narcissistic personality disorders, a number of whom have developed neurotic integrations.

Terms describing states of integration refer to an assessment of the state of ego organization and structural differentiation. In the psychotic, "there is among the ego's defenses a regressive alteration of reality testing" (Arlow and Brenner, 1964, p. 175). A borderline integration is characterized by poor anxiety tolerance, poor frustration tolerance, and poor impulse control, as well as by a predominance of defenses such as projection, denial, denial in fantasy and a resultant splitting. Superego and ego-ideal structuralizations are incomplete and prone to chronic externalization. Many of these patients show a preference for the mode of seeking narcissistic perfection in the external object. Their quest is typified by a profound sensitivity to disappointments in the object that interferes with their maintaining relationships. Typically their involvement is characterized by intense idealization, followed by intolerance for, and rage in response to, the perception of any imperfection in the object, all resulting in the eventual denigration and desertion of the object.

Kernberg (1975) conceived of splitting, the "keeping apart

[of] introjections and identifications'' (p. 29), as the ''essential
defensive operation of the borderline personality organization''
(p. 29). However, splitting as thus defined can be encountered
in a spectrum of less sick patients particularly as a regressive
defensive experience in response to conflict. In this classification,
the designation borderline emphasizes those aspects of ego integration that Kernberg (1975) referred to as ''non-specific ego
weakness'' (p. 22).

The majority of patients considered narcissistic personality
disorders do not demonstrate ''non-specific manifestations of ego
weakness'' and will not be designated borderline in this classification. The integrations of their egos fall within a spectrum
which bridges the borderline and neurotic diagnostic categories.
Their egos possess considerable capacity for sublimation, as well
as for regressions with borderline features. Such regressions may
occur when these subjects are confronted with a threat to their
integrations of narcissistic perfection. A narcissistic injury may
provoke a regression characterized by defensive activity, anxiety,
fluctuation of mood, and loss of sublimatory potential. At such
a moment, when the subject feels his survival is threatened,
feelings of concern for others, as well as guilt and empathy,
become of secondary importance.

Many patients considered narcissistic personality disorders
do not experience *chronic* feelings of emptiness. Rather, they
experience shifts in mood, self-esteem disturbances, and feelings
related to emptiness that can all be correlated with the success
or failure of their defensive quests for the illusion of narcissistic
perfection. A successful middle-aged man described his perception of life as gray and bleak when he attempted to relinquish his
compulsive pursuits of perfection in the conquest of women and
the stock market. With regard to these patients the issue of vari-
ability of disorder at different times and under various circumstances is being stressed. Often their egos are capable of
interacting with their environments to restore a sense of narcis-

sistic perfection to their self-representations, and this results in a reintegration and a diminution of manifest borderline features.

The term *neurosis* as employed in this classification refers solely to a state of ego integration and structural differentiation. A neurotic integration of narcissistic investment is typified by (1) a character organization whose predominant defense mechanism is repression and which, in addition, may employ reaction formation, isolation, undoing, and regression with some capacity for sublimation; (2) some significant and often long-standing object relationships; and (3) a considerable degree of superego and ego-ideal differentiation and structuralization. The superego of the neurotic narcissistic personality disorder is more prone to defensive externalizations than that of the neurotic suppliant personality disorder, who represents the more traditional neurotic character organization.

THE TYPICAL NARCISSISTIC
PERSONALITY DISORDER

The concept of a dynamic spectrum of integration is fundamental here. Within the designations borderline and neurotic, there exists a distribution of pathology of psychic structure. The sicker borderline patient is vulnerable to diffuse, free-floating anxiety and depersonalization, as well as to a variety of serious symptoms and disordered object relations. It seems likely that a number of so-called sicker borderlines are unanalyzable latent psychotics. Their defenses, be they narcissistic, masochistic or whatever, defend against psychosis. A healthier borderline character integration is more vulnerable to structural regression in response to conflict. Within the neuroses, one can find a similar spectrum from mild to serious character impairment and symptomatology.

There is also a spectrum of integration of one of the two modes of narcissistic investment along a continuum from psychotic to normal.

The term narcissistic personality disorder, as it is presently employed, refers to a more limited spectrum of patients who, on the sicker extreme, are borderline; on the healthier, neurotic. (This spectrum correlates with Wilhelm Reich's description of a range of integrations found in phallic-narcissistic characters.)

The classification delineated here stresses two perspectives: the mode of investment and the state of integration of a subject's narcissism. Because of the importance of additional features in patients considered narcissistic personality disorders, a sketch of a typical narcissistic personality disorder is indicated. In this description an attempt will be made to delineate the differences between patients considered narcissistic personality disorders and those considered neurotics. It must be emphasized that these differences are often distinctions of degree rather than of kind. As Annie Reich (1960) pointed out, "narcissistic disturbances" include a spectrum of patients with a spectrum of characteristics; the boundary between who is a narcissistic personality disorder, and who is a neurotic is a vague one.

The typical patient considered a narcissistic personality disorder is characterized by an integration less than that of a neurotic and by an associated predominant mode of narcissistic investment in the self-representation. Such patients pursue their narcissistic investments in a more frenetic manner than do neurotics. A life-felt imperative is often associated with their quests.

Mahler, Pine, and Bergman (1975) have emphasized the intensification of disappointment not only in the parent(s) but also in the self at the "rapprochement crisis": "The junior toddler gradually realizes that his love objects, his parents, are separate individuals with their own interests. He must gradually and painfully give up both the delusion of his own grandeur and his belief in the omnipotence of his parents" (p. 228). Patients typically considered narcissistic personality disorders struggle more tenuously to retain the delusion of their own grandeur.

The question of why a particular person integrates his narcissistic investments in a particular mode and state of integration is as difficult to answer today as it was in 1913 when Freud grappled with the question of why "this or that person must fall ill of a particular neurosis and of none other'' (p. 317). In 1937 Freud explored the question he had raised in 1913:

> The aetiology of every neurotic disturbance is, after all, a mixed one. It is a question either of the instincts being excessively strong—that is to say, recalcitrant to taming by the ego—or of the effects of early (i.e. premature) traumas which the immature ego was unable to master. As a rule there is a combination of both factors, the constitutional and the accidental. The stronger the constitutional factor, the more readily will a trauma lead to a fixation and leave behind a developmental disturbance [p. 220].

The answer to the question why some toddlers are more compelled than others to pursue investments of narcissistic perfection for their self-representations while being more reluctant to accept the limits of the self and the object is to be found in some combination of ''constitutional and accidental'' factors.

Freud (1937) emphasized individual constitutional differences that significantly influence the fate of every analysand: ''Each ego is endowed from the first with individual dispositions and trends'' (p. 240). Weil (1970) defined these dispositions as ''the basic core'' (p. 442) and described and elaborated them with data obtained by the direct observation of infants. This core significantly influences a toddler's experience of the quality of his object world. Weil elaborated a spectrum of inherited dispositions and proposed three types of basic cores: Type A (healthy), Type B[1] (hyperactive), and Type B[2] (hypoactive). The Type B[1] infant has a ''very low threshold and is extremely hyperactive'' (p. 447). ''Excitability implies an imbalance between the protective barrier and the infant's capacity to deal with and integrate stimuli'' (p. 449). Mahler (1971) states that ''optimal maternal availability'' (p. 410) is helpful in facilitating the toddler's progression through the rapprochement crisis. Weil (1970) had emphasized that an ''ordinary devoted'' (p. 446) mother's capacity for responsiveness may be strained by a toddler who is born with a hyperactively imbalanced basic core. Such an infant may more tenaciously pursue his mother's "attention and participation" (Mahler, Pine, and Bergman, 1975, p. 228) and more defiantly resist integration of the painful perceptions of limits implicit in the rapprochement crisis. Type B^1 infants who are serendipitously nurtured by exceptionally available, empathic mothers may have a better chance of negotiating a stormy rapprochement crisis and of developing a more normal character integration. Family legends about how difficult a particular analysand was as an infant or toddler and about how his mother felt about him at that stage of development may prove useful in the reconstruction of why a particular analysand became a narcissistic personality disorder.

In addition to possibly possessing such constitutional factors, most patients typically considered narcissistic personality disorders have experienced some actual significant disappointment in one or both parents. Their disappointments are usually of a more serious nature than those experienced by neurotics. This generalization can be helpful in understanding this group of patients. With any given individual, disappointment may be negotiated without impairment and may even occasionally contribute to an exceptional adaptation. Constitutional differences, as well as compensating fortunate events, may contribute to a less serious response in any individual case. Why a person becomes what he is remains uncertain. Nevertheless it is important to emphasize the nature of the real disappointments that these patients have often experienced. These disappointments may be referrable to a disorder in the quality of maternal or paternal relatedness as well as to some specific parental failure or disappointment.

Disorders in maternal relatedness—ranging from self-involved hostility through cold, extractive narcissistic investment to unrealistic, adulating, indulgent, excessively gratifying involvement—may serve as phase-inappropriate disappointments. Fluctuating and inconsistent maternal, and paternal, relatedness is common, and it is my impression that corporal limit-setting is common. In addition, parents' pleasure in humiliating is not an uncommon real experience of a number of "typical" narcissistic personality disorders. The traumatic quality of the parental objects' personalities can make a subject's experience of normal developmental narcissistic injuries—that is, the perception of separateness, the limits of socialization in general, and toilet training and the oedipal situation in particular—more intensely felt. Specific events, such as a father's leaving to fight in a war, his death by suicide or natural causes, or his failure in marriage or business, can serve as a traumatizing nidus to the organization of a narcissistic personality disorder. Those maternal disappointments that contribute a serious formative hindrance to early ego development often result in more serious ego impairment of a borderline or psychotic nature. Cases in which the predominant disappointment was in the father and/or which occurred in later phases of development (oedipal, latency, and even adolescence) usually have more integrated egos and may have experienced a regressive dedifferentiation of their superego and ego-ideal structuralizations that resulted in a narcissistic personality disorder. Many cases have experienced both kinds of disappointments.

It is important to stress that each patient has had a variety of disappointing experiences, associated with painful, frightening, and often disorganizing affects. For example, a mother's unempathic self-involvement during her toddler's rapprochement subphase confronts the toddler with the perception of her unavailability. This perception is associated with acute feelings of anxiety and rage. Mother's chronic unavailability leaves her child feeling lonely, depressed, and perhaps anxiously empty. Father's failure during his son's oedipal or latency phase may stimulate feelings of rage. The chronic perception of father's impotence stimulates feelings of guilt, castration anxiety, sorrow, and disappointment. A father's premature death can leave his son feeling a limitless depression and longing as well as an anxiety derived from his identification with a dead man. Father's death terrifyingly and prematurely confronts a boy with his mortality.

Such experiences contribute to an intensely ambivalent attitude toward one or both parents. Rage is frequently repressed or is expressed in displaced and subtly sexualized sadistic fantasies, attitudes, and activities. This rage is a response to festering disappointment. They struggle with wishes for revenge, with wishes to undo their traumatic disappointment, as well as with fantasies of creating a world for themselves within which they will never again be vulnerable to a recapitulation of their formative disappointment. The content of a particular quest for narcissistic perfection often derives defensively from such a traumatic disappointment. If the subject can be perfect in a particular way, he will not be disappointed or will not suffer the fate of the disappointing parent with whom he is identified.

Rage at the disappointing parent or parents may contribute to the development of a character trait of defiance. Freud (1917) noted that defiance was the result of a "narcissistic clinging to anal erotism" (p. 130), adding that "as a rule, infants do not dirty strangers" (p. 130). Defiance is reflective of an underlying disorder in superego integration. Because the parent is experienced as disappointing and not admirable, the superego structuralization is relatively deficient of sublimated homosexual libido (Freud, 1914, p. 96) or of a loving investment in the object representations from which it is derived. The superego is perceived as a vengeful, frustrating implementor of limits. This leaves these patients feeling that limits exist only because of the malevolence of the frustrator. Even death, the ultimate limit, is anthropomorphized in this manner. The subject has the fantasy that he can maintain narcissistic perfection for his self-representation if he just can beat the external frustrator.

Although a variety of affective signals can provoke narcissistic investments, these patients all struggle with anxiety that heralds the destruction of their self-representation. The toddler is enraged at his mother in response to the frustrations implicit in his state of separateness. He feels his mother is to blame for this state of affairs, and when she is destroyed in fantasy for it, the toddler anticipates her retaliation. Such ubiquitous developmental events have been more intensely felt in patients typically considered narcissistic personality disorders because of the quality of their basic cores, the personalities of their parents, and/or the exigencies of their lives. As a generalization, mothers of patients typically considered narcissistic personality disorders were angrier at their children for frustrating them than were mothers of subjects who developed normal or neurotic character integrations. The actual angry nature of the maternal object intensifies the toddler's fear of being separate and his fear of maternal retaliation. The toddler's rage in response to the limits implicit in his state of separateness is reinforced and exaggerated by his perception that his mother also resents his separate existence. She would like him to exist to gratify her. Because his individuation elicits her anger, it intensifies the anxiety the subject experiences in the process of separating. These perceptions and the feelings they elicit contribute to the elaboration of the separation-individuation processes as self-destructive murderous acts by these toddlers. They are convinced that the rage these processes of differentiation stimulate will destroy their mothers and themselves. Subsequent frustrations are associatively experienced as recapitulations of the original separation experience.

There are three often observed, noteworthy characteristics of these patients' elaborations of their separation experience as a fantasied act of self-destructive murder. First, these subjects do not clearly distinguish between fantasy and action. They behave as if thinking will imminently be translated into action. If they perceive themselves or their objects feeling angry, they are convinced annihilating physical violence will ensue. Second, these self-destructive fantasies of murder are done and undone. Representatives are killed, but they are just as quickly revivified by virtue of their primary process investment. Third, the fear of imminent retaliation is reinforced by their frequent formative experience of parents who actually lost control. Their parents' penchant for physically expressing their anger influences these patients to believe that feelings really are dangerous.

In defense against the threatened destruction of their representational world (a self- and object-loss anxiety [Freud, 1926, pp. 137–138]), these subjects attempt to remove frustrations and to restore a sense of narcissistic perfection to their self-representations. This restoration serves to create the illusion that there are and will be no frustrations and/or that the self-representation is safe from the murderous rage of the parental introject.

Any frustration reminds the subject that the sense of narcissistic perfection has been lost. The sense of perfection is constructed of narcissistically invested self, object, and self-object memory traces. Any narcissistic injury stimulates separation anxiety because it heralds the dedifferentiation of the narcissistically invested structures that derive from percepts of these representations. Narcissistic rage is a secondary defensive response that attempts to find someone or something that can be blamed for the insulting loss of perfection. This rage is analogous to the rage the toddler felt toward his mother in response to his original perception of the limits of his emerging self-representation. The anxiety deriving from fear of destroying the object, and fear of the object's retaliation, may provoke other defensive efforts to deny the injury or to restore a sense of narcissistic perfection to the subject's self-representation. When structured, narcissistically invested defenses are prominent, often central, features of an individual's character organization, he is designated a "typical" narcissistic personality disorder. If these defenses function, the subject feels safe.

This discussion has stressed preoedipal factors in the genesis of narcissistic defenses and narcissistic personality disorders. Preoedipal factors and fixations are the *elemental* building blocks of all narcissistic structures. However, oedipal factors can significantly influence a subject's pursuit of narcissistic perfection for his self-representation. For example, a paternal failure may evoke fear of paternal retaliation and intensify a boy's castration anxiety.[2] Such a situation may contribute to a boy's motivation to strive to acquire phallic-narcissistic perfection for his self-representation.

Annie Reich (1960) has defined these patients' ego ideals as "crudely sexual" (p. 128). There is a spectrum of arrested ego-ideal development that can be correlated with the arrest in the integration of these patients' narcissism. Sicker narcissistic personality disorders are devoid of an ego ideal in the traditional sense of the word (Freud, 1914). They do not delegate narcissistic perfection to their ego ideals. Instead their superegos are devoid of abstraction and remain fixated upon concrete self- and object representations. Their ego ideals are similarly composed and fixated upon distinct, cohesive, archaically and narcissistically invested self-representations (Sandler and Rosenblatt's "ideal self-image," Kohut's "grandiose self") and upon distinct cohesive, archaically and narcissistically invested object representations (Kohut's "idealized parent imago"). There they exist as standards for their actual self-representations. Their egos engage in activities that can be conceptualized as attempts at identification with their archaically and narcissistically invested self- and object representations. If the subject can be like his narcissistically invested self- and object representations, he momentarily feels he has restored a sense of his original narcissistic perfection to his actual self-representation. Thus imbued he feels safe from the traumas that left him fixated at this level of structural development.

Most, if not all, cases are associated with a very significant,

[2] Annie Reich (1960) has emphasized these patients' "unbearable castration fears" (p. 218), their need to ward-off "feeling[s] of catastrophic annihilation" (p. 224), and their equation of castration with object loss (p. 223). Her important work emphasizes the relationship between castration anxiety and anxiety that portends the destruction of the self-representation, as well as the association of phallic conflicts with formative "pregenital losses and injuries" (p. 223) frequently experienced by these patients.

and often strongly repressed, homosexual transference potential and feminine identification. This is influenced by a number of factors. It reflects the often unresolved nature of their oedipal situations. For example, to compensate for a traumatic disappointment in his father, a male narcissistic personality disorder may long for an admirable father to love and be loved by; in addition, the sought-for father to love will compensate for the formative disappointment in maternal relatedness. Finally, homosexual negative oedipal strivings may defend against castration anxiety derived from a seductive, excessively stimulating, positive oedipal experience. A similar situation may be described in female narcissistic personality disorders.

The orientation of the narcissistic personality disorder toward himself and his object world often does not permit him to seek help with the same kind of self-awareness and motivation for change which is found more frequently in well-organized neurotics. The narcissistic personality disorder commonly seeks analytic help because his personality organization is no longer able to maintain a view of himself as perfect. Therefore, it is no longer able to maintain the flow of narcissistic supply and its resulting narcissistic equilibrium. The patients who *seem* to have the best prognosis are those who have some awareness that their system does not bring them happiness and who, therefore, would like to change. However, this is never a pure motivation and they simultaneously wish the analyst would somehow restore their narcissistic equilibrium. The kind of motivation we would like to see is usually only observable after significant analytic work. A related point is that since acting-up is a characteristic of these personality disorders, acting-out will be an inevitable component of successful analytic work with many of them.

Significant analytic work facilitates an integration of the defensive nature of these narcissistically imbued pursuits. This increases a tolerance for threatening situations and the painful, frightening, and disorganizing affects associated with them. It allows an analysand to gain some distance from his imperative use of objects, resulting in an increased motivation for growth and analytic work. Ultimately it permits an integration of the relative passivity, helplessness, and vulnerability implicit in the human condition, allowing these analysands a greater potential to experience intimacy and love. These issues will be elaborated and commented upon with reference to the question of analyzability of narcissistic personality disorders in chapter 5.

PREOEDIPAL VS. OEDIPAL FACTORS

There is a significant controversy about the importance of phallic-oedipal versus pregenital or preoedipal fixations in the genesis of these character disorders. Kernberg and Kohut stress the importance of the former. For Kernberg, the postseparation traumatic quality of the maternal object results in a regressive refusion of self- and object representations. Kohut (1971) emphasizes the importance of the *"personality* of the parents (especially the mother)'' (p. 65).

Both preoedipal and oedipal factors are, however, important in the genesis of these disorders and there are a number of cases in which oedipal factors are of major importance. In all cases, the interplay of the subject's basic core and the personality of the preoedipal maternal object results in ''a point of fixation'' to which the ''function may regress'' (Freud, 1913, p. 318). Mahler, Pine, and Bergman (1975) emphasized the importance of preoedipal fixations on the emerging oedipal experience: ''The infantile neurosis becomes manifestly visible at the oedipal period; but it may be shaped by the fate of the rapprochement crisis *that precedes it*'' (p. 230). The rapprochement crisis is associated with an emerging stability of the representational world. It is probable that defensive attempts to restore a sense of narcissistic perfection to the self-representation are significantly influenced by these differentiations. The original fixation point can be correlated with these structuralizations. In more disturbed narcissistic personality disorders, this fixation may result in an alteration of the ego that profoundly interferes with all subsequent development. There are, however, a number of healthier patients considered narcissistic personality disorders whose "fixation point" is less distorting to ego development. Their pursuits of narcissistic perfection for their self-representations, while always associatively linked to the original fixation point, are significantly, if not definitively, influenced by later events.

In every case, preoedipal, oedipal, even postoedipal factors *can* all significantly influence the subject's pursuit of illusions of narcissistic perfection for his self-representation. All influences need to be analyzed. The emergence of one or another trend can represent both a valid focus for analytic exploration, as well as a resistance. I have seen a number of cases in which the traumatic nature of the oedipal situation left a profound impact on the subject's character organization. In three cases the male analysand's father had died suddenly (one from suicide when the analysand was five years old and two from natural causes during these patients' latency and adolescence, respectively). In another case, the parents separated when the analysand was four years old. In each of these cases the subject experienced significant disappointment in his father. This interfered with superego and ego-ideal structuralization, resulting in a dedifferentiation of these structures and regressive pursuits of narcissistic perfection for the self-representation. These pursuits can be conceptualized as multiply motivated. First, anxiety derives from an identification with a dead or degraded (by mother) father. The subject believes that if he can restore a sense of narcissistic perfection to his self-representation, he will be safe from death and/or mother's denigration (which he may believe killed his father). Second, castration anxiety derives from fear of retaliation by a regressively elicited, archaically and narcissistically invested paternal object representation structured as an introject within "self-as-place." Third, there is a wish to bring father back to life. The loss of the paternal object at later stages of development is linked to the loss of the object associated with emergence from the symbiotic phase. Fourth, there is a wish to repeat the gratifying (confusing and

frightening) experience of winning mother who was often seductively overvaluing of the child and subtly (or not so subtly)
devaluing of her husband. The issue of the role of oedipal factors
in the genesis of narcissistic personality disorders will be elaborated in chapter 3.

Kohut (1971) would not place as great an emphasis on the
influence of these traumatic events. In reflecting upon the factors
that influence the genesis of such character disorders, he stated:

> The interplay between inherited psychological propensities and
> the *personality* of the parents (especially of the mother) is of
> vastly greater importance than the interplay between hereditary
> factors and gross traumatic *events* (such as the absence or death
> of a parent), unless the gross external factors and the parents'
> personality disturbances are related (as, for example, when
> there is divorce of the parents, or in the case of a parent's
> absence due to mental illness or of his or her loss due to suicide
> [p. 65].

Kohut conceptualizes traumatic loss as functioning primarily to
deprive the child "of the chance of freeing himself from the
enmeshment through the gradual withdrawal of narcissistic cathexes" (p. 82).

I am in basic agreement with Kohut that the personality of
the parents (particularly the mother) is probably the single most
important factor in most cases in the genesis of a narcissistic
personality disorder. The difference presented in this chapter is
a difference of emphasis. The four patients alluded to above all
had parents whose personalities were less than optimal. Their
mothers' narcissistic investment in them as "His Majesty the
Baby" was excessive. They were treated as phallic-narcissistic
objects to undo their mothers' sense of want. Three of the four
were first-born or only children. Their fathers' relationships to
them were less than optimal; the fathers' personalities certainly
left much to be desired. Nevertheless, loss of the father was an

acute trauma that these children's egos were ill equipped to integrate. Their immature egos were unable to mourn (Wolfenstein) this loss. This fact profoundly influenced the effect of the loss on their development. It potentiated a disruption of processes of internalization associated with superego structuralization, and it intensified their castration anxiety. Kohut's (1971) emphasis on preoedipal factors and on the formative influence of the parents' personalities results in what I believe is a somewhat one-sided perspective. These acute traumas are presented as no more than interferences to processes of "transmuting, structure-forming internalization" (p. 82). He stated:

> The period which follows the sudden interruption (through an external event) of a child's chronic narcissistic enmeshment with a pathological parent is indeed crucial. It may determine whether the child will make a renewed effort toward maturational progress or whether the pathogenic fixation will now become ingrained. The absence or loss of the pathological parent may be a wholesome liberation if the child's libidinal resources enable him to move forward and, especially if the other parent, or a parent substitute with a special empathic interest in the threatened child, jumps quickly into the breach and permits a temporary re-establishment of the narcissistic relationship as well as its subsequent gradual dissolution [p. 82].

These traumatic events are more than losses of an opportunity to facilitate the development of "idealizing libido." Even in the best of situations they represent profoundly important object losses with very significant dynamic and structural consequences. The loss of a parent or of an intact family need not necessarily result in serious distortions of character development. The effects of such an event can be compensated for, to some significant degree, by a parental surrogate and development can proceed. However, these losses are real and cannot be undone. The specific dynamic meanings of the loss, as well as the mourning of the lost object, are important subjects for analytic exploration and working through in patients typically considered narcissistic personality disorders.

Most neurotic patients have been more fortunate. Their basic cores, their parents' personalities, and/or the exigencies of their lives have better facilitated their ego development. Their healthier ego-ideal development derives, in part, from having had admirable parents whose representations could sustain a delegation of their original narcissistic perfection. Although a patient with a neurotic narcissistic personality disorder strives to recapture illusions of narcissistic perfection for his self-representation, he does so to a lesser degree. His ego strives to integrate these pursuits with his abstract, depersonified ego ideal as well as within the constraints of his reality. The success of such effort is associated not only with a sense of safety, but also with a more modulated sense of well-being and self-worth. It is worth noting that neurotics are predominantly motivated by castration anxiety and/or superego anxiety.

THE "NORMAL" NARCISSISTIC PERSONALITY

Kernberg (1975) quite correctly adds the qualification "who come for treatment" (p. 333) to his statement that his second group of narcissistic personalities is the type most commonly seen in his practice. It is possible that the population of an author's practice potentiates one or another view of the distribution of various integrations within a diagnostic category. Few, if any, analysts see many patients they would diagnose normal. Yet, in agreement with, and in extension of, Freud (1914), Wilhelm Reich (1933), and Kohut (1971), it is a premise of this book that modes of narcissistic investment are ubiquitous and that what is different is the prevalence of one or another mode and its state of integration. Therefore, sketches of a normal narcissistic personality disorder and a normal suppliant personality disorder seem indicated. As has been noted, one might object to this diagnostic designation finding it contradictory. One might ask, ''How can one be 'normal' and 'disordered?' '' This apparent contradiction is something of a paradox. Most, if not all, human beings distort their perception of themselves in relationship to reality. Their pursuit of illusions of narcissistic perfection in one or another mode contributes to that distortion, and it is this ubiquitous potential that the term *disorder* emphasizes.

Normal narcissistic personality disorders and normal suppliant personality disorders reflect the predominance of one or another mode of investment within a normal ego organization. Normal narcissistic personality disorders are more self-involved and interested in their own aggrandizement than are normal suppliant personality disorders. Simultaneously, they enjoy relatively rich, full, object-related lives often pursuing the narcissistic aggrandizement of their self-representation in a humanistic, object-related context. Their superegos are relatively tolerant and realistic, while their ego ideals and egos are both tolerant of their realistic limits and capable of facilitating considerable degrees of sublimation.

The normal suppliant personality disorder is less interested in self-aggrandizement. He or she is usually more interested in the aggrandizement of a superior, institution, or cause. The sense of narcissistic fulfillment comes from gaining a sense of synchrony with the ego ideal. They may recapture some sense of narcissistic perfection for their self-representation by achieving a position of some power and responsibility within an organization or movement.

This chapter has reviewed the relevant contributions to the theory of narcissism in order to clarify the diagnostic category narcissistic personality disorder. The definition of narcissistic personality disorder presented here attempts to elucidate this heuristically valuable diagnostic designation while preserving an appreciation of the ubiquitous nature of narcissism in the ''character'' of the ego. Narcissistic personality disorders are defined by their preferred *mode* of attempting to restore a sense of narcissistic perfection to their self-representation and by the *state of integration* of narcissism by their egos. This definition, proposed in the framework of a classification of narcissism within the ''character'' of the ego, is intended to complement other diagnostic considerations that reflect non-narcissistic issues.

3

Entitlement, Self-Destructiveness, and the Fear of Humiliation

This chapter focuses clinically upon three character traits frequently encountered in narcissistic personality disorders: their ego attitude of entitlement,[1] their self-destructiveness and their fear of humiliation. These often dynamically interrelated characteristics contribute a chaotic quality to such subjects' lives in general and their analyses in particular—analyses aimed at facilitating the "assimilation" of the multiplicity and alternation of irrational motives in their lives. Since most recent authors have stressed, I believe to an excessive degree, the preoedipal determinants of these issues, oedipal factors will be emphasized in this explication in order to redress this imbalance and stress the multidetermined nature of the genetics and dynamics of these character constellations.

Narcissistic personality disorders feel entitled to have what they want when they want it just because they want it. What they want is often narcissistically invested. They feel entitled to pursue it, no matter how they do so or whom they hurt. The foundations

[1] Levin (1970) distinguishes between excessive, normal, and restricted entitlement. I use the term *entitlement* here as Levin used *excessive entitlement*. Applying this term solely to its pathological excesses allows for greater clarity.

67

of this defensive ego attitude, employed especially against painful, affectively laden perceptions, are internalizations that derive
from the quality of the primary caretaking object (usually the
mother). This internalization of the self-as-agent receives rein-
forcement and/or regressive revivification by subsequent life
events. The oedipal constellation, particularly the nature of the
relationship with the negative oedipal object, may be important
in the genesis of this character trait in selected narcissistic personality disorders.

Guilt in response to oral, cannibalistic rage at the frustration
of the narcissistic personality disorder's sense of entitlement is
commonly defended against—and therefore not consciously experienced—by processes of externalization. This preoedipal,
"edible" guilt, together with oedipal factors, contributes to the
narcissistic personality disorder's self-destructiveness. The pursuit of perfection, coupled with a penchant for experiencing limits
as humiliations, often causes such patients to risk more than is
prudent and frequently results in calamity. Limits are typically
felt to be imposed by harsh frustrators who force the subject to
passively submit. A limit may be experienced as a passive, homosexual submission associated with intense castration anxiety. In
defiant flight from the active frustrating aggressor, the subject
insists upon pursuing behavior that in reality is self-destructive.
In so doing, he proclaims that he has not submitted. Such self-
destructive tendencies function, in part, to preserve the subject's
sense of perfection for the self-representation. A frustration or
limit to the self-representation is thus not perceived as inevitable,
but as passively endured at the hands of a frustrator. A representation of this sado-narcissistically invested, malevolent, archaically elaborated frustrator is structured as an introject in self-
as-place. A maladaptive variant of an "identification with the
aggressor" (A. Freud, 1936) takes place, as does a resultant split[2]

---

[2] This resultant split in the self-representation is a fundamental aspect of
masochistic phenomena. These processes and their relationship to narcissism
are discussed in more detail on pp. 125, 128-129 of *The Structural Hypothesis:
An Evolutionary Perspective* (A. Rothstein, 1983).

in the self-representation. The subject experiences annihilation anxiety in response to the perceived limit, but rather than be passively destroyed, the self-as-agent identifies with the frustrator and imposes the frustration on the self-as-object. This identification momentarily restores an illusion of narcissistic perfection to the self-as-agent. When the constellation is oedipal, the self-as-agent identifies with a regressively revivified superego precursor that is similarly structured in self-as-place and implements a punishment on the self-as-object.

A number of narcissistic personality disorders have experienced confusing and contradictory oedipal situations that were simultaneously and/or alternatingly gratifying, frightening, and disappointing. Such experiences strain even exceptional "assimilative" capacities. When a narcissistic personality disorder experiences a relatively positive oedipal victory, tainted by a serious disappointment in the negative oedipal object, this situation contributes to disorders of ego-ideal (A. Reich, 1960) and superego structuralization that are characterized by intrasystemic conflict and a penchant for defensive externalization. The oedipal constellation remains active and unresolved, characterized by a spectrum of feelings—elation, intense castration anxiety, and guilt, as well as disappointment in their negative oedipal object and hunger for a victorious, admirable negative oedipal figure.

Although I have stressed the dynamic relatedness of the narcissistic personality disorder's ego attitude of entitlement, self-destructiveness, and fear of humiliation, these factors will be explored separately here for heuristic purposes. Such a separation parallels aspects of these subject's analytic experience. Most sessions and periods of the analysis focus on one or another of these factors, while particular sessions are more synthetic, facilitating the analysand's integration of the over-determined nature of his experiences.

ENTITLEMENT

An understanding of the genesis of the ego attitude of entitlement can help in analyzing its defensive elaborations. Often these patients are successful in work and play and come to analysis because of difficulties in their ability to love other human beings. Analysis of their ego attitude of entitlement can facilitate their attaining greater tolerance for the object and enable them to experience more significant degrees of intimacy. As long as they feel entitled, the object is viewed as existing only to gratify them. If they can slowly mourn this attitude of self, they become progressively more able to experience the object as separate and to tolerate desires on the part of the object that do not complement their own.

The entitled subject feels he should get what he wants. Those who do not feel free to coerce the world to respond to their inner percepts are depressed when they are frustrated. These subjects are narcissistic personality disorders with a neurotic integration of their sense of entitlement. Patients more typically referred to as narcissistic often feel freer to manipulate the object world to conform to their representation of how it should be. When frustrated, these patients are more often enraged than depressed. They are enraged at the frustrator, but may become depressed if they are unable to remove the frustration.

What vicissitudes of early development result in distortions of self-as-agent, leaving it with a feeling of entitlement? How much is the ego attitude of entitlement subject related, that is, related to a maturational sequence? To what extent is it object related, that is, influenced by the quality of mothering? Certainly, there is a spectrum of biologic endowments, a range of "basic cores" (Weil, 1970). In the language of psychoanalysis, this translates to the intensity of drive and its relationship to the organizing capacities of the primordial ego. The infant endowed with a more intense drive must feel a greater discomfort, or tension, as discharge gratification is awaited. It is as if the primordial self-as-agent were a blank sheet to be written on by the experience of one's biologic self—the increasing discomfort or tension of drive discharge demands in relationship to the qualities of early mothering.

The gratifying moments when a child is being overvalued provide the experiences which serve as the anlage for the feeling of entitlement. Such early preindividuated, parental attitudes are incorporated into the germinal self-as-agent. Freud (1914) aptly characterized them in *On Narcissism:*

> The child shall have a better time than his parents; he shall not be subject to the necessities which they have recognized as paramount in life. Illness, death, renunciation of enjoyment, restrictions on his own will, shall not touch him; the laws of nature and society shall be abrogated in his favour; he shall once more really be the centre and core of creation—'His Majesty the Baby', as we once fantasied ourselves [p. 91].

In order for the infant to develop without a defensive view of self-as-agent as entitled he must appropriately separate: "The dominance of the pleasure principle can really come to an end only when a child has achieved complete psychical detachment from its parents" (Freud, 1911b, p. 220n).

The appropriate weaning of the narcissistic position, thus preventing the development of the defensive ego attitude of entitlement, requires parents with a capacity for empathic relatedness, who have integrated the limitations in their lives, including their finiteness. In *On Narcissism,* however, Freud (1914) referred to parents' nonintegration of their own limitations as a ubiquitous motivation for their investment of the infant as a narcissistic object and his endowment as "His Majesty the Baby":

> The child shall fulfil those wishful dreams of the parents which they never carried out—the boy shall become a great man and a hero in his father's place, and the girl shall marry a prince as a tardy compensation for her mother. At the most touchy point in the narcissistic system, the immortality of the ego, which is so hard pressed by reality, security is achieved by taking refuge in the child [p. 91].

Freud emphasized here the ubiquitous nature of parents' narcissistic investment in their children. It is a premise of this work, however, that the degree to which the infant is treated as a narcissistic object significantly influences the tenacity with which he attempts to retain his imagined entitled position as "His Majesty the Baby." When this phase-appropriate narcissistic investment is excessive, for whatever reasons, there is a greater potential for the subject to struggle to retain his crown.

There is a spectrum of disappointment resulting from the quality of parenting. A mother may be hostile, cold, and rejecting at one moment, while at another she may be overvaluing of her narcissistically invested object. The infant subject internalizes memory traces of those gratifying moments into self-as-agent; they form the core of the ego attitude of entitlement and defend against reawakening of memories of painful and frightening responses to mother's hostility and self-involvement.

The preceding discussion dealt with some of the factors of preindividuated experience that influence the degree of narcissistic fixation and the corresponding strength of the ego attitude of entitlement. However, overvaluing parental attitudes often continue and influence the ongoing development of distortions within the self system. I will now elaborate factors that interfere with separation-individuation—and the concomitant relinquishment of feelings of specialness—as well as factors that result in a regressive reactivation of the attitude of entitlement.

Easser (1974), Kernberg, (1967), Kohut (1966, 1968, 1971, 1972), Murray (1964), and, implicitly, Mahler (1971) have all emphasized the importance of less-than-optimal maternal availability in the genesis of narcissistic character pathology. A number of problems of maternal relatedness are subsumed under the rubric of maternal availability (see Mahler, 1971, p. 410). Mothers may be unempathic, cold, hostile, anxious, or overinvolved and excessively gratifying. Often mothers are inconsistent and alternate between one or another of these attitudes. What seems similar in all less-than-optimal situations is that the relationship to the child is not motivated by a wish to nurture in a phase-appropriate manner, but rather seems to be more self-oriented. All these patients have experienced moments of being overvalued by their mothers as narcissistic objects. A representation of an endowing and overvaluing smile is internalized within self-as-agent. Structured there, it forms the core of a sense of omnipotently endowed entitlement. "Optimal maternal availability" implies a mother's propensity to respond with a phase-appropriate balance of frustration and gratification (Mahler, Pine, and Bergman, 1975). A mother who relates to her child primarily out of her own needs is more likely to engender defensive attitudes of self. The quality of her unavailability and of the subject's post-individuated experiences with other objects within the family influence these developing attitudes of self.

Mothers who engender an ego attitude of entitlement use the child to fill an inner void. Appropriate behavior by the child fills the mother with positive feelings. She smiles at him and infuses him with correspondingly gratifying affects. This contributes to a feeling of prolonged fusion between mother and child. The greater the maternal object's narcissistic investment, the more painful will be the loss of the fusion experience. At times, the toddler feels excessively gratified; at others, when the mother is unempathic and self-involved, he feels disorganizing anxiety.[3] When the child cannot narcissistically gratify his mother, she will be disinterested and/or depressed; the child will feel enraged and alone, humiliated and mortified at his lack of power to stimulate her interest. He is enraged with this frustrating, narcissistic, unempathic bad mother and would like to chew her up.

The individuating toddler confronted with one or another aspect of disordered maternal availability disavows the perception and defends against it and the resulting intense anxiety and rage

[3] A description of the quality of the toddler's affective state is at best an approximation of what he actually experiences. These descriptions are based on analytic reconstruction as well as on direct observation of infants and toddlers.

that threaten to disorganize his immature ego with the defenses of denial and denial in fantasy. He denies his perception of the unrelated, frustrating aspects of the maternal object. His developing attitude of entitlement is a fantasy that facilitates the denial by reassuring the subject that he will find an all-gratifying, narcissistically invested maternal object. This attitude is expressed by the feeling that all objects should conform to his wishes for pleasure. Any perception to the contrary has to be defended against or the result is depression.

The attitude of entitlement protects him from the humiliating narcissistic injury that he cannot control mother. It defends him from the realization that mother cannot love him for himself, but rather that she loves him primarily as a reflection of herself. At this early stage of development, the child's ego attitude of entitlement defends him against his rage at his mother's lack of relatedness, and against his perception of his inability to change her. It also defends against the disorganizing object-loss anxiety and secondary depression implicit in the feeling that mother is absent when she is not gratified. Entitlement helps maintain a split that interferes with the integration of the angry disappointment felt in the unrelated aspects of his experience of his mother. This split interferes with what Freud called "psychical detachment" and what we today call separation-individuation. For people who feel entitled, any frustration is perceived as a loss of the self-object bliss which their defensive ego attitude of entitlement attempts to preserve.

All frustrations are perceived by the toddler as a self-object differentiation. The resulting anxiety, when intense, is experienced as a "catastrophic annihilation" anxiety (A. Reich, 1960, p. 224)[4] signaling the ego that the integrity of the self is threatened. Such experiences are frequently related in metaphors of death and are associated with rage, humiliation, and depression. The ego attitude of entitlement defends against these painful feel-

---

[4] For a more detailed discussion of the anxiety of patients typically considered narcissistic personality disorders, see pp. 54–56.

ings. The child hungers for fusion experiences with an all-good mother, and the ego attitude of entitlement maintains the view that that is what the object world owes him. The analytic task is to help these patients integrate and accept the inevitability of frustration as part of the fabric of life rather than as a symbolic threat to their existence. Frustrations are experienced as life-threatening assaults because they challenge the integrity of the entitled self-as-agent. As the attitude is assimilated, the self-representation that feels entitled is transmuted and the inevitability of frustration is integrated.

The development of frustration tolerance is profoundly influenced by the quality of parental relatedness. Of particular importance is the quality of limit-setting experiences, especially the parental rage expressed in these interactions. This development is, however, also influenced by a number of primary, autonomous ego functions. The biologic intensity of the id and the integrity of those primarily autonomous components of the primordial ego influence the quality of the subject's pursuit of gratification from the object, as well as his experience of its frustration. It is a well-known clinical fact that a small percentage of individuals seem to be able to tolerate very significant degrees of early deprivation and still develop well.

As the child separates, he more clearly perceives the distinction between self and object. The object is the frustrator. If the parent's lack of relatedness manifests itself in the process of limit setting through the excessive expression of anger, corporal violence, or excessive attempts at control, the outer world is perceived as frightening. This perception may stimulate a defensive regression to a more narcissistically invested view of self as entitled that enables the subject to avoid confronting the implications of the frightening object. The frightening object may be mother or father.

If the child is left with an excessive amount of unneutralized oral aggression resulting from the interaction of his endowment with his experience of a relatively unavailable mother, the rage may be projected onto representations of the parents and influence the toddler's perception of them as more dangerous than they actually are. If the parents are frightening and employ corporal means of limit setting, the child's fantasies will be reinforced by his experience of reality. Accidents and surgical procedures may also contribute to a postindividuated perception of the world as frightening. One or all of these factors will influence the quality of oedipal castration anxiety which often contributes to a defensive regressive reactivation of these attitudes.

The narcissistic patient struggles with fluctuating affective states. When the external world seems to conform to his entitled attitude, he feels elated. This feeling recaptures memories of original experiences of narcissistic perfection. Postindividuated experiences of mother's approval of him—for his performances or simply for existing as a repository for her wishes—reinforce his feelings of specialness. Alternating with these ''highs'' are moments of anxiety and rage when his ego attitude of entitlement is frustrated by some aspect of himself (self-as-object)[5] or by the external world.

As the child develops, the father is an important source for the formation of the superego. In return for the father's love, the child relinquishes some of his omnipotent wishes and attitudes. As Freud has pointed out in *On Narcissism,* a vestige of this narcissism is preserved in the ego ideal. Representations of the father's love are structured within the ego ideal and are reexperienced when self-as-agent conforms to the standards and sanctions of the ego ideal and superego. An illusion of security is concomitant with this structuralization. If the child performs in relationship to the standards of his ego ideal and superego, he feels he will be loved and cared for.

A traumatic disappointment in a parental object may result

---

[5] The entitled subject treats the frustrating aspect of himself as if it were an external object. Self-as-agent, the ''I,'' is enraged at self-as-object and would like to rid itself of the frustrating aspect of self in order to restore a feeling of perfection to the self.

in dedifferentiation of superego structuralizations and a defensive reactivation of the ego attitude of entitlement. A father's failure in business or his death may serve as such a disappointment. During superego formation, the child delegates some of his omnipotence to his ego ideal and to representations of his father. These perceptions of his father as strong and as capable of surviving fuel identifications with the father. Emulating the father invokes the illusions and promise of survival. If a major insult occurs to this ongoing identificatory process prior to a firm and independent identity formation, a defensive narcissistic regression may occur. In the absence of a respectable and admirable paternal representation, the boy regresses to primordial grandiose views of self and the associated attitude of entitlement.

A particular kind of behavior is not uncommon among fathers of entitled individuals. These fathers, often failures in their own or their wives' eyes, nevertheless, felt entitled. They were often angry and jealous of the children's untainted futures; they themselves would have liked to start again and envied their children's more age-appropriate expressions of narcissism. These fathers often set inconsistent and insincere standards, so that their children experienced them as saying, "Do as I say, not as I do." The superego is an important modulator of narcissistic equilibrium. In the absence of idealized representations, the mourning of entitled attitudes is impaired. Anger at father may fuel defiant maintenance of these attitudes. Simultaneously, maternal preference for the child as a narcissistic object and denigration of the husband may reinforce the child's disappointment in his father and his own feelings of specialness.

In *Some Character-Types Met With in Psycho-Analytic Work,* Freud (1916) described as "exceptions" people who would not "submit" to "the doctor's guidance . . . to make the advance from the pleasure principle to the reality principle by which the mature human being is distinguished from the child" (p. 312). He postulated that the particular motivation for this character resistance was that "their neuroses were connected with some experience or suffering to which they had been subjected in their earliest childhood, one in respect of which they knew themselves to be guiltless, and which they could look upon as an unjust disadvantage imposed upon them.'' His two examples were of a woman suffering from a painful organic illness of congenital origin and a young man who was ''the victim of an accidental infection from his wet-nurse'' (p. 313). Freud stressed that the injustice was felt to be the result of a chance event and that the subjects' feelings of specialness derived from their experiencing the handicap as unjust.

Two clinical situations seem to contradict that premise. First, there are individuals with handicaps who mature without a distorted view of self as entitled. Second, there are many narcissistic patients who have not suffered an obvious unjust event yet, nevertheless, feel entitled to be treated as exceptions. A premise of this book is that the quality of early mothering is most responsible for the defensive attitude of self referred to as the ego attitude of entitlement. In my work with deaf children and adolescents, I have been impressed with the fact that they do not all see themselves as exceptions entitled to special privilege. Those who do have usually been experienced by their parents as a narcissistic injury to their own capacity to produce a normal, or even exceptional, child.[6] These parents have also been deprived of a repository for their narcissistic fantasies. Such parents are often enraged; in an attempt to defend against this rage, they treat their damaged child as special and attempt to spare him frustration. The child is often enraged at his parents who he feels should have omnipotently spared him his fate. He feels cheated and treated unfairly. He uses that feeling, reinforced by his parents' guilt, to extractively maintain his position of special entitlement. His feeling of entitlement is related to the degree he has been treated

---

[6] The vast majority of hearing parents of deaf children learn that their children are deaf when they are older than eight months of age. This affords the child the possibility of an earlier experience of maternal overvaluation with which he can construct an ego attitude of entitlement.

as a narcissistic object by his parents. Their capacity to empathically respond to his pain is impaired in direct relation to their investment of him as a narcissistic object.

The deformed child, experienced as a narcissistic injury by his parents, may be subtly rejected. The narcissistic character is rejected when he does not fulfill the narcissistic fantasies of his mother. The handicapped child thus has a concrete impairment around which he integrates his feelings of defectiveness. Many narcissistic patients experience their selves as defective and yet cannot adequately explain why. I am suggesting that this feeling is an attitude of self that is derived, in part, from internalizing the mother's narcissistically deflated or depressed, disinterested or inappropriately angry facial representation into the germinal self-as-agent. This representation of defectiveness can function as another defense against experiencing rage at mother's unavailability. The ego of the toddler is not sufficiently developed to integrate the perception that mother is in some way not optimally available; this perception would be disorganizing and would stimulate overwhelming anxiety. It is as if the subject feels, "No, mother can't be like that; it must be my fault. If I could do the right thing, if I could be perfect, then mother would love me. If mother doesn't love me it must be because I am defective."

Many male patients who struggle with an ego attitude of entitlement also feel deep mistrust and simultaneous "hunger" for women. They are often promiscuous and hypersexual. Affairs and mistresses are common to their experience. Their affairs are overdetermined and often represent symbolic enactments of oedipal crimes. From the perspective of their ego attiude of entitlement they feel entitled to pursue their hunger for a sense of unity with a maternal object. Their formative experience of painful, enraged helplessness to control their mothers' affections leads them to struggle to find the ideal woman whom they will not have to feel like killing and whose imagined destructiveness they need not fear. It is important for them to experience their fear of a woman's dissatisfaction. They often treat an angry, frustrated

woman as inscrutable and terrifying. They may feel simultaneously enraged at women and yet be unable to communicate their
feelings. The very act of communicating would violate their feeling of entitlement. They feel entitled to a woman who intuitively
perceives their wishes and who is all-gratifying. They fantasy
that, if they could find her, they could avoid their painful experience of frustration with its concomitant feelings of helplessness, anxiety, and rage.

Selected aspects of an analysis will demonstrate these issues.
Mr. C sought help in a crisis atmosphere after an impulsive second
marriage. He felt he had been intimidated into this marriage and
that he was unable to definitively terminate a relationship with
another woman.

Mr. C is a first child many years older than his only sibling.
To this day he is his mother's favorite. Although he enjoys the
gratification of his special position, he has had a growing sense
that her love is intimately related to his performance. As a toddler,
he experienced painful situations of helplessness. He remembers
being tied to a tree outside his home so his mother could ''keep
him out of her hair.'' His parents separated during the height of
his oedipal experience. He was both left alone and overstimulated
by his mother. He has pleasurable memories of sitting at her side
looking up her legs at her exposed genitals. During latency he
would crawl under tables at parties and attempt to look up
women's dresses. As an adult, he enjoys looking at a mistress
exposing her genitals.

The early years of his first marriage were relatively pleasant.
His main investment in those years was the pursuit of professional
success. His entitled view was that his wife was to put him first
in all important choices and live to support his efforts. Her view
was somewhat different. She seemed to have viewed him as a
provider who was to impregnate her and provide her with the
''finer things of life.'' Conflict was inevitable. After ten years
of marriage, he had a professional opportunity in another city.
She refused to move. He was hurt and enraged, yet he felt helpless

and unable to express his feelings. He complied with his wife's wishes despite his feeling he was entitled to something better. He lamented, "There must be a situation where I would feel better." Impelled by a spectrum of impounded painful feelings and a hunger for gratification, he pursued his quest for pleasure extramaritally. This led to his divorce and to a number of involvements.

He viewed his current marriage as a relationship that was to provide him only with pleasure. He felt entitled to it. His wife should always be available and should intuitively and enthusiastically gratify him. To have to ask for anything was depressing because it confronted him with his separateness and with the loss of his narcissistically invested view of himself. If he asked, he would have to face the possibility she might say "no." His fear of being frustrated, and of feeling enraged, impelled him to pursue his entitled position with other women.

His avoidance of asking, his fear of communicating, implicitly, his fear of women, their rage and his own, and his use of other women as a defense against these painful and frightening issues were explored analytically. This enabled him to mourn progressively his defensive view of himself as entitled and to perceive his wife more realistically as a separate object with her own needs.

His attitude of entitlement also manifested itself in the transference. He assumed that the analyst would be happy to wait for payment of his bill. If he felt like purchasing an expensive object the analyst would not mind waiting for his check. He was aghast at the suggestion he should consider the analyst's needs. He experienced the issue as simply a "cash flow problem." People and situations could be manipulated to provide him with a maximum of pleasure. As his ability to experience the analyst as more than a need-satisfying object increased, so did his ability to tolerate frustrations in other relationships. As could be expected, he felt entitled to perfect hours and to the analyst's perfect availability. The analyst should be absolutely punctual and should listen with total attentiveness. These wishes reflected the quality of his entitled expectations of those he felt were his objects. If they were perfect, he could be spared all pain. The subject who feels entitled attacks the object for its imperfections. If the frustrating object is seen as inscrutable and terrifying, a replacement is sought. The attitude of entitlement contributes to the perpetuation of this process. Since the problem is experienced as residing in the imperfections of the external object, the subject feels entitled to pursue a new object. This interferes with the ego's integrating its inevitable limits and vulnerabilities.

SELF-DESTRUCTIVENESS

Self-destructiveness is a common, but not ubiquitous, characteristic of narcissistic personality disorders. It is motivated, in part, by intense castration anxiety and parenticidal guilt. In a number of patients, these painful affective signals derive from the fact that they experienced intense and confusing oedipal situations that have remained active and unresolved. Usually, an aspect of their oedipal situation was experienced as a relatively positive oedipal victory. Their dilemma is associated with a spectrum of feelings: elation, intense castration anxiety, guilt, as well as disappointment in and longing for a victorious, admirable father.[7]

Preoedipal events significantly contribute to these oedipal conflicts and their associated feelings. Oral aggressive cannibalistic urges to devour the relatively unavailable maternal object are an important component of these preoedipal conflicts. One patient slipped and referred to his guilt as "edible guilt." The quality of preoedipal development results in fixations or developmental interferences that influence the oedipal experience. These patients usually struggle with an admixture and alternation of oedipal and preoedipal issues. Both aspects need to be ana-

---

[7] The clinical material that follows derives from the analyses of a number of men with narcissistic personality disorders. It is probable that similar experiences occur in the genesis of certain female narcissistic personality disorders. Such women may long for an admirable mother.

lyzed, and each can act as a resistance to impede the analysis of the other. From the perspective of their self-destructiveness we can explore the oedipal constellations of a number of narcissistic personality disorders.

Fifty years ago, Freud attempted to integrate various clinical experiences that seemed to contradict the pleasure principle. These data influenced *On Narcissism, Beyond the Pleasure Principle, The Ego and the Id,* and *Some Character-Types Met with in Psycho-Analytic Work.* The latter paper dealt with clinical material that today would be classified under the rubric of narcissistic character pathology. In Section III, "Criminals from a Sense of Guilt," Freud (1916) described patients with a propensity to act out during analysis. He explained that this activity "was accompanied by mental relief" (p. 332) because it was motivated by and relieved a "sense of guilt derived from the Oedipus complex and was a reaction to the two great criminal intentions of killing the father and having sexual relations with the mother" (pp. 332–333). The crucial word is "intentions." A number of the patients considered here have experienced a reality which comes closer to actualizing these intentions. There appear to be three general ways that these patients' oedipal situations are different from those of neurotics. First of all, they were born into families in which the father was viewed as a failure by the mother. In many instances he was an actual failure. Second, these mothers treated their boys predominantly as narcissistic objects by overvaluing them as long as they promised to undo the humiliation of father's failure. Third, these boys experienced an actual seduction by their mothers. In addition to these three, three other frequent factors are that these boys were only children, their fathers were physically abusive employing corporal means of limit-setting and their mother and/or father enjoyed humiliating them. Such experience intoxicates, frightens and infuriates the child. He is intoxicated by that aspect of his oedipal situation experienced as an implied victory, and this further interferes with his mourning his grandiose self. He is frightened and enraged at his mother for treating him extractively. He is terrified she will denigrate, humiliate and destroy him if he does not perform adequately. In addition, he fears father's retaliation for his symbolic oedipal victory. Both factors contribute to his intense castration anxiety.

How often are these oedipal factors found in so-called narcissistic patients? I have seen them in five cases. These factors also appear to be relevant to the history of Kohut's (1971, p. 60) Mr. A, and to the first case Murray described in his paper "Narcissism and the Ego Ideal."[8] The following case illustrates these points.

Mr. B was an only child. He sought analysis to save a deteriorating marital situation. His father had died suddenly when the patient was nine years old. His father had been prone to violent outbursts and employed corporal punishments. Once when the boy angered the father, he was hit across the back with the handle of a hammer. In reality his father was a failure; however, his mother created a family mythology which portrayed the father as a man of great promise who never realized his potential, primarily due to the malevolence of others and luck. She believed luck skipped generations; the boy would be the lucky one and gratify her wishes while fulfilling his preordained destiny.

After his father's death, the mother gave the boy the parents' bedroom so he would better be able to study. One night, during the first year of her mourning, she entered the boy's bed clad in a nightgown and rubbed her feet against his. She told him not to tell anyone about this because they might not understand. The boy was able to inform her it made him uncomfortable. However, for the next two years, prior to her remarriage, she would often

---

[8] Murray's (1964) patient is described as having had "an intense oedipal era" in which he was his mother's favorite, . . . the major source of her emotional expressions and fulfillments." Concomitantly mother devalued his father and brother. Finally, the boy experienced a "physical relation with mother." Until he was six, she would allow the child to get into bed with her and half lie on her while he toyed with the soft lobe of her ear" (pp. 484—485).

rub his back at bedtime. Mr. B fondly remembered this gratifying, less overtly incestuous, experience.

Mr. B remained his mother's favorite after she remarried, when he was eleven years old. Although his mother slept with his stepfather, Mr. B continued to sleep in the bedroom, while the adults slept on the convertible sofa in the living room. His stepfather envied the boy's special position. When the boy was thirteen, his stepfather attempted to sanction him for dirtying a towel with paint. An argument ensued. His mother supported Mr. B. This led to his stepfather's leaving home for a month. His mother allowed her husband to return contingent on his tendering a humiliating apology to the boy. This adolescent experience recapitulated that aspect of his oedipal situation that had been experienced as a victory, while simultaneously reinforcing his fear of humiliation at the hands of a dissatisfied woman. The victorious aspect of the experience further reinforced his sense of specialness.

In a number of patients considered narcissistic personality disorders, we see a spectrum of very real maternal seductions and paternal failures. Although none of these men were, in fact, guilty of incest or paricide, they all had life experiences that more closely approximated what Freud called "the two great human crimes." This aspect of the patient's oedipal situation was experienced as an oedipal victory and contributed to intense castration anxiety (A. Reich, 1960), patricidal guilt, and eventually to self-destructive behavior. It should also be noted that these oedipal situations were usually complicated by being simultaneously or alternatingly gratifying and disappointing in addition to being contradictory and confusing. Their positive oedipal victories were tainted by negative oedipal disappointments. Their victories were relative and imperfect. Their favored positions, as mother's overvalued narcissistic objects, made perceptions that she slept with other men more intensely felt narcissistic injuries. This aspect of their oedipal situation was often experienced as an infidelity, and as a disappointment, both in their mothers and in themselves. Rather than experience rage at their mothers, they often focus on their own inadequacy. Mother's infidelity confronts them with the humiliating perception that they have a child's body. In a number of male narcissistic personality disorders, the overvalued position as mother's favorite narcissistic object contributes to an intensification of the ubiquitous narcissistic injuries of the oedipal situation.

What effect does the traumatic quality of life experiences have on character development? A number of authors—most notably Wilhelm Reich (1933), Jacobson (1954), Annie Reich (1960), Kohut (1966, 1968, 1971, 1972), Kernberg (1967), and Easser (1974)—have written about the genetics of narcissistic character pathology. They stressed both preoedipal and oedipal factors. With the exception of Wilhelm Reich most stressed preoedipal factors. Jacobson described early maternal deprivation with resultant defensive fusions of self- and object images. Kernberg stressed the role of excessive oral aggression with resultant fusion of ideal self-, ideal object, and actual self-images. Easser stressed a lack of maternal empathy. Annie Reich pointed to early experiences of helplessness, anxiety, and rage in relationship to the primal object who could not be controlled. In addition, she emphasized the importance of early primal scene experiences.

Kohut (1971) stressed the importance of preoedipal and oedipal genetics. His patient Mr. A's superego structuralization was disrupted by his father's failure during his latency. He had been rendered vulnerable to this disruption by the "unreliability of the empathic responses of his mother" during infancy and by his "father's extreme, sudden, and unpredictable mood swings during the preoedipal and oedipal period" (p. 60).

Kohut's ideas concerning oedipal and postoedipal factors in the genesis of a narcissistic personality disorder underwent a radical transformation. In 1971, in regard to Mr. A, Kohut stated:

The reactive as well as the primary hypercathexis of the grandiose self were predominantly related to early oedipal fixation points [p. 68].

In 1977:

In retrospect, the explanation given with regard to the move of patient A. toward his father [reference deleted] was inexact. . . . I would now assume that the intensity of Mr. A.'s idealization of his father (and thus the traumatic disappointment in him) was due to his earlier disappointment in the mirroring self-object, not to his disappointment in a more archaic idealized one [p. 11n].

Kohut (1977) has reduced the genesis of these disorders to a unifactorial disappointment in the "mirroring self-object." Although Kohut's work has contributed to an aappreciation of the importance of the real nature of the preoedipal maternal object, his reductionistic construction can be employed, in selected cases, as an intellectual resistance against remembering and reexperiencing the real nature of the oedipal and postoedipal maternal and paternal objects. In some analysands mourning of oedipal and postoedipal (A. Freud, 1958) narcissistic investments is of central importance to their analytic experience.

Narcissistic personality disorders demonstrate a spectrum of pathology that appears to have been influenced by preoedipal and oedipal factors. Both preoedipal and oedipal factors are relevant in the developmental investment of narcissistically tinged self- and object representations as well as in the resulting narcissistic character integration. In both sexes, a spectrum exists in the degree of preoedipal genetics which form the substrate for this pathology. Naturally, these preoedipal issues occupy an important and often central position in the analyses of these patients. Let us, however, for a moment focus on what appear to be important oedipal factors in the histories of a number of male patients with narcissistic character integrations. In addition to the importance of preoedipal factors in these patients there were sessions and periods of their analyses in which the material was clearly oedipal and required being responded to as such. There are also some subjects in whom narcissistic issues and narcissistic transference phenomena represent regressive attempts to integrate intense castration anxiety deriving from what are primarily oedipal conflicts.

Father's failure in reality, but especially in mother's view of things, in business, in the bedroom, or through death, combined with a degree of maternal seduction, leaves these boys with a feeling that they have won the oedipal battle. This contributes to the preservation of a narcissistically invested view of self and an inordinate sense of guilt combined with an ever-present fear of retaliation by the defeated father. This fear of retaliation by an object representation of the father—who was in reality prone to violence and is now represented as enraged—contributes to the intense castration anxiety so nicely described by Annie Reich (1960). To the degree they believe that their omnipotent wishes have destroyed father, they fear his retaliation.

A preoedipally colored view of mother as extractive and as having been responsible for father's destruction adds fuel to the child's intense castration anxiety. This preoedipal view of a biting, castrating mother contributes a counterphobic quality to these men's negative oedipal interests in fellatio. Their phallic grandiosity, again described by Annie Reich, can be seen as, in part, defensively motivated in relationship to these parental object representations. Their intense castration anxiety is often experienced as a threat to their survival. This stimulates defensive activities whose purpose is to diminish the anxiety by restoring a sense of narcissistic perfection to their threatened self-representations.

The victorious aspect of the oedipal experience is exaggerated, not only by virtue of mother's realistic, seductive overvaluation, but also in defense against, fear of, rage at, and disappointment in his parents.

In *On Narcissism,* Freud elaborated two factors in the development of the ego ideal. First, it is a reservoir of the infant's primary narcissism. Second, it derives from an idealization of the boy's relationship with his father. Preoedipal disturbances of maternal relatedness lead to excessive narcissistic investments not only in self-images, but also in the ego ideal. The factors emphasized here, namely, the father's failure and the boy's relative victory, interfere with later aspects of ego-ideal and superego formation. Freud has stated that the superego is the heir of the oedipal struggles. A stable, internalized superego structuralization requires a respected father who has won the oedipal struggle. This is a necessary motive for the boy to repress his longings for the mother and identify with the father.

These patients suffer not simply because they have been defeated. They have also experienced a partial primal victory. Their ego ideal lacks the sublimated homosexual libido (Freud, 1914, p. 96) which is derived from a loving relationship with a victorious and admired father. The absence of an idealizable paternal object interferes with the oedipal aspect of ego-ideal structuralization. Instead, the subject attempts to restore his originally felt narcissistic perfection to his self-representation. His relatively positive oedipal victory and negative oedipal disappointment reinforce his sense of entitlement and fuel his self-destructive behavior. Since the superego is lacking internalizations derived from identification with a loving, respected father, the subject contends with fears of submission to and attack by a paternal representation that exists as an introject, tenuously internalized within self-as-place, where it conveys primary-process qualities that threaten castration. The superego in such a patient will have both punitive and permissive standards. A punitive paternal representation may be derived, in part, from childhood experiences of corporal limit setting by a father who was often enraged at his son for his preferred position in the wife's affections and for his untainted future. The maternal representation derived from the same experience may often encourage the crime. This results in significant intrasystemic conflict. Because the patient felt that retaliation was inevitable, he may have actively sought a lesser punishment rather than passively waited to be destroyed by a father represented as castrating, enraged, jealous, humiliating and/or retaliating. This contributed to the superego externalization, so frequent in these patients.

At their core, these patients have an incompletely mourned grandiose self that feels entitled. When their feeling of entitlement is frustrated, they reflexively wish to chew up their frustrator. Their superegos punitively and mistakenly judge the wish to be equivalent to the act and, implementing talionic law, threaten to devour the subject. Their potential to feel that their wishes are equivalent to acts is reinforced by aspects of their oedipal experience.

These patients are left with an oedipal situation that is still active and unresolved. They experience a number of conflicting longings and fears. They hope to maintain their positive oedipal victory and the feeling of omnipotence derived from it, but they fear a castrating paternal retaliation. Their negative oedipal constellation is similarly active, but is often subject to more intense repression because of its homosexual implications. They long to be loved by a man whom they can love and respect. Intertwined with these significantly unresolved oedipal dynamics, a festering fear of humiliation may be observed.

FEAR OF HUMILIATION

Fear of humiliation is a central affect-laden fantasy in certain narcissistic personality disorders. Individuals with narcissistic personality disorders live in terror of losing their sense of perfection, and some experience that loss as a humiliation. Fear of humiliation has many dimensions. In this chapter, I shall explore one aspect of response to that fear—fantasies and actions deriving from identification with a humiliating introject. This defensive identification, like all others, is always, in part, a narcissistic identification. This is so because the self-representation-as-agent that fantasizes itself undoing a trauma by doing it to an object and/or the self-representation-as-object is narcissistically invested. The self-representation-as-agent that felt humiliated and fears humiliation is humiliating.

While the genesis of this character defense is overdetermined, I emphasize its development in these individuals in response, in part, to a particular kind of perception and experience of their parents. As little children these patients were repeatedly humiliated by their parents. Humiliation was more likely to occur when they failed to live up to their parents' narcissistically invested fantasies for them, or when their existence challenged their parents' other narcissistically invested pursuits. In addition, they were exposed to their parents' more general penchant for humiliating those who failed them. The case of Mr. C illustrates the importance of the fear of humiliation for this "typical" narcissistic personality disorder.

Midway in his analysis, Mr. C, a successful fifty-one-year-old married man, missed his Wednesday morning analytic hour, the second session of the week. This week was noteworthy in that Mr. C was about to be left by the analyst for two weeks. This patient typically had difficulty consciously experiencing feelings associated with being left by the analyst, and it was not unusual for him to leave for business trips prior to being left by the analyst. He had responded to interpretations of these resistances with incredulity and denial. He began the following session on Thursday evening by stating that he had felt "lousy" on Wednesday morning and just did not feel like coming to the session. He had spent the night in a hotel room with a beautiful and "fantastic" woman in her early twenties. He related that she was very sexy and they had had "great" sex, but he had not slept well.

Similar sequences of events had occurred many times before and were understood from a number of perspectives. As a child Mr. C had been overvalued and seduced by his mother who had presumably unwittingly, exposed her genitals to him. This seduction, as well as the failure of his parents' marriage and their temporary separation when he was five years old, contributed to his experience of the inevitable limits of the oedipal phase as an intensely felt mortification, which influenced his addictive interest in forbidden women. He was especially fascinated by younger women and was thrilled when he looked at their vaginas. As a latency child, he had enjoyed hiding under tables and looking up women's dresses. Although he had enjoyed sex with his wife prior to their marriage, he no longer found her interesting.

Mr. C's behavior had been understood and interpreted as a symbolic enactment of an oedipal crime associated with a sense of defiance of, and then confessional submission to, the analyst as the externalized representative of his superego. He understood that because he orchestrated and controlled this enactment, it was narcissistically gratifying. Our work to this point had focused on the fact that these sequences of events had enabled him to both gratify symbolic, positive, oedipal longings and to defend against the guilt associated with these gratifications.

However, Mr. C had come to understand that his behavior served multiple functions. It enacted an overdetermined identification with his maternal grandfather who was revered by his mother. This identification defended Mr. C against memories of the mortifying (Arlow, 1980) disappointments of positive and negative oedipal longings. His maternal grandmother had died when his mother was an infant, and his grandfather, a sea captain, had never remarried. Family legend, perpetuated by his mother, portrayed her father as an almost God-like figure who, however, had "a woman in every port." Mr. C's identification with his grandfather defended him against his fear of ending up like his father, humiliated by his mother for failing her, locked out of her bedroom, impotently pounding on her door.

This late latency memory served a screening function (Murphy, 1961) for oedipal primal-scene traumata in which Mr. C had experienced the door shut in his face. In addition, from a descriptive perspective, Mr. C had come to understand that his dissatisfaction with his life and his unhappiness with his sexual activities were masochistic and subtly self-destructive. While these insights had diminished his self-destructiveness and associated painful fantasies of imminent disaster, and had contributed to his ability to pursue professional success more assertively, they had neither altered his compulsive attraction for young "forbidden" women nor enabled him to feel satisfied with his life.

On the Thursday evening mentioned above, the analyst once again focused on the transference implications of Mr. C's having missed his Wednesday morning hour. Mr. C said that he just did not feel like coming to the session and "facing himself." The phrase "facing himself" reflected some integration of the defensive externalizing function of his acting out. In response to the analyst's query as to whether he had thought of informing the analyst prior to the missed session, the patient said that he had, but did not want to deal with his feelings and "What's the difference, anyway? I thought I pay for the hour and you can read your paper." The analyst suggested that by not working more successfully on his personal life he was gratifying the fantasy of humiliating not only himself but the analyst by "keeping the analyst waiting" for him to change his behavior. Because Mr. C's acting out protected him from consciously experiencing feelings in the transference associated with being left by the analyst, the analyst had attempted to deal with the more displaced expression of his sadistic pleasure in "keeping the analyst waiting." The patient's associations confirmed this interpretation in the transference and in all his important relationships.

In the following session, Mr. C recalled his sense of humiliation as a child. He remembered his embarrassment when his mother chastised him for "shitting in my pants."[9] He recalled

---

[9] In addition to being chastised for anal indiscretions, a number of other humiliating memories festered as traumatic nidi in Mr. C's mind and recurred in his associations. He recalled being tied to a tree, probably when he was two, to "keep me out of my mother's hair." Mortifying oedipal and early latency memories recurred painfully in his associations: his mother insisted he wear a bobby pin in his hair when he went to school; his father spanked him for breaking Christmas tree ornaments; his mother shut the door in his face, as she had in his father's face, to be with a male friend.

that when he was three years old, a tall, terrifying, white-haired gardener, who looked like a giant, had yelled at him for walking on flowers. He described running away and feeling intense discomfort. An adult might say he sounded ashamed and mortified. He remembered that when he was four years old he had climbed a tall wall, carrying a salad bowl, in order to have lunch with a friend. When the friend was not there, Mr. C remembered calling his name to no avail and feeling lonely and alone. He noted that his pursuits of perfection in himself and in women created the illusion of protecting him from disappointments, which he experienced as humiliations.

He began his first session after the analyst's vacation by expressing his feelings of humiliation when he looked at his "childish way of life" in the analyst's presence. His pleasure in humiliating and being humiliated was all he thought about when the analyst was away. He remarked, "I feel if I give up feeling humiliated I also have to give up sexual highs. Somehow they're linked together." In clarification of his sadomasochism, the analyst noted the sequence of seduction followed by humiliation that characterized Mr. C's heterosexual relationships. The analyst interpreted Mr. C's identification with his seductive and humiliating mother in an oedipal context: "You do to them [women] what you felt your mother did to you as a child. You felt she built you up to be number one and then shut the door in your face and slept with other men." Mr. C remarked, "I see my mother's legs opening to me." He expressed terror at the thought of relinquishing his need to feel special to women. His associations bore witness to his awareness that he derived masochistic gratification from feeling humiliated by "forbidden" women. He interpreted this masochistic pleasure as the price he paid in expiation to his sadistic superego for gratifying narcissistically invested, positive oedipal longings. The analyst's interpretation was intended, in addition, to facilitate Mr. C's appreciation of the sadonarcissistic pleasure he experienced in humiliating others.

In the ensuing weeks, analytic work focused on Mr. C's

tendency to both fear humiliation and to impose it on himself and others. He became increasingly aware that he experienced as humiliating any limitations of the self or of the object. In addition, he deepened his appreciation of the defensive function of his narcissistic investments. These investments protected him from feeling disappointed, impotently enraged, and humiliated like his father. In that sense, his narcissistic investments kept Mr. C from remembering painful disappointments in his father and from fears of being like him.

Analysis at this time focussed on the negative oedipal transference. Mr. C's wish for a relationship with a strong, respectable, protective and loving father-analyst was interpreted. The fantasied humiliation of the analyst and himself in frustration of this wish was interpreted, as was the defensive function of the sadomasochistic regression. The analyst interpreted, "This [Mr. C's fantasied humiliation of the analyst] allows you to maintain our relationship (with the implicit hope of gratification) and to express your anger." Mr. C expressed the wish to be the analyst's friend, to talk to him for hours and to share activities, but he felt humiliated by these feelings. He expected the analyst to disappoint him as his father had, and recalled his mother's sadistic pleasure in humiliating. When his associations shifted to heterosexual conquests, these were interpreted as a defense against the homosexual implications of the father transference. Mr. C then associated to the humiliating gardener, and the screening function of this memory was interpreted. This work was associated with Mr. C's further assimilation of his defensive superego externalization.

In conjunction with work on paternal trends, Mr. C recalled that his mother was "a great humiliator." He remarked, "I learned to hate it [humiliation], but saw its power." Mr. C's work on his defensive pursuit of the "perfect cunt" and his fear of the humiliating experience of women closing their legs in his face facilitated his enjoying his wife sexually for the first time since their marriage. Prior to this time, he had expressed his dissatisfaction with his wife's imperfect vagina, manifest in the presence of her diaphragm and the smell of her chronic monilial infection. He had been able to enjoy her sexually when they got high and pretended to have an affair.

Within the context of this theme, Mr. C began a session noting, "A strange thing happened this weekend. I'm getting horny about Varenka [his wife] even with a rubber. My attitude is everything. I had such a nice time. I had an intense *dream*. There were many women: a mulatto secretary, seductive and forbidding, flashing her cunt at me; Brigette in black panties flashing her cunt at me. I was at a carnival, the lights were so intense." He associated to the lights, "They're so intense, awe-inspiring." He paused and said, "I look at them but can never touch them, like my mother's cunt." He remarked that sex with Varenka was "great," but not what he wanted. In the next session he expressed his wish to be "free."

Mr. C's work on his experience of oedipal disappointments as humiliations enabled him to sufficiently relinquish his quest to undo these mortifications so that he was able to enjoy his wife. However, Varenka was not his mother. Pleasure with Varenka reminded Mr. C of the disappointments of his childhood and of the inevitability of disappointment in his adult life. He believed that if he let himself be happy with Varenka, he would end up with her legs shut in his face and, like his father, impotently frustrated by a humiliating woman, and dead. Within this context, the analyst interpreted his desire to be "free" as representing a fantasied state of existence in which Mr. C would never be disappointed or feel sadistic and murderous rage. It connoted an imagined way of life in which he could pursue his pleasures and not feel humiliated as he had when his mother shut her legs and her door in his face, or feel abandoned as he had when his father went away. "Free" meant he could pursue symbolic oedipal gratifications that magically undid the humiliations of his oedipal experience, without feeling anxious or guilty.

About a month later, Mr. C began a session by reporting

a dream that facilitated a more complete construction of his oe-dipally organized fear of humiliation. "I was with a blonde. We were making love. It was sensual, and I come back and she's making love with another guy—licking his ass. I call her a whore and she says, 'That's who I am.' " Mr. C said he felt closer to Varenka, was sharing more of his financial successes with her, and felt less afraid of her. He had fantasied that if he divorced Varenka she would take all his money. His association to the blonde woman led him to a lady friend, Denny, who had on occasion licked his anus. He noted, "sexually it's very special, base and degrading," and remarked on the linkage of his sexual pleasures and her humiliation.

In response to the preceding work, the dream and its asso-ciations, the analyst offered the following construction: "As a very young child you felt you were the only one and very special to your mother. Then you perceived there were others and that they had sexual relations with your mother. You felt humiliated by this perception and by the inadequacy of your body. As a result, you fear a recapitulation of these events with any woman you become involved with—you fear a loss of a special rela-tionship and experience her rejection and infidelity as a humili-ation. You defend against this fear by identifying with your grandfather, maintaining relationships with a number of women, and humiliating them and yourself. You experience any woman you can't have as a humiliation, while any perception of limits of your body evokes anxiety because it reminds you of your humiliating experience of the limits of your body as a young child." In that regard, Mr. C had been obsessed with growing older and had been seriously considering a face-lift and hair transplant.

The fear of humiliation has many dimensions and finds expression in relation to narcissism, masochism, and sadism. In chapter 1, I define narcissism as the experience of pleasure in illusions of perfection. Freud (1905, p. 157) defined masochism as both pleasure in pain [what he noted Schrenck-Notzing referred to as "algolognia"] and as "pleasure in any form of humiliation or subjection" after Kraft-Ebbing's emphases on the masochist's passive posture in relation to the active sadist. Masochists gain narcissistic pleasure from illusions of actively eliciting and controlling the sadist's humiliation of them, which they experience passively (Eidelberg, 1959; Bergler, 1961).

Patients with narcissistic personality disorders considered here actively enjoy sadistically humiliating others in identification with their humiliating superego introjects. In addition to the distinction between the narcissist's penchant for activity and the masochist's passive proclivity, it is important to note that masochistic characters are more often pessimistic and defend against their fear of humiliation by fantasied seduction of the humiliator (Loewenstein, 1957; Eidelberg, 1959). They seek humiliation, in part, to gain the unconscious narcissistic gratification of controlling the insult they feel to be inevitable. Those with narcissistic personality disorders are typically more optimistic. Although they may fear humiliation, they have the sense that they can master this fantasied danger by active identification with the humiliator. This defensive identification motivates them to fantasize and/or enact the humiliation of others.

Mr. C would be considered a "typical" narcissistic personality disorder. Enactments and acting out were characteristic of his personality "armor" and might influence Kohut (1977) to consider him a "narcissistic behavior disorder" (p. 193). The enactments were importantly related to Mr. C's fear of humiliation, which was a fundamental, organizing, affect-laden fantasy of his character. I am suggesting that real humiliating qualities of his parents have been internalized, and archaically elaborated and structuralized as humiliating superego introjects. These introjects provide part of the impetus for defensive sadistic, masochistic, and narcissistic identifications with the introject, particularly with the humiliating introject. This mechanism of *identification with the humiliator* is an elaboration of A. Freud's (1936) concept of "identification with the aggressor" (p. 117), subsequently elaborated by Berliner (1958) as "identification with the hater" (p. 40), by Sandler (1960) as "identification with the introject" (p. 155), and by Segal (1969) as "identification with the doer" (p. 485). These humiliating superego introjects are integrated in a less than optimal manner and are prone to defensive externalization. In addition, their internalized presence provides an aspect of the unconscious motivation for defensive sadistic acts toward others, as well as the self, and for the subsequent undoing and expiation of these acts.

Freud's dissatisfaction with the actual seduction theory, as well as his self-analysis and concomitant discovery of infantile sexuality, influenced him to develop a model of the mind that emphasized the wish for gratification (discharge) and inevitable conflict concerning those wishes. This perspective led him (1926) to propose an ontogeny of dangers related to phase-appropriate conflicts concerning the wish for gratification. Within Freud's final model of anxiety the primal danger is internal economic imbalance, the " "danger' . . . of non-satisfaction, of a *growing tension due to need,* against which it is helpless" (p. 137). Freud suggested that "the *content* of the danger it fears is displaced from the economic situation onto the condition which determined that situation, viz., the loss of the object" (p. 138; italics added). Then "castration anxiety develops into moral anxiety—social anxiety" (p. 139) and finally into "the fear of death (or fear of life) which is a fear of the superego projected onto the powers of destiny" (p. 140).

The emphasis of Freud's formulations influenced his conception of the development of the superego. He stressed that it was a structure essentially derived in response to conflicts with the drives. Freud proposed that the superego is definitively structured in response to internalizations associated with the child's relinquishing of its oedipal wishes. The superego's hostility and sadism derive significantly from the person's own aggressive drive and ultimately from Thanatos. The development of Freud's ideas, and of psychoanalysis in general, is characterized by the discovery and excessive emphasis on one factor and the corollary deemphasis of other factors. Within Freud's developing structural perspective, conflict was seen to derive primarily and interminably from the insatiability of the id. The deemphasis of the influence of the real object on developing structure is seen in Freud's (1926) suggestion that "the loved person would not cease to love us nor should we be threatened with castration if we did not entertain certain feelings and intentions within us" (p. 145); yet it is interesting to note that prior to Freud's disillusionment with the actual seduction theory, he had emphasized the importance to ego development of ubiquitous perceptions of the hostile object. He (1895) stated:

> There are in the first place, objects (perceptions) which make one scream because they cause pain; . . . a perception . . . emphasizes the *hostile* character of the object and serves to direct attention to the perception. Where otherwise, owing to the pain, one would have received no clear indications of the quality of the object [p. 423].

Toward the end of *The Ego and the Mechanisms of Defense,* A. Freud (1936) shifted her focus from an emphasis on the ego's defensive responses to the id to those of the external world. She delineated defensive identifications deriving from the person's ubiquitous internalization of frustrating and frightening perceptions. Her seminal concept of "identification with the aggressor" provides an important theoretical construct for consideration of subjects' responses to traumatic external experiences. She proposed that identification with the aggressor reflects "the reversal of roles of attacker and attacked" (p. 123), and noted:

> Identification . . . combines with other mechanisms to form one of the ego's most potent weapons in its dealings with external objects which arouse its anxiety [p. 117].

Treatment of difficult character disorders and negative therapeutic reactions have contributed to a shift of emphasis that integrates the quality of real parental objects' contributions to developing psychic structure. Such work[10] has increasingly emphasized defensive identificatory processes in response to terrifying perceptions. The theories of Loewenstein (1957), Berliner (1958) and Segal (1969) are particularly noteworthy in this regard. Loewenstein (1957), viewing masochistic behavior from the perspective of "survival" (p. 230) rather than "drive development" (p. 230), conceived of it as a "weapon of the weak—i.e., of every child—faced with danger of human [parental] aggression" (pp. 230–231). I have suggested that:

Identification with the aggressor can be viewed as a narcissistic identificatory alteration of the self-representation as agent in response to a frightening, angry, sadistic and/or [humiliating] parent that becomes internalized and elaborated by the primary process in the developing superego [Rothstein, 1981, p. 442].

Loewenstein (1957) discovered the masochistic complement to this process in his description of "seduction of the aggressor" (p. 216). He noted that "essentially it is very different than a defensive ego mechanism . . . [it] consists of behavior which seeks and frequently achieves to change an unloving to a loving attitude in the parent. And while mobilizing libido in both, *it wards off anxiety in the child and aggression in the parent*" [p. 216; italics added].

---

[10] In the ensuing discussion of theory, support for my hypotheses is quoted from authors who are usually considered to have nearly irreconcilable views. This is so because it has been typical in discussions of psychoanalytic theory to focus upon and emphasize differences. In a larger sense, from an evolutionary rather than a revolutionary view of the process of development of theory (see Rothstein, 1983), I have found it valuable to ferret out similarities in colleagues' contributions. This has particular heuristic merit when exploring a deemphasized aspect of a subject, in this case, the influence of qualities of the real parental object on developing psychic structure.

Berliner's (1958) reminder that "the ill-treating parent does not belong to the dim prehistoric past" (p. 43) is in striking contrast to Freud's (1926) comparison of the loving parent and the wolf. Berliner proposed that "the introjection of another person's sadism [is] the essential pattern" (p. 41) in masochism. He delineated the mechanism of "identification with the hater" (p. 49) and noted that "the original traumatic situation is re-enacted by identification" (p. 48). Segal (1969) described "identification with the doer" (p. 485) as a defense mechanism encountered in some patients with a tendency to act-out. He related this penchant to their efforts to master the trauma of intense unexpected stimulation. Segal stressed real primal scene experiences, separations and abandonments as frequently encountered traumatic determinants of such defensive identifications.

My focus here is on one factor in the experience of certain patients with narcissistic personality disorders: their fear of humiliation. This fear is exaggerated and, as mentioned earlier, develops as a fundamental, organizing, affect-laden fantasy, partly in response to the internalization of qualities of their parents. While it is true that the child's experience is a fantasy elaborated by a child's mind, and different children perceive and elaborate similar events differently, some have real experiences with parents who enjoy humiliating them. These real experiences, as well as other, complementary experiences, such as parents' narcissistic investment and overvaluation of them, contribute to the children's elaboration of these experiences and to their fear of humiliation.

Influenced by their own fantasied pursuit of perfection, the mothers and fathers who typically overvalue their children at the same time compete with, envy, and at times enjoy humiliating them. This propensity to sadistically humiliate is accentuated and intensified when such parents feel their children fail them as narcissistic objects. A primal fear that persons with narcissistic personality disorders have is the dread of such humiliation; they defend against it by actively attempting to be their parent's successful narcissistic objects. Because this is rarely possible and because limits, experienced as humiliating failures, are inevitable, such individuals defend against their fear of humiliation by identifying with their humiliating superego introjects.

In a related vein and from the perspective of "beyond the pleasure principle," Eidelberg (1959) described "external humiliation as the final aim of a masochist" (p. 280). He suggested that "perhaps the best defense against humiliation is self-humiliation or humility" (p. 277). He proposed that this masochistic defense is motivated by a wish "to eliminate the memory of a narcissistic mortification imposed upon him by somebody else" (p. 276) and, in that sense, "to deny the *presence* of an unconscious internal narcissistic mortification" (p. 287; italics added). Eidelberg proposed, as had Bergler (1961), that masochistic defenses were in fact narcissistic. It is as if the masochist were saying, "I can always succeed in provoking a humiliating defeat and retain in that way my infantile omnipotence" (p. 283). Cooper (1977) has elaborated Bergler's contribution and has highlighted the ubiquitous relationship of masochism to narcissism.

I would add that Eidelberg is elaborating Loewenstein's (1957) conception of "seduction of the aggressor" (p. 216) and implicitly proposing the more specific "seduction of the humiliator" as a structured presence in the masochist's superego.

Because I have discussed the relationship of narcissism to masochism in *The Structural Hypothesis: An Evolutionary Perspective,* I will limit my comments here to aspects of their relationship that are relevant to a discussion of the fear of humiliation. While these two phenomena are quite different pleasurable experiences, masochism being the experience of pleasure in pain and narcissism the experience of pleasure in illusions of perfection, both are associated with the fantasy of the presence of the narcissistically invested object. It is also important to note the frequent, if not ubiquitous, occurrence of narcissistic and masochistic defenses and resistances in the analysis of the fear of humiliation. In the analysis of narcissistic personality disorders, masochistic resistances and defenses will appear after significant working through of narcissistic defenses has been accomplished. A similar process occurs in the analyses of many masochistic characters; after considerable working through of the predominant masochistic defenses has been accomplished, narcissistic resistances may appear. In addition, I would add that if their analyses are successful, both types of character disorders will experience depression in the later phases of the work, after their narcissistic and masochistic resistances have been analyzed and worked through to some significant degree.

Nevertheless, there are striking differences between masochistic characters and narcissistic personality disorders in general, and specifically with regard to their fear of humiliation. Masochistic characters are pessimistic and defend against their fear of humiliation, as Eidelberg and Loewenstein suggest, by fantasied seduction of the humiliator. They seek humiliation as one of their aims and gain the unconscious narcissistic gratification of controlling the insult they feel is inevitable. Persons with narcissistic personality disorder are consciously more optimistic. Although they fear humiliation, they have the sense that they can master this fantasied danger by active identification with the humiliator. This defensive identificatory process motivates these analysands to fantasize and/or enact the humiliation of others.

An attempt to hypothesize and reconstruct an ontogeny of the fear of humiliation transcends data that are truly analytic, and calls upon psychoanalytically-oriented observations and theories of early development. From that more speculative perspective it is probable that those who will develop narcissistic personality disorders, as toddlers emerging from the rapprochement crisis and on the way to self and object constancy, were more definitively confronted with their parents' occasional sadistic pleasure in humiliating them. Maturation and development confront these young children with their parents' requirement that they be narcissistically perfect and with humiliating rejections when they fail. These perceptions are internalized and structured in their ego ideal and superego. They feel they must be narcissistically perfect to be lovable and safe, and believe they will be humiliated when they are not. The more these attitudes are characteristic of the mother in early phases of development, the more likely the occurrence of serious sadomasochistic and negativistic character pathology. Thereafter, the fear of humiliation is an expectation ubiquitously associated with any narcissistic injury. It is transferentially active and lends a paranoid quality to the object relations of such individuals.

It is important to note, however, that in certain cases mothers may be more adulating than humiliating, while fathers may be the more active humiliators, particularly within the competition of the oedipal phase. In the foregoing discussion of self-destructiveness, I suggested that it is not uncommon for certain men with narcissistic personality disorders to have been firstborn sons, adulated by mothers who denigrated and humiliated fathers experienced as failures. I stressed that such fathers, nevertheless, felt entitled. They were often angry and jealous of the children's untainted futures; they themselves would have liked to start again and envied their children's more age-appropriate expressions of narcissism. In a related vein, I (1980) have suggested that:

> The oedipal child seeks a particular kind of confirmation from the negative oedipal object. The little boy seeks more than paternal mirroring as a compensation for deficiencies of preoedipal maternal empathic responsiveness (a Kohutian construct). The oedipal boy requires the approval and encouragement of his father for his oedipal competitive strivings. When a father is unable to enjoy his son's strivings and is hostile to them, the negative oedipal constellation is intensified. This constellation is usually associated with an idealizing transference as well as with more deeply repressed homosexual transference trends [p. 450].

The vulnerable father, whose own narcissistic conflicts inhibit his pleasure in phase-specific affirmation of his son's competitive oedipal strivings, often enjoys actively humiliating his son's assertive phallic pursuits. These sadistic humiliations are internalized as paternal superego introjects. Such paternal images may complement maternal introjects derived from a panoply of perceptions, including observations of mother humiliating father. These superego introjects provoke a number of defensive processes that include identification with the humiliator.

It is of interest that Erikson (1954) delineated such a dynamic-genetic constellation in Freud's development. He (1954, p. 41) quoted Freud's (1900) statement:

> One evening before going to bed I had disregarded the dictates of discretion, and had satisfied my needs in my parents' bedroom, and in their presence. Reprimanding me for this delinquency, my father remarked, "that boy will never amount to anything." This must have been a terrible affront to my ambition, but allusions to this scene recur again and again in my dreams, and are constantly coupled with enumerations of my accomplishments and successes [p. 216].

Erikson (1954) remarked that this memory "suggests not onnly an individual trauma, but also a pattern of child training" in which "fathers . . . humiliate[e] them [boys] before others, and especially before the mother" (p. 42). He suggested that for Freud and boys raised in this manner "the inner humiliation [is] forever associated with the internalized father image" (p. 43). Erikson quoted from Freud's associations to the dream of Count Thun. Freud's associations to that dream inform us that on the dream day he had experienced envy of powerful and privileged government officials. He had been particularly envious of their possession of first-class lavatory facilities and had sarcastically suggested to the railroad conductor "that he should at all events have a hole made in the floor of the compartment to meet the possible needs of passengers" (p. 209). Freud then reported,

"In fact I did wake up at a quarter to three in the morning with a pressing need to micturate, having had the following dream" (p. 209). The last part of this long manifest dream involved Freud, an old man, and a urinal. Freud dreamt, "So I was a sick-nurse and had to give him the urinal because he was blind" (p. 210). Freud's associations and interpretation of the dream emphasize that perceptions of the dream day of powerful Count Thun and the "government bedfellow" (p. 209) had reawakened festering memories of childhood humiliations and of numerous narcissistically invested defenses, among them identification with the humiliator. As Freud's associations approached the "deeper layers" (p. 213) he recalled "a very peculiar competition [concerning] . . . the production of *flatus*" (p. 213). Freud related being "reproached" (p. 216) by his father for bedwetting when he was two. He concluded that the scene quoted by Erikson provided the material for the final episode of the dream, in which, in revenge . . . *the roles were interchanged*. The older man (clearly my father . . .) . . . was now micturating in front of me, just as I had in front of him in my childhood. . . . Moreover, I was making fun of him" [pp. 216–217; italics added].

Freud's dream work reflects the mechanism of defensive sadonarcissistic identification with the humiliator, in which Freud gratified his wish to humiliate his father as he had felt humiliated by him. It is of interest that the manifest content of Freud's latency conflicts with his father concerned urinary and/or anal "indiscretions." Similarly, the first childhood humiliation that Mr. C recalled was of his mother chastising him for loss of control of his anal sphincter. In the context of these associations from the here-and-now experience of fear of humiliation in the transference, Mr. C did not immediately recall primal scene humiliations regarding the inadequacy of his penis in the context of his mother's rejection of him for adult men. It may be that experiences of narcissistic injuries of toilet training, which are associated and temporally synchronous with the more definitive perception of the limits of the self and objects, are the contents of the more fundamental humiliations of development. On the other hand, the little boys' (Freud's and Mr. C's) experience of oedipal mortifications are subject to repression. In addition, I am suggesting that boys like Freud and Mr. C, who were overvalued firstborn children of adulting mothers, find it easier to get angry at their fathers than their mothers. To recall oedipal mortifications is to feel murderously angry at their mothers. Murphy (1961) has pointed out that "a trauma in the present can serve as a screen for those in the past, and past traumata can serve as a secondary screen for traumata of more recent origin" (p. 522). From Murphy's perspective, anal traumata can serve a screening function for the traumatic quality of later oedipal experiences. The reverse may also be true.

In addition to considering Murphy's emphasis on the screening function of traumatic memories, it is similarly important to recall Brenner's (1974) suggestion that anal fantasies may be displacements employed to express more repressed oedipal wishes. Brenner stated:

Oedipal fantasies are often expressed in oral and anal terms, not necessarily as a result of regression. It is often more appropriate to speak of regression with respect to an oedipal child's fantasy of anal birth, for example, or of oral impregnation. The fact that a wish or fantasy is expressed in oral terms is not proof, nor always a good indication, that its origin was pre-oedipal. It is often assumed that oral and anal wishes must have originated during the oral and anal phases, i.e., that they must be pre-oedipal in the literal, historical sense. It cannot be too strongly emphasized that this assumption is incorrect. Oedipal wishes are often expressed in oral and anal terms. The instinctual mode in which a wish or fantasy is expressed is not a sure guide to its time of origin in infantile development [pp. 28–29].

Successful analytic work with some patients who have narcissistic personality disorders requires resolution of their fear of humiliation, their penchant for experiencing any limit as a humiliation, as well as their proclivity for sadonarcissistic and masochistic defensive identificatory responses to humiliating superego introjects. This means that they must assimilate the disappointments of the formative humiliations of separation-individuation, weaning, toilet training, oedipal phase development, socialization in general, as well as the uniquely individual disappointments and losses from all stages of life. For Mr. C, the disappointments of his oedipal phase are stressed because the unique exigencies of his life resulted in their exaggerated distortion. His mother's seductiveness and the failure of his parents' marriage made the frustration of positive oedipal wishes a more intensely felt disappointment. His father's departure within the context of his failed marriage, and his self-involvement and interest in other women, contributed to Mr. C's experience of his father's departure as a traumatic abandonment. His parents' pleasure in humiliating contributed to this experience of these disappointments as humiliations.

What is being emphasized in this chapter is that some patients with narcissistic personality disorders are particularly prone to experience limits as humiliations, in part because of their painful perceptions of their parents' enjoying the activity of humiliating them. These painful perceptions are undoubtedly exaggerated and distorted by projections and the primary-process qualities of the child's mentation, which results in superego introjects of a more terrifying nature than the original parental object. These archaically-elaborated humiliating introjects are the contents of the externalizations the analyst will experience in the transference.

While countertransference is a tool of the analyst and inevitable, the responses stimulated by analytic work with "typical" narcissistic personality disorders are noteworthy and will be discussed in more detail in chapter 4. In the context of this chapter's emphasis, provocative defiance and sadistic and perverse enactments by such patients may evoke a countertransference wish to make these analysands humiliatingly submit to "the exigencies of life." The analyst may unconsciously envy his analysand's narcissistic and sadistic gratifications and, in identification with sadistic aspects of his own superego, enjoy humiliating him or her. Such a countertransference potential is also encouraged by these patients' unconscious masochistic wishes, which may intensify their potential to fear and feel humiliated by the analyst.

It would be a fallacy to think of fear of humiliation as the psychological "bedrock" of any individual's character organization. The pursuit of narcissistically invested explanations has influenced some colleagues intent on making their point to make unifactorial statements. Thus, Berliner (1958) could say that masochism is "the introjection of another person's sadism" (p. 51), Eidelberg could suggest "external humiliation [is] the final aim of a masochist" (1959, p. 280), and Bergler (1961) could propose that "a masochistic solution . . . constitutes that 'basic neurosis' " (p. 63). The patient with a narcissistic personality disorder pursues defensive narcissistic, sadistic, and masochistic identifications as components of the defensive configuration of his character armor. The predominance of narcissistic defenses contributes to the diagnosis of narcissistic personality disorder. These defenses are employed in the ego's attempts to assimilate current narcissistic injuries as well as the interminable residues of formative conflicts and traumatic experiences. Behind these patients' identifications with the humiliating superego introject are overdetermined fears of humiliation associated with a panoply of festering, humiliating memories.

It is worth emphasizing that the fear of humiliation, far from being a road to psychological bedrock, itself serves defensive functions. This fear, coupled with defensive identification with the humiliator, is based on the illusion of the presence of a superego introject. Such a presence serves multiple purposes, among which is the provision of an illusionary object for an assortment of fantasied gratifications. In the context of the emphasis on this chapter, I am stressing that this fantasied presence serves several protective functions. It shields the subject from perceiving his own and the object's murderous rage as well as associated archaically elaborated fantasies of their destructive potential; from experiencing the disorganizing affect that A. Reich (1960) cogently referred to as "feelings of catastrophic annihilation"; and from a sense of loss and depression associated with the assimilation of more realistic perceptions of himself and others.

It is important to reemphasize the multiplicity of these patients' determinants and the seemingly contradictory aspects of their experiences. From a descriptive perspective their sense of entitlement and the resulting behavior can be characterized as the entitled pursuit of pleasure. However, its driven quality underlines its defensive and conflictual nature. These pleasures are symbolically experienced as oral-narcissistic and oedipal defenses and gratifications. They are, however, also simultaneously and/or alternatingly experienced as "edible" and/or oedipal crimes. The term *edible* has been employed here to connote a sense of crime derived from oral-cannibalistic urges toward the maternal object. Patients typically considered narcissistic personality disorders often experience individuation as a crime. Their pursuit of a pleasurable existence that violates their mother's view of the way they should be (a narcissistically invested repository of her fantasies) may stimulate intense anxiety derived in part from fear of her humiliating and ultimately annihilating retaliation. Such symbolic elaborations stimulate guilt and anxiety (an aspect of which is the fear of humiliation), contributing to these patients' self-destructive behavior. This behavior is often influenced by three additional factors. First, their murderous rage at any frustrator is particularly intense when they are frustrated by those they love most dearly. Second, guilt in response to rage, experienced as resulting in the actual death of a loved one, contributes to self-destructive expiation. Such patients may pursue a self-destructive course rather than acknowledge and accept a reality that contradicts their entitled sense of specialness (this factor is elaborated in chapter 8). Third, the pursuit of perfection is, in itself, self-destructive. This quest is often stimulated by the perception that the subject is achieving real happiness. Because real happiness may symbolically represent a positive oedipal victory it stimulates castration anxiety and depression. These affects are maladaptive signals of their unresolved oedipal situation. They reflect fear of a retaliating parental representation, as well as a more realistic acceptance of parents as they really were. The subject is motivated to defend against the pain of these affectively laden representations by pursuing illusions of perfection. Because these illusions are unattainable, their addictive pursuit dooms the subject to an unhappy fate, satisfying his "unconscious need for punishment."

The panoply of affective, dynamic, and genetic determinants of these patients' behavior provides a challenging and difficult task in their analytic management. Successful analyses require analysands with good psychological aptitudes. These aptitudes will often be relatively unavailable at the beginning of the analytic experience. First, a good working alliance must be established within which the analysand trusts that the analyst is not attempting to prohibit his pleasurable pursuits or control his choices. This is no easy task. A more detailed discussion of aspects of these issues of introductory-phase analytic process of narcissistic personality disorders is presented on pp. 115-118. Second, the analysand must gain some understanding that his pursuits are not motivated simply by pleasurable wishes. When this is accomplished, the analyst has the task of acquainting the analysand with the multiply determined nature of his experiences.

4

Countertransference

My purpose in this chapter is to explore countertransference proclivities experienced at various phases in the analytic work with
patients considered narcissistic personality disorders. However,
because narcissistic investments are ubiquitous, narcissistic resistances occur in a broad spectrum of patients from healthier to
sicker ones. Therefore, the countertransference reactions described here with narcissistic personality disorders may occur at
varying points in all analyses.

In chapter 2, narcissistic personality disorder was defined
by the predominance of narcissistic defenses in a person's character "armor" and by the state of the ego's integration of its
defenses. Thus, before proceeding with a discussion of countertransference, it is important to note that most analyzable patients
with narcissistic personality disorders employ, in addition to their
narcissistic defenses, other defenses including denial of narcissistic injury, projection of rage, externalization of superego introjects, as well as defensive masochistic and sadistic identifications.
However, in evaluating these subjects' analyzability, the issue
is not dynamic (i.e., not the pursuit of illusions of narcissistic
perfection for the self-representation); it is structural and functional. The issue is not the presence of narcissistic defenses but
the state of their integration.

The analyzable patient with a narcissistic personality disorder will have an analytic experience characterized, in part, by mourning of illusions of narcissistic perfection for the self-representation-as-agent and by their ego's progressive relinquishment of its defensive narcissistic pursuits. Such patients have a view of themselves as perfect in some way and, implicitly, as being admired for that state of perfection. The aspect of their analytic experience being considered here concerns the understanding of current dynamic and genetic roots of these investments, their defensive functions, and their relinquishment in so far as it is possible. Because the total relinquishment of these defenses is probably impossible, it is particularly the working through of their maladaptive aspects that is desirable. Considering this process as akin to mourning is helpful because the subject experiences it as a loss of an illusionary aspect of the self-representation, and underlying this, as the loss of the illusion of an admiring object. This mourning process and the associated experience of painful depression is characteristic of aspects of successful mid-phase work with such analysands.

Patients with narcissistic personality disorders who are unanalyzable, in contrast, are unable to relinquish and mourn their narcissistic defenses. They tenaciously cling to their investments as to a life preserver. Analytic zeal may provoke transient psychotic regressions characterized by disturbances of the reality testing and judgment functions of their egos, serious acting out and/or disorganization. For these subjects a reality-oriented, affirming psychotherapy that facilitates mutative internalizations is indicated, rather than analysis. Many of these patients require an interminable tie to the therapist, which may be of varying intensity.

In this chapter, I will explore countertransference encountered in the analysis of narcissistic defenses at various stages of analytic work with narcissistic personality disorders. I am suggesting that there is a predictable process to the analysis of these defensive investments that can be correlated with common countertransference responses. In the introductory and early mid-phases of work with patients considered narcissistic personality disorders, the tasks with such analysands are: (1) to be able to tolerate and even enjoy,[1] as a parent enjoys a child, his analysand's narcissistic defenses, (2) to allow the analysand the opportunity to fantasize a panoply of potential transference gratifications associated with these defenses, and (3) to facilitate the shared elaboration of these fantasies in words.

Analysands considered "typical neurotics" have a significant quotient of narcissistic investments allocated to their ego ideals. Their analytic work revolves around the analyst as object of their sexual and aggressive fantasies, significantly derived from and organized on an oedipal level of development. These transference trends afford the analyst the subtle sexual and narcissistic gratifications of being the center of the analysand's attention. The analyst working with a patient considered a narcissistic personality disorder is deprived of these gratifications until the work is well into mid-phase and some working through of narcissistic defenses has been accomplished.

Countertransference vulnerabilities in response to tasks of the introductory phase will depend, in part, upon the presentation of a subject's narcissistic investments and their defensive elab-

---

[1] The phrase "and even enjoy" is intended to suggest that the analyst's ability to identify with his patient's narcissistic defenses, when associated with a mildly positive affective tone, might be a positive prognostic indicator concerning the analyst-analysand collaborative match. This may be what Stone (1954) had in mind when he stated: "The therapist's personal tendencies may profoundly influence the indications and prognosis" (p. 593). In considering qualities of the "analyst himself" (p. 592), he suggested that "special predilections, interests, emotional textures may profoundly influence prognosis . . . a therapist must be able to love a psychotic or a delinquent and be at least warmly interested in the 'borderline' patient (whether or not this feeling is *utilized* technically), for optimal results" (p. 592). Conversely, following Loewald's (1973) critique of Kohut, it is important not to enjoy one's analysands' narcissistic pursuits excessively, thereby infantilizing them, encouraging their acting-out and avoiding the task of analyzing the defensive function of their narcissistic investments.

orations. Some patients will present as basically inhibited [Ko-hut's (1977) "narcissistic personality disorder proper"], others as more prone to enactment. Such inhibited patients anticipate disappointment and protect themselves from the pain of expected rejection and humiliation by keeping their fantasies to themselves. They may, like McDougall's (1980) "anti-analysand" (p. 213), be well behaved and conform to the structure of the analytic situation. However, they do not allow the analyst into their representational space to become an "analytic-introject" (Meissner, 1981, p. 170) to be actively identified with. They do not trust the analyst sufficiently to become involved with him in a manner that would facilitate their active pursuit of productive insights and growth-enhancing internalizations. Instead, they stay within themselves.

It is in the analysis of this type of presentation of narcissistic defenses that Kohut (1971) has taught us a great deal. He has taught us that our boredom and rage may be a response to our frustrations in general and to our not being the center of the analysand's attention in particular, and he has emphasized the importance of recognizing the repressed or suppressed grandiose fantasies that underlie the presenting inhibition.

However, Kohut's description of boredom in response to the mirror transference is like so much else in his contribution: it is correct but inevitably incomplete, and in that sense, a misleading hypothesis. Kohut suggests a unifactorial explanation for the analyst's experience of boredom. Boredom is conscious and, therefore, only the manifest content of the analyst's experience. Although in selected situations it may reflect a countertransference response to the emergence of an analysand's wish for an affirming, confirming and/or admiring response, it also may reflect, as does any conscious manifest experience, a symptomatic expression of other countertransference conflicts. While this analyst has experienced boredom in response to mirror transference phenomena, it has also occurred in response to process that reflects conflicts concerning homosexual trends.

Within the rubric of the mirror transference, Kohut (1971) has helped us to understand and facilitate the progressive expression in words of the analysand's longing for a special kind of responsiveness, whereas in the idealizing transference the analysand fantasizes that the analyst possesses particular qualities by which he longs to be sustained, to internalize, and with which to identify. In regard to the latter transference trend, Kohut has emphasized the analyst's unconscious and unresolved narcissistically invested longings as responsible for his countertransferential response, a premature disavowal of the analysand's overidealization of the analyst.

There are patients considered narcissistic personality disorders who are not so inhibited. These patients are prone to manifest enactments of their ego-syntonic, entitled pursuit of narcissistically invested gratifications. These more provocative analysands may evoke countertransference envy from their more socially well adapted and, in that sense, inhibited analysts. Such analysands may evoke a sadistic countertransference response that derives from the analyst's defensive ego identifications with his own sadistic superego introjects. This type of response may manifest itself in activities of judging and labeling the analysand with an array of pejoratively-toned labels and diagnostic designations such as "pathologic" narcissism, or worse, may motivate the analyst to attempt to control and/or humiliate the analysand.

It is helpful to think about these action-oriented adults' behavior as analogous to children's play. One such subject emphasized this point when, after purchasing "the best sailboat," he told me in a sarcastic and self-deprecating manner, "You judge a man by the price of his toys." If the analyst thinks about these analysands as playing and accepts the futility of giving them advice, he may be able to help them recover and understand the unconscious fantasies behind their playful and, at times, sadistic and self-destructive behaviors.

Conversely, an analyst may experience a narcissistic and sadistic identification with his less inhibited analysand, and enjoy and subtly encourage his enactments. Loewald (1973), in his review of Kohut's first book, implied that Kohut's work might be influenced by just such a countertransference proclivity.

The major task of the mid-phase of analytic work with these patients is the analysis of the defensive functions of their narcissistic investments. This work mobilizes archaically elaborated introjects and what A. Reich (1960) described as "catastrophic feelings of annihilation" (p. 224). In addition, the temporary relinquishment of these defenses is associated with the recovery of painful, conflict-laden memories from all stages of development, as well as new experiences of closeness and intimacy that are both gratifying and frightening. Since this aspect of treatment inevitably evokes resistances, their analysis is another important function of the mid-phase. Although any resistance may be employed, acting-out, externalization of superego introjects, and sadistic and masochistic identifications are not infrequent as these analysands struggle to restore a sense of perfection to their self-representation-as-agent.

Externalization is common for a number of reasons. The often unresolved oedipal conflicts of these patients leave their superegos prone to dedifferentiation as they lack the enforcing presence characteristic of optimal oedipal-phase resolution (Freud, 1933). It is as if these analysands externalize their superego introjects, in part, to repair the maladaptive introjection of representations of their disappointing parent(s), and thus provide an admirable presence that will allow the oedipal phase to be more adequately resolved and their development to proceed. In addition, externalization of superego introjects allows the individual to avoid the experience of profoundly painful guilt and to maintain the fantasy that frustrations are not inevitable but exist only by virtue of the external presence of a frustrator. If this frustrating superego introject can be fooled, manipulated, defeated or destroyed, the person can maintain the illusion that any gratification is possible. This illusion is inevitably associated with a fantasied sense of perfection for the self-representation-as-agent.

A brief vignette is presented to emphasize these subjects' tenacious penchant for externalization of superego introjects. A forty-year-old married man, Mr. P, was referred to this analyst for a fourth attempt at analysis. His first analysis ended in his successful provocation of his analyst to angrily criticize his behavior. His second analyst died during the first year of their work. His third analysis ended in his interminable waiting for his analyst to "make me do something." Mr. P's life and his analyses were characterized by procrastination.

Mr. P began his fourth attempt at analysis under the pressure of his wife's confrontation that he make decisions about their marriage and having children. His was an action-oriented, narcissistic personality disorder. He pursued illusions of narcissistic perfection in the in-love states, which characterized a succession of extramarital affairs. He avoided the full impact of his guilt and the painful loss of his illusions by relating to his wife as if she were a father-policeman. Mr. P began his fourth analysis with the consciously-stated fantasy that his latest liaison was with the brightest, warmest, sexiest of women with whom he could painlessly have a child. He employed the analyst as the externalized representative of his superego. These defensive functions of his externalization were repeatedly interpreted. In particular, its purpose of creating the illusion that limits existed only by virtue of the external presence of a frustrator was emphasized. The working through of this defense facilitated this patient's acceptance of limits in general, and in particular, the limit explicit in attempting to relinquish his pursuit of illusions of perfection for the self-representation-as-agent.

As Mr. P's analysis progressed his proneness to externalization was understood to reflect, in addition to the above-described defensive functions, an aspect of his "success neurosis." He experienced aspects of his narcissistically invested pursuits as oedipal crimes that could be undone in fantasied masochistic submission to an externalized representative of his superego.

Sadistic and masochistic defenses are common alternatives

sought as narcissistic defenses are relinquished. This is so because masochistic defenses are associated with unconscious narcissistic gratifications.[2]

This mid-phase work is associated with all the countertransference vulnerabilities of the earlier work. In addition, the mobilization of painful and frightening memories, and the analysand's experience of deepening depression, may evoke an analyst's wish to soothe his pain-ridden patient. I am suggesting that this countertransference wish to soothe may contribute, in part, to technical recommendations that resemble corrective emotional experiences and/or supportive psychotherapy.

Deepening depression is characteristic of successful mid-phase work with such subjects. Its analysis requires that the analyst be able to live with the depression and the verbal and non-verbal hostile, negativistic and masochistic trends often associated with it. A 36-year-old surgeon, Dr. T, in the fifth year of his second analysis, had been complaining of deepening depression for two years. He had attempted with numerous activities to mute the pain of his depression and to coerce the analyst into soothing him with supportive comments. Most dramatic was his putting himself on the antidepressant imiprimine and in that way gratifying the fantasy of denigrating the analyst and threatening the integrity of the analysis.

More recently, in the context of analytic work on the negative, oedipal, homosexual transference elements in his current depression, the patient had expressed the fantasy that he might choose to miss some sessions and even quit his analysis. These threats evoked anxiety in the analyst, alerting him to possible countertransference and motivating him to think about Dr. T after the hour. He was anxious at the thought of Dr. T's not being at the next hour and considered interpreting the patient's fantasy of leaving him as both an expression of and defense against his

---

[2] I have explored this relationship in a chapter on masochism in *The Structural Hypotheses: An Evolutionary Perspective* (Rothstein, 1983).

anger at the analyst. The patient arrived at the next hour and began to elaborate his fantasy that his depression meant that his analysis was failing and that he was a failure to the analyst. The analyst interpreted this in the positive oedipal transference as a reflection of Dr. T's wish to be a success and a star to the analyst, as he felt he had been at moments to his mother.

The above interpretation derived from recent work on Dr. T's relationship with his mother, and at that moment felt correct. However, the analyst also informed Dr. T that his depression was part of his analysis and, paradoxically, might reflect successful progress. At the time this seemed a reasonable educative intervention. It was only later, after the hour, that the analyst recognized that his countertransference wish to "soothe" the analysand had motivated the supportive, and in that sense, non-analytic intervention. This countertransference wish to soothe may be encouraged by too rigid fealty to concepts such as "holding," "mirroring" and/or "containing."

As the analysand is helped to experience increasing depression he will become enraged at the analyst for not soothing and restoring him to a fantasied state of perfection. He may attempt to project his depression onto the analyst (Olinick, 1964) and to destroy the analyst and the analysis. At this point, the potential for negative therapeutic reaction may become manifest and challenge the analyst's narcissistic investment in being successful.

Consistent interpretation of these resistances, when successful, results in the analysand's increased capacity to experience pain, anxiety and depression, and is associated with the progressive reorganization of past, repressed, archaically-elaborated experiences in conscious, secondary process mentation. The tendency toward "catastrophic feelings of annihilation" and the sense of disaster is replaced by more organized signal affective experiences and an increased capacity for the experience of depression and socializing guilt.

As this work progresses, the analysand increasingly appears more like a neurotic, and his termination phase is not significantly different from those in successfully conducted analyses. What requires emphasis is that the tasks of termination in regard to the working through of narcissistic defenses are associated both with the subject's integration of insights into the ubiquity of narcissistic investments and their defensive function in denial of the limits and vulnerabilities of the self, the object and life. It is particularly important that the relinquishment of the narcissistic identification with the analyst be worked on in the termination phase. Patients will struggle against this working through by maintaining an overvalued view of their analysts.

In contrast to Kohut, I (1980) have emphasized that the incomplete working through of the idealizing transference interferes with the progressive individuation and autonomy associated with more optimal termination. This is especially insidious and profoundly important in the termination of training analyses. The countertransference tendency to disavow the archaic delegated idealization of the introductory phase gives way in the termination phase to the countertransference pleasure of the neophyte's more modulated admiration and overevaluation, not only of the training analyst but also of his narcissistically invested institutions. If the training analyst is working with a candidate who shows "great" promise he may be seduced into reciprocating his analysand's overevaluation. Although such narcissistic investments are interminable, the analysis of their resistant and defensive functions facilitates the mourning and growth so central to the work of successful terminations. Such productive efforts are harbingers of progressive postanalytic self-analysis and individuation, including the potential for independent and creative experience.

In conclusion, it is worth noting that contributors to the field of countertransference in narcissistic investments have often found themselves the subject of comments concerning their countertransference proclivities. In that regard Freud wrote of himself, in response to a letter from Binswanger, "the eye that sees cannot see itself" and warned colleagues against their temptation to put themselves in the "role of prophet" (1923, fn., p. 50) to their patients. Interestingly, Kohut (1977), the discoverer of the converse countertransference to idealizing transferences, described Freud's aversion to narcissistic gratifications. Loewald (1973), while remarking on the value of Kohut's first book, cautioned against regarding it as the final word and suggested that Kohut's work might be limited by a countertransference identification with his analysand's narcissism.

Kohut's (1971) description of the analysis of resistances to the expression and experience of fantasies associated with narcissistic transferences are of considerable heuristic value (Rothstein, 1980). However, his (1977) differentiation between a narcissistic personality disorder proper and a narcissistic behavior disorder, based on a distinction between the former's preference for sadistic fantasy and the latter's preference for sadistic enactment, might reflect a countertransference to activity and the more direct expressions of aggression. Finally, associates of Kohut have implied that Kernberg's preference for early confrontation and interpretation might reflect countertransference in the broader sense. There is some truth in all these statements. However, they remind us that all contributions are inevitably limited, emphasizing the need for continued communication between contributors.

There has been a tendency in psychoanalysis in general, and in discussions of narcissistic personality disorders in particular, to place unifactorial emphasis on contributors' dynamic-genetic constructions. I (1983) have suggested that creators' narcissistic investments in their theories contribute to these tendencies. To the degree that these investments are dogmatically held, although not formally considered countertransference, they contribute a rigidity to the analytic ambience and a tendency to stereotyped interpretations of data. To the extent that theories are divested of these investments, they better accommodate the resonant influences of all stages of development as well as the relative influence of endowment and environment on each individual analysand.

5

The Analyzability of Narcissistic Personality Disorders

Any inquiry into the analyzability of narcissistic personality disorders is tentative at best. All studies of analyzability demonstrate that the analyst's ability to predict the outcome of an analysis is quite imperfect. Accuracy and agreement are often easier to obtain when considering prospective analysands at the sicker and healthier extremes of the spectrum of character integration. Since the patient typically diagnosed a narcissistic personality disorder falls into the midrange of the spectrum of character integration, his analyzability is more difficult to assess. It is not unusual for an analysand diagnosed as a narcissistic personality disorder who begins an analysis with a guarded prognosis to become a subject who works well and accomplishes a great deal. In many cases a judgment of analyzability and prognosis may not be possible after an initial consultation. A six-month to two-year trial of analysis may be necessary. In that regard a consultation can be thought of as attempting to assess suitability for a trial of analysis. The induction phase is often particularly difficult with these patients. Attention to the clinical suggestions of Modell (1976), Kohut (1971), and Gedo (1975) may be helpful in this regard.

It is probable that a number of patients typically considered more "narcissistic" and less "neurotic" who, prior to analysis,

125

were prone to impulsivity with externalization of superego function and little apparent sense of guilt or experience of depression, are ultimately analyzable. In regard to motivation, it is common for narcissistic personality disorders to seek help when their narcissistic equilibrium is threatened and to be primarily motivated by a wish for magical repair via oral incorporative internalization of the idealized analyst. Their capacity for introspection and reflection may be compromised by their agitated state and may not be clearly present for a number of years. Thus, the early presence of a relatively conflict-free therapeutic alliance is unusual in the typical narcissistic personality disorder. The analysis is more often enmeshed in their emerging idealizing transference.

Before proceeding it is important to note that different authors bring to their work a variety of competing theoretical perspectives that contribute to the meanings they derive from their clinical data. Most theoretical orientations encourage an either-or perspective. In addition, the terms ''analysis,'' ''analytic process'' and ''analyzability'' have different meanings for practitioners of varying points of view. In regard to the genesis of a narcissistic personality disorder, some authors stress a developmental arrest of the ego while others emphasize a fixation point to which regression from later conflict clusters. Finally, some of the difference of opinion regarding prognosis, suitability for an attempt at analysis and analyzability derives from the application of the diagnostic category of neurosis and the resulting conception of analytic process. In the evaluation of analyzability of subjects diagnosed as narcissistic personality disorders, different aspects of character organization and analytic process must be emphasized.

Although this chapter focuses upon the analysand's character organization, the question of the personality of the analyst with whom a narcissistic personality disorder will work is particularly germane to the question of analyzability.[1]

---

[1] This perspective is in the tradition of Stone (1954) in contrast to that of Eissler (1953). Stone considered that a particular analyst would be more or less able to establish a working alliance with a particular analysand.

Kohut's (1971) emphasis on specific countertransference potentials to these patients may be of considerable clinical value in helping an analyst create an ambiance where analytic work with narcissistic personality disorders can proceed. He has elaborated common countertransference potentials, particularly boredom, to these analysand's self-involvement and to their efforts to obtain the analyst's attention and participation in their emerging grandiosity. Kohut (1971) and Gedo (1975) have elaborated countertransference potentials to these analysands' penchant for delegated idealization. Analysts who are more comfortable with and tolerant of these tendencies, and who perhaps, as Schafer (1978) implies, are themselves better able to respect and enjoy the penchant for acting-up, -in, and -out and for superego externalization, will be more likely to conduct successful analyses with narcissistic personality disorders.

The literature concerning these patients is characterized by strikingly different opinions on their analyzability and prognosis. In discussing the analyzability of "phallic-narcissistic characters," Wilhelm Reich (1933) described a range of difficulties from those of a better integrated group of patients who "in spite of their narcissistic preoccupation with their selves . . . often show strong attachments to people and things outside" (p. 201) to those of a more troubled group that includes "addicts, particularly alcoholics" (p. 205). He was quite optimistic about their prognosis:

> The analytic treatment of phallic-narcissistic characters is one of the most thankful tasks. . . . The analysis is always successful if one succeeds in unmasking the phallic-narcissistic attitudes as a defense against passive-feminine tendencies and in eliminating the unconscious tendency of revenge against the other sex [p. 206].

Annie Reich (1960) also referred to a wide spectrum of "narcissistic pathology" (pp. 215–216), but did not specifically comment on analyzability. She did, however, make two points that are relevant to these considerations. Like Wilhelm Reich she noted that "notwithstanding the severity of the disturbance, large areas of the personality usually remain intact and are not involved in the pathologic process" (p. 231). Second, she implied that the degree of "successful modification of body narcissism depends primarily upon the ego's capacity for sublimation and . . . deaggressivization" (p. 224) and can be correlated with prognosis.

Kernberg (1970a) described a small group of patients (rather than a broad spectrum) with varying degrees of narcissistic difficulties, whom he referred to as "a pure culture of pathological development of narcissism" (p. 51) and designated "narcissistic personalities." The pathognomonic finding in these patients is "a fusion of ideal self, ideal object, and actual self images" (p. 55). He considered the prognosis of this narrow group to be poor, but stated that it "improves with patients who preserve some capacity for depression or mourning, especially when their depression contains elements of guilt feelings" (p. 73).

Eisnitz (1974) made one of the more detailed and extensive comments on prognosis to be found in the literature. His discussion assumes that these patients fall within a neurotic category.

> It is most important to evaluate motivation, i.e., the patient must come for himself. At least to some extent, treatment should be for a "me," rather than for a patient who is acting solely as an extension of a parent or mate or someone else. Secondly, his treatment goal preferably should involve some conscious desire for realistic change, rather than simply the fulfillment of a narcissistic goal. He must show some capacity for reflection and insight.
>   . . . there should be indications of internalization of superego function, with some capacity for guilt [reference deleted] and relatively stable ideals, as opposed to a predominant emphasis on pleasing, fearing punishment from and borrowing

ideals from external sources. The more indications of conflict at the oedipal level, the better the prognosis. While it is to be expected that there will be significant fluctuations in self-esteem, it is preferable that some estimates of the peaks and valleys be made, so that they are judged to be within the limits which can be sustained during an analysis. . . . Extreme rage reactions or indications of strong destructive feelings toward the self are not good signs.

. . . there should be some capacity for sustained object relations. These might be found on a relatively good level with work colleagues . . . or . . . with his or her children [pp. 285–286].

In regard to responses to loss or "significant narcissistic frustration," he stated that "it is a good prognostic sign if there is some constancy of ideals and ego style which survives such an event" (p. 286). Finally, although Eisnitz acknowledged the elegance of Kohut's descriptions of the narcissistic transferences he emphasized that "recognition of these or other transference elements, however, is not sufficient; the sooner there are indications of some level of therapeutic alliance, the better the prognosis" (p. 286). Eisnitz's considerations can be described as quite correct, but conservative. He and Kernberg share the view that the more like a neurotic the subject is the better the prognosis. He does note two important positive indications that deserve emphasis and elaboration: the presence of oedipal factors and islands of good object relationships.

Kohut's views of prognosis are generally quite optimistic. In his earlier work *The Analysis of the Self*, Kohut (1971) described a broad spectrum of "narcissistic personality disorders" who are neither psychotic nor borderline, but who represent "specific personality disturbances of lesser severity whose treatment constitutes a considerable part of present-day psychoanalytic practice" (p. 1). These patients are characterized by their ability to experience narcissistic transferences. In striking contrast to

Eisnitz, Kohut believes these transferences potentials to be the sole criterion of their analyzability.

In 1977, Kohut distinguished between two types of analyzable narcissistic disorders: the narcissistic personality disorder and the narcissistic behavior disorder (p. 193). The former is characterized by "autoplastic symptoms . . . , such as hypersensitivity to slights" and "hypochondria or depression," as well as by a preference for sadistic "fantasies"; the latter, by "alloplastic symptoms . . . , such as perversion, delinquency, or addiction," and by a penchant for sadistic "behavior" (p. 193). Although Kohut considered narcissistic behavior disorders analyzable, he felt that their ability to enact their sadistic fantasies reflects underlying superego pathology; this he believed renders the prognosis considerably more guarded.

Kohut's distinction between narcissistic behavior disorders and narcissistic personality disorders suggests a number of questionable implications. Foremost among these is that narcissistic behavior disorders are sicker and more difficult to treat. A judgment of health or illness should derive from an assessment of the subject's integration of his narcissistic investments, not from his preference for defensive fantasy versus defensive behavior. One often observes narcissistic personality disorders with both defensive behavior and fantasy. Similarly, one may observe healthier narcissistic personality disorders whose narcissistically invested pursuits express themselves primarily in behavior, while sicker patients, particularly those with schizoid characteristics, pursue illusions of perfection primarily in fantasy. One important and typical technical challenge with these patients is the analysis of their behavior and its ultimate translation into fantasy.

As Kohut's ideas developed, he proposed a new paradigm that progressively emphasized analysis as a reparative object relationship of a predominantly preoedipally-derived developmental arrest. Interpretation in general, and conflict in particular, were gradually deemphasized. Kohut believed that analyzability cannot be determined in consultation but is only assessable in an analytic situation, and that if a process characterized by mirroring and/or idealizing transferences can be established, the patient is analyzable. Increasing experience within this paradigm influenced Kohut to emend his sweepingly optimistic formulation and to focus on subjects' ability to enter into such a reparative relationship. Gedo (1979, 1981), until recently a collaborator of Kohut, has developed a theory of analytic process that retains an emphasis on interpretation but which places greater importance on learning. He states, "The therapeutic limits . . . actually coincide with the individual's capacity to acquire new knowledge" (p. 80). His (1981) view is similar to Kohut's in that what the analysand learns is conceived of as repairing preoedipally-derived developmental "deficits [of] . . . symbiotic attachments" (p. 221). Like Kohut, the only contraindications to analysis are overt psychosis and the threat of serious psychotic regression. Any person who can enter into a collaborative learning relationship with the analyst is potentially analyzable. According to Gedo, analysis is "the treatment of choice for all chronic personality disturbances . . . psychoanalytic psychotherapy is now *indicated* only in situational crises or as a supportive measure for persons threatened with disorganizing experiences" (p. 16). The "limits of analyzability [are]: first, the emergence of actual states of helplessness in the course of treatment; second, the continuing influence of unalterable but disavowed convictions" (p. 78).

While I am in basic agreement with Kohut and Gedo about the broad applicability of analysis as the treatment of choice for nonpsychotic personality disorders, in my experience it is not the ability to establish stable, narcissistic, transference configurations or to learn about their preoedipal roots that renders a subject analyzable. Rather, it is the analysand's ability to work these through.

For a subject to be analyzable, he has to be able to establish and maintain a collaborative alliance with a particular analyst whose personality affords a matrix within which that subject's neurotic transference potential can be focused. Finally, and of central importance in resolving the transference neurosis, is the role of insight gained through interpretation that results in progressive individuation and autonomy. Although identification with the "analyst-introject" (Meissner, 1981) is an important component of the process, it is not the unique mode of therapeutic action of the analytic endeavor. This point is relevant because there are subjects who can accommodate to an analytic situation but who rarely develop past a regressive internalization of the analyst as a reparative, narcissistically invested introject characteristic of mid-phase analytic process. Nonetheless, these subjects may experience significant therapeutic benefit from such a relationship. However, where reparative or "transmuting" internalization gained in the nonverbal "mirroring," "holding" or "containing" ambiance is the primary mode of therapeutic action, a "therapeutic" rather than "analytic" result has been achieved.[2]

The diagnostic category "narcissistic personality disorder" includes a large number of patients who exhibit a broad spectrum of character integrations of their narcissistic investments—integrations vulnerable to significant regressive dedifferentiation. Kohut's "narcissistic behavior disorder" stresses sadistic behavior as an activity of such importance as to require a separate diagnostic category. Wilhelm Reich's (1933) focus on the wish for "vengeance on the strict mother" also emphasizes that sadism, in one form and stage or another of integration, is a characteristic of this diagnostic category. However, just as a broad spectrum of integration exists in narcissistic personality disorders in general, so their penchant for sadistic activities is variously integrated. Playful, sadistic teasing or overt, pleasurable, and often reciprocally experienced sadistic foreplay has quite different prognostic implications from cold sadistic behavior which dominates an experience and is often the only component of impor-

---

[2] For further elaboration of this point, see Rothstein, 1980, pp. 445–450.

tance in a transient encounter with an object. Patients who exhibit the latter have a more guarded prognosis.

The question of why there has been, and still is, considerable controversy about the question of analyzability and prognosis cannot be definitively answered. Stone (1954) noted that personal factors in the analyst may be of critical importance.

The transference neurosis and character disorders of an equivalent degree of psychopathology remain the optimal general indications for the classical method. While difficulties increase and the expectations of success diminish in a general way as the nosologic periphery is approached, there is no absolute barrier; and it is to be borne in mind that both extranosological factors and the therapist's personal tendencies may profoundly influence the indications and prognosis [p. 593].

These "personal tendencies" influence analysts' intellectual opinion. An analyst with a penchant for working with these patients is more likely to express an intellectually organized optimistic opinion concerning their analyzability. Conversely, an analyst who finds these patients difficult, offensive, or boring is likely to be more pessimistic about their analyzability. Stone felt that more needed to be understood about process and prognosis: "With the progressive understanding of the actions of psychotherapeutic admixtures or of large scale parameters in the psychoanalytic method, now so largely intuitive in their application, we can hope that such success will be more frequent" (p. 594).

Kohut's work represents a systematic attempt to fulfill Stone's expectations. In 1968, he noted:

There are thus certain analysts who are said to be exceptionally gifted in the analysis of "borderline" cases. . . . But . . . as our knowledge about the narcissistic disorders increases, their treatment becomes the work of analysts who do not employ any special charisma but restrict themselves to the use of the

tools that provide rational success: interpretations and recon-
structions [pp. 102–103].

He delineated a developmental schema of narcissism, its characteristic expression in the analytic situation, and common countertransference vulnerabilities to the narcissistic transferences.
His recent resynthesis of these constructions within a new paradigm and his disavowal of the structural hypothesis reflect his
view that traditional metapsychology restricts an analyst's responsiveness to and comprehension of these patients. It is probable that with patients referred to as narcissistic personality
disorders the genesis of their character organization has contained
more real deprivation than has that of neurotics. Therefore their
analyses have a more reparative quality than those of typical
neurotics. The analyst serves as a new object (Loewald, 1960),
particularly during the "holding environment" (Modell, 1976)
aspect of the introductory phase. This facilitates reparative internalizations that are in many ways analogous to Kohut's (1971)
transmuting internalizations and Strachey's (1934) mutative interpretations. These structuralizations then facilitate midphase process more typical of the analyses of traditional neurotics.

A number of questions about the current distinction between
neurotics and narcissistic personality disorders can facilitate our
inquiry into the analyzability of these patients: (1) Is there a
definable difference between neurotics and narcissistic personality disorders? (2) Are criteria for analyzability and prognosis
difference from those for neurotics appropriate to narcissistic
personality disorders? (3) Is a distinction between psychoana-
lytically oriented therapy and psychoanalysis with these patients
possible and heuristic? These questions facilitate the drawing of
distinctions—distinctions that are always relative since the boundaries between narcissistic personality disorder and neurosis, as
between psychoanalysis and psychoanalytic psychotherapy, are
neither rigidly nor clearly defined.

In chapter 2, the term *narcissistic personality disorder* describes one of two universal modes of narcissistic investment, while *neurosis* refers to a state of integration of such investment. However, because this synthesis is new it seems heuristic to discuss the analyzability of patients now diagnosed neurotic or narcissistic personality disorder from the perspective of commonly accepted usage. That is, patients typically considered narcissistic personality disorders are thought to have less well-developed psychic structures than neurotics. Patients usually considered neurotic have more internalized superego structuralizations and more typically delegate their narcissistic investments to object representations. In the terminology of chapter 2, such a neurotic would be considered a suppliant personality disorder with a neurotic ego integration of his narcissistic investment.

As Modell (1976) has noted, "our theory of therapeutic change in psychoanalysis may itself be constantly changing due to the changing nature of the neuroses" (p. 285). A number of contemporary social factors have contributed to this "changing nature of the neuroses." Modern mores permit a wider range of gratification. Normal adolescence (Blos, 1962) is prolonged for increasing numbers of people as educational opportunities become more available and as successful adaptation requires increasing years of formal preparation. Groups within society encourage "acting-up" (A. Freud, 1968), thereby facilitating superego dedifferentiation and externalization. Indeed some patients designated narcissistic personality disorders today might well have been considered neurotic twenty-five years ago.

Let us return to the first question: Is there a definable distinction between patients typically considered narcissistic personality disorder and those patients typically considered neurotic? Neurotics struggle primarily with intersystemic conflicts and have ego ideals characterized by a degree of depersonification. Narcissistic personality disorders struggle primarily with conflicts and responses to their quest to restore a sense of narcissistic perfection to their self-representation (annihilation anxiety, rage, depression, elation, etc.). Their ego ideals (A. Reich, 1960) and

their superegos are characterized by aberrations of structuralization. This does not mean that these patients are missing something, that they have an incapacity or a defect, but rather, that
their superegos and ego ideals are characterized by a penchant
for regressive dedifferentiation and externalization in response
to conflict and by intrasystemic conflict between poorly integrated, often contradictory, object representations. Most patients
struggle with a combination of these difficulties, and a given
diagnosis at any point in the analysis reflects the analyst's consideration of the relative importance of the issues to that subject's
character integration: a subject may be considered neurotic only
to appear more narcissistic after defense analysis or transference
regression.

In analytic work with narcissistic personality disorders,
questions of analyzability and prognosis relate to defining the
nature and goals of the analysis and the indications for its termination. These issues of criteria revolve around the ability of
the analyst and analysand to create an environment and relationship within which the analysand can mourn his defensive pursuit
of illusions of narcissistic perfection for his self-representation,
particularly those that are maladaptive. Eisnitz's emphasis on the
evaluation of a subject's response to previous loss and narcissistic
injury is particularly relevant to evaluating his potential to tolerate
the narcissistic injuries associated with an analytic experience.
It must be stressed that the analysand's manifest capacity to mourn
may significantly increase after a number of years of "mirroring"
(Kohut, 1971) within an ambience Modell (1976) had described
as a "holding environment."[3]

[3] Bach (1977) succinctly described the essentials of this environment in
his critical comment on one analysand's previous analytic experience: "It
seemed to me that the previous analyst had neglected this crucial area of tension
management and that his oedipal interpretations, while 'true', were premature
and had only served to enrage and frighten the patient who, like an over-excited
child, needed to be calmed before he could be reasoned with. This tension
regulation was . . . the provision of the specific type of narcissistic object
relationship needed at that time to enable the analysis to proceed" (p. 227).

Resiliency, flexibility of response to narcissistic injury, and talent—three complex characteristics of the ego—can facilitate the mourning experience characteristic of analytic work with these patients.

Resiliency, the ability to spring back or recover, as from depression, reflects an internalized sense, within self-as-agent, that "I" can make it. It usually derives from a well-integrated primary maternal identification that analytic work should increase and render more autonomous.

Resiliency, flexibility of response to narcissistic injury, and real talent, when combined, facilitate opportunities for adaptive narcissistic gratifications that assuage the insult of the loss of one's original narcissistic perfection. These qualities provide the building blocks out of which a more realistic life can be established as compulsive pursuits of illusory narcissistic perfection for the self-representation are relinquished.

The analysis of narcissistic elements has been characterized as a mourning experience. The analysis of neurotic elements can be characterized by a degree of conflict resolution both inter- and intrasystemic in nature and by a diminution of the severity of the superego. Again, it is worth stressing that most analyses have elements of both kinds of processes occurring in alternating or complementary fashion. The relative prevalence of one or another type of material determines the diagnosis. It is not an uncommon experience for a diagnosis of narcissistic personality disorder to be followed by many years of analytic work characteristic of this diagnostic category only to subtly shift to a process characteristically neurotic. In such cases the analysand's pursuit of perfection for his self-representation had probably been a lifelong defensive attempt to find a conflict-free nirvana that would protect him from the perils of preoedipal, oedipal and postoedipal longings, disappointments, and dangers—all perceived as life-threatening.

The distinction between psychoanalysis and psychotherapy certainly is heuristic and although full discussion of this subject is beyond our present scope, an aspect of it is relevant to the question of the analyzability of narcissistic personality disorders. In 1977, Kohut described a process of analytic termination that most analysts would consider psychotherapy. He described a patient, Mr. M, who, "abandoned by his natural mother . . . had been in an orphanage until he was three years old" (p. 25). His adoptive mother was emotionally distant and died when he was twelve years old. These life experiences resulted in a "serious structural defect" (p. 20), the healing of which occurred through the "analysis" of his mirror transference.

Difference of opinion arises in response to Kohut's description of Mr. M's termination as analytic. Fundamental issues remained unanalyzed, leaving a central and repressed sector of Mr. M's character organization unaffected. In Kohut's judgment to do so "might bring about a perhaps irremedial disintegration of the self" (p. 19). Kohut felt that "behind these layers of frustration there hovered always a nameless preverbial depression, apathy, sense of deadness, and diffuse rage that related to the primordial trauma of his life" (p. 25). Most analyses benefit from some unanalyzed identification with the analyst as new object. However, where there is the *primary* mode of therapeutic action, throughout the process, and where it remains unanalyzed at termination, the process should be considered a psychotherapy. Profound early deprivations and the resulting disturbances may necessitate a judgment that analysis would result in serious disorganization and therefore that a subject is not analyzable.

The question of analyzability is clearer when dealing with more seriously disturbed patients such as those that Wilhelm Reich described. In the presence of poor impulse control, poor frustration and anxiety tolerance, and minimal sublimatory potential, it is relatively easy to arrive at a judgment of guarded prognosis. However, it is my impression that many analysands diagnosed as narcissistic personality disorders are ultimately analyzable, but present clinical pictures similar to those of other narcissistic personality disorders whose analyses ultimately fail.

All analysts like some analysands more than others. Liking a prospective analysand who is a narcissistic personality disorder is one factor that contributes to a favorable prognosis. A less-than-positive attitude often reflects a subtle countertransference potential toward the prospective analysand's particular quests to restore a sense of narcissistic perfection to his self-representation (perversions, for example). Such a countertransference potential has at least two disadvantages. First, it potentiates these analysands' penchant for superego externalization. They prefer to manipulate, argue, and fight with an external judge than to experience internal conflict with its associated guilt and depression. Second, subtle dislike of an analysand intrudes on an analyst's ability to create an analytic situation within which the collaboration and tasks characteristic of introductory phrase process can be experienced.

Potential analysands may exhibit a number of characteristics that also make for a more guarded prognosis. These include: (1) a history of recurrent experiences of overwhelming anxiety (probably associated with fragmentation or dedifferentiation of the self-representation), often linked to chronic maladaptation or serious drug addiction; (2) serious psychosomatic illness; (3) chronic, rather than transient, feelings of deadness, sometimes associated with anhedonia; and (4) paranoid and projective mechanisms as the predominant defensive response to narcissistic injury.

In regard to the process of assessing prognosis, suitability for analysis, and analyzability, there are a number of subjects seeking help who at evaluation do not appear psychotic, but are vulnerable to serious psychotic regression in the transference and are probably not analyzable. It is often quite difficult to distinguish unanalyzable and analyzable narcissistic personality disorders before a trial analysis. Certain unanalyzable narcissistic personality disorders can develop narcissistic transferences associated with salutary reparative internalizations but cannot work them through. Interpretive attempts to facilitate a working-through process can evoke psychotic regressions or serious acting

out, sometimes including rapid disruption of the working relationship.

I have described narcissistic personality disorders by the
prevalence of their narcissistic defenses and the pursuit of a panoply of narcissistic investments for their self-representations.
These investments are integrated by their egos in a spectrum from
psychotic to normal. As I discussed in chapter 4, most analyzable
narcissistic personality disorders employ, in addition to their narcissistic defenses, other defenses including denial of narcissistic
injury, projection of rage, externalization of superego introjects,
as well as defensive masochistic and sadistic identifications.
However, in evaluating analyzability, the issue is not dynamic
(i.e., the pursuit of illusions of narcissistic perfection for the self-
representation); it is structural and functional. A consideration
of other structural and functional characteristics of ego organization is required when attempting the difficult and precarious
task of assessing analyzability. Analysts are left with the awareness that among a large group of subjects considered "typical"
narcissistic personality disorders, some will have optimal analytic
experiences while others will accomplish much less. Paradoxically, it is worth emphasizing that an individual with an unanalyzable narcissistic personality disorder may experience significant
therapeutic gain from an incomplete analytic endeavor.

At this point, two very different unanalyzable narcissistic
personality disorders will be described to highlight structural and
functional aspects of their ego organization that made analytic
work with them impossible. The integration of their self-representations were rigidly maintained and vulnerable to de-differ-
entiation associated with psychotic regression. They were inflexible
in response to narcissistic injury, rigidly clinging to their narcissistic investments in their self-representations as to a life preserver. They possessed a penchant for enactment, and little genuine
interest in or capacity for fantasy or self-observation.

Mr. M, a 31-year-old lawyer, and recently divorced father
of a preschool son, sought analysis with the stated wish to be

close to and committed to a woman and to have a family. In retrospect, it seems more probable that this presenting complaint reflected his view of what a good patient should say in order to be accepted. Mr. M was more sincerely motivated to find out what it was about him that resulted in his difficulty in keeping a secretary. He told a heart-rending story of life and his Herculean efforts to overcome his past. His mother was typical of the mothers of narcissistic personalities described by Kernberg (1970a): cold, enraged and profoundly unempathic. His father was prone to violent outbursts, was a ne'er-do-well alcoholic, and died when Mr. M was preadolescent.

A vignette from his late latency emphasized the lifelong impact of his mother's disturbed personality. Mr. M was at school with a strep throat and 103° temperature. He called his mother, who insisted he walk the four miles from school because she didn't have the time to get him and wished to save the cost of the gasoline for the four-mile trip. Mr. M recalled his literally crawling part of the way home. In adolescence, Mr. M spent most of his waking hours away from home, and when he was 17 he quit school to join the Army. In the Army he was a model soldier, obtained a high school equivalency degree and some college credits. After an honorable discharge he worked his way through college and law school. In addition to his stated wish to improve his relationships, his only other complaints were of frequent headaches and a functional bowel disorder.

During the process of establishing the analytic situation, Mr. M expressed the conviction that he did not have the time to be in a four-sessions-per week endeavor. I agreed to begin work with him at a frequency of three sessions per week, conceiving of this as a "modification" of the introductory phase of his analysis. In retrospect it was the beginning of his psychotherapy. Initiating treatment in this manner seems to have reflected Mr. M's need to control the analyst and not to be treated do in what he perceived to be the analyst's way. He would receive an analysis but it would not cost him as much in time or money as it did

other mortals, who he felt were "suckers." The analyst came to
appreciate that for Mr. M any sense of not being in control of
the object was rigidly experienced as a *real,* rather than a symbolic, threat to his life.

Mr. M was very active and somewhat hypomanic; however,
his affect was inappropriately bland. He worked long hours and
pursued his pleasures with a similar ardor. It was not unusual for
him to work a 65 to 70-hour week and drive 12 hours to ski 15
hours on weekends. His relationships were both extractive and
self-centered. Objects were easily idealized, expected to be all-
gratifying, and quickly devalued when they were not. On one
occasion his penchant for defensive denigration failed him. In a
jealous rage he lost control and fractured a lady friend's jaw. He
felt no sense of guilt or remorse, only fear of the legal implications
of his act. A session from the third year of his therapy reflects
the profound nature of the disturbance in his object relations. He
referred to women as "things" or as devalued members of his
"stable." He began a session speaking of the frustrations he was
experiencing with a lady friend, Laura, who was "a great cook
but a lousy fuck." Then he reported a dream:

I was somewhere, not in the United States, in a foreign place,
in an open-air whorehouse. I selected a woman and started
screwing her. She was bad. I complained and she told me to
start the fucking machine. I put my cock in it. It vibrated. It
was good. I came. I was happy.

Mr. M became silent and after about five minutes the analyst
commented, "People are frustrating; machines appear to be frustration free," to which Mr. M responded, "It didn't talk back,"
and became silent once again. After a few minutes I reminded
him that he hated his mother "talking back." He said, "Right."
He went on to conjecture that he could complement his relationship with Laura, who was a great cook, with Cookie, who had
lots of orgasms.

It is important to emphasize that although the transference implications of Mr. M's associations are obvious to any analyst, he tenaciously avoided working in the transference. He was capable of intense rage reactions; however, these were never experienced in the transference. Mr. M demonstrated a profound denial of feelings and was often unable to experience or understand what he was feeling. In response to the analyst's inquiry, "What are you feeling?" he would reflexively say, "No," as if the analyst's question was experienced as a threatening intrusion. He would withdraw into silence and, on occasion, into sleep.

The analyst's attempts to explore these regressions and their transference implications were met with impenetrable rationalizations. In response to the analyst's suggestion that his falling asleep on the couch might have something to do with his feelings toward the analyst, Mr. M suggested that he was tired because he had been screwing all night. In the fourth year of analysis, Mr. M began the session prior to the analyst's leaving him for a winter vacation by informing the analyst that he had had a very disturbing dream.

> I was with Howard at a ski area. Each of us was with a woman. We agreed to meet at a particular time to ski together and he came in ski clothes and said he decided not to go, and I was enraged. It was dangerous to ski alone. It was a tremendous betrayal.

He associated to conflicts with senior partners over his vacation, and remarked that he couldn't think of another reason for the dream. The analyst commented, "Maybe it's a response to my leaving you." Mr. M responded, "No, it has to do with the firm; they're going to insist and I'm going to walk out. There is just a limit as to how much they can push."

After four years of work, Mr. M felt that he had profited a great deal from his experience. He could now keep his secretary and was able to avoid many potentially self-destructive interactions with his associates. However, his manner of relating with women was basically unchanged. He would become intensely involved, and after months of disappointment he and his friend would end the relationship. His treatment experience focused almost entirely on his real-life involvements. He almost never spoke of the analyst except in idealized terms.

At the beginning of the fifth year together, we discussed his situation. He expressed a wish to work on his difficulties with women. The analyst suggested that these problems revolved around issues of intimacy and could be dealt with in his relationship to the analyst. The analyst suggested that to do this Mr. M should consider increasing the intensity of his relationship to the analyst by coming four times per week and attempting to experience and express his feelings, thoughts, and fantasies about the analyst. Mr. M agreed, but within a month felt that the exigencies of his professional responsibilities necessitated the termination of formal treatment. He felt no more than a week was necessary to deal with his feelings about leaving. He could have comfortably stopped without any additional sessions.

I hypothesized privately that Mr. M chose to interrupt his formal work because to deepen it was to feel like murdering the analyst and/or being destroyed. The analyst chose to respect his decision because in the analyst's judgment Mr. M was unable to experience or reality-test this unconscious fantasy. Mr. M left, expressing his gratitude, secure in the knowledge that the analyst was there and that he could resume therapy if he felt he needed to.

At the present time, Mr. M continues to prosper professionally and socially. His personal life remains much the same. He calls the analyst about once a year for a referral for his current lady friend. During these phone conversations he talks about his life and expresses the wish that the analyst find his friend an analyst as wonderful as his analyst. Such an analyst would undoubtedly be able to change his friend so that they might be happy together.

It is important to emphasize that Mr. M experienced a transient and profound disorder of the reality-testing and judgment functions of his ego. He has been capable of exposing himself and others to very significant danger, armed with a conviction of his own omnipotence and invulnerability. These misconceptions derive from a rigidly maintained investment in illusions of narcissistic perfection in his self-representation, an investment that at those life-threatening moments appeared to be psychotically integrated. On one occasion, Mr. M risked his life in a successful effort to stop an armed robbery. He scoffed at the analyst's concern and suggestion that he was endangering his life. Although Mr. M was undoubtedly gratified by the analyst's statement, ''I am concerned that you might seriously hurt yourself or even be killed,'' his sense of reality was seemingly unaffected by this intervention.

Mr. Q, a successful businessman in his early fifties, had been in analysis or psychotherapy, pursuing a magical cure, most of his adult life. He had had three five-year analyses with competent analysts, as well as an experience with family therapy just prior to beginning work with this analyst more than seven years ago. At that time he was recently bankrupt, divorced after a marriage of 14 years, and had just had a gastrectomy because of a life-threatening ulcer. It is possible that these events were significantly motivated by unanalyzed psychotic transference (Searles, 1963) to the family therapist. He was depressed and felt hopeless about his ability ever to find work satisfying to him. He had numerous idealized fantasies of finding nirvana in one or another state of retirement. Despite these profound difficulties, Mr. Q possessed a charm and likeable quality and communicated a tenacious motivation to ''beat'' all his difficulties.

Mr. Q's charm and characterological desire to please had undoubtedly influenced his previous analysts to work with him. His first analysis was terminated with the analyst informing Mr.

Q that, while there was some unfinished business, he felt that Mr. Q had had a successful analysis. His second analysis was begun a year later in response to anxiety concerning his prospective marriage. This analysis ended in an acting out, with Mr. Q quitting. He recalled that when he telephoned on Monday to apologize for having quit on Friday, his analyst told him he had filled his hours.

After a number of years, Mr. Q shared a secret with me. He had a secret fantasy life that he had never shared with his analysts. He had performed for them, assuming that his reward would be a cure. I have little doubt that if I had seen Mr. Q 25 years earlier, as a young, anxious, successful businessman, I would have considered him potentially analyzable.

Mr. Q was the first of two boys born five years apart. His mother's behavior toward him was inconsistent. She was depressed, hypochondriacal, and suffered from migraine headaches that left her bedridden for two to three days at a time. At other moments she overvalued and adulated her beautiful child. She communicated a message to Mr. Q that he was special and would get whatever he wanted just by smiling. His father was a successful businessman, proud of his ability to cheat his customers and his wife. He flaunted both his illegal business practices and his mistress. Although his parents repeatedly told Mr. Q that they loved him and only wanted the best for him, he never believed them. As a child he suffered multiple hypochrondriacal concerns and was constipated. Bowel movements were infrequent and painful, facilitated by fantasied battles between competing armies. He had difficulty in school but was able to leave home to attend and graduate college. He subsequently lived with his parents until his marriage at the age of 28.

For the past seven years this analyst has worked with Mr. Q in a psychotherapy of varying intensity with significant "modifications" (Stone, 1954). Adjunctive treatment with 300 milligrams per day of imiprimine was employed during the fifth year and reinstated in the sixth year of work. During these years Mr.

Q was able to marry and assume responsibility for his new wife's children. In addition, his enjoyment of work increased and he achieved significant success. Following a minor surgical procedure which necessitated withdrawal of imiprimine, Mr. Q became hypomanic, interrupted treatment, and seriously threatened his second marriage, which has since ended in divorce. Five months later he resumed treatment.

Mr. Q has serious problems in the areas of anxiety and frustration tolerance, and has a chronic sleep disturbance. He has been chronically afflicted with feelings of worthlessness, despite significant success. He had treated these difficulties with alcohol, and more recently with diazepam, to which he became addicted.

The analyst's view of Mr. Q is of a person struggling valiantly to "assimilate" (Waelder, 1936) an everpresent sense of disorganization. Mr. Q has experienced frank paranoid transference responses that seriously threatened the therapeutic alliance and limited work in the transference. His conflicts and defensive responses to rage mobilized in the transference have necessitated major modifications of technique to have any effect on his rigidly integrated defenses. A barely disguised dream reflects Mr. Q's exquisite sensitivity to the frustrations of the therapeutic situation experienced as a humiliation. Mr. Q was chronically enraged at the forty-five minute duration of his sessions. He was anxious the entire session in response to his constant awareness that the session would soon end. He dreamt:

I came for the doctor and he wasn't there. His secretary didn't know where he was and suggested that I come back at 6:00 o'clock and I'm annoyed. The doctor finally arrived. I'm very angry but I couldn't confront him. He wouldn't listen to my suggestions. He tried to reason with me, but there is no dealing with me.

In response to conflict with his business partners Mr. Q dreamt *of killing his cousins, the grotesque nature of their dead bodies, and his fear of being caught.* He enthusiastically brought this dream to the analyst, stating, ''This dream is one of the most important I've ever had because it emphasizes my fear of being caught. Prior to this dream I always thought it was castration anxiety, but it's not. It's anxiety in response to my fear of being caught for my wish to kill anyone who frustrates me. I'm stuck with my partner, like with a relative, and I can't get rid of him.'' Although Mr. Q gained considerable insight into the relationship between his rage, anxiety and defensive narcissistic investments, imiprimine proved more effective than insight or the therapeutic relationship in diminishing Mr. Q's anxiety.

In the second year of work, in response to the analyst's identifying the extractive nature of his relationship with his fiancée, Mr. Q became outraged, stood up, paced the room and accused the analyst of having devious and criminal intentions. In the ensuing years attempts to work in the transference often resulted in a psychotically integrated ''identification with the aggressor'' (A. Freud, 1936, p. 117). Anna Freud described this defense as a ''reversal of roles of the attacker and attacked'' (p. 123). Behaving like the analyst, Mr. Q interpreted that the analyst was projecting his problems onto Mr. Q. The analyst identified the difficulty of working in the transference and suggested that the patient limit his exploration to issues of current reality. This resulted in some gains but was limited by his misperception of his object world.

In response to the perception that he was destroying his body, Mr. Q stopped drinking. Diazepam replaced alcohol as his anti-anxiety agent. The quality of his rage seemed to diminish, and he requested another attempt at working in the transference. Mr. Q reminded the analyst that he was aware of his difficulties in getting closer to his wife and of the fact that working in the transference offered a potentially safer and less self-destructive area within which to experience these difficulties. He suggested a modification designed to deal with his poor frustration tolerance and paranoid mistrust. He felt that twice-a-week, tape-recorded, triple sessions were the answer. This evoked two questions of potential countertransference in the analyst. Could the analyst tolerate: (1) the patient uninterrupted for two hours and fifteen minutes, and (2) the helpless exposure of being recorded by the patient? The analyst decided there was no danger to Mr. Q in his suggestion and was intrigued by the possibilities of the experience.

Mr. Q recorded the sessions. He then took the tapes (i.e., the analyst) with him on his weekends. He listened to the tapes and returned after a few weeks, stating, ''I'm crazy! How do you tolerate me? I'm really paranoid.'' This arrangement continued for several weeks, gradually changing to two 90-minute sessions per week. This work resulted in some tentative diminution of Mr. Q's suspicious, projective inclination to feel attacked and criticized as well as in his becoming somewhat calmer, more able to remain in contact with the object, and to listen to, rather than compete with and control, the analyst and/or his wife. This modification of technique also seemed to enable Mr. Q to impose on himself the narcissistic injury of the transference interpretation, thereby mitigating his psychotic transference potential. However, his exquisite sensitivity and tendency to experience the transference as real continued to seriously limit analytic work. Although he was able to be more self-observing and self-critical at some concrete distance from the object, especially when the analyst (recording tape) was totally in his control, his penchant for projective distortions of reality remained unaltered.

At the present time, if the integration of Mr. Q's narcissistic investments is seriously threatened by the analyst, his proneness to disavow reality becomes more manifest. If the analyst persists in interpretive efforts, Mr. Q attacks and/or leaves the analyst in order to maintain his integration. As long as he is able to restore his sense of control, his distortions of reality are transient. In conclusion, Mr. Q remains vulnerable and rigidly defended in denial of his conflicts and disavowel of painful and terrifying perceptions. He withdraws into idealized fantasies created to support his denial and defend him from awareness of his rage at the inevitable limits of the self, the object, and of life.

In order to facilitate an inquiry into analyzability, I will discuss these two, very different, unanalyzable narcissistic personality disorders from four complementary perspectives: (1) the relationship to ego development of formative experiences with their parents, with particular emphasis on the integration of the self-representation and the development of the capacities for fantasy, self-observation and sublimation; (2) the influence of process versus shock trauma in the genesis of character pathology; (3) the development of trust in relation to a variety of alliances with the analyst; and (4) the question of diagnosis.

Stability in the integration of the self-representation is an essential prerequisite for an analytic process. In selected unanalyzable narcissistic personality disorders their narcissistic defenses protect against psychosis. They cling to their defenses and/or the analyst to protect against disorganization. In analyzable narcissistic personality disorders, the stability of the self-representation is associated with their ego's potential for assimilation of the defensive function of their narcissistic investments in relation to traumatic formative experiences and attempts at conflict resolution. Such an analytic process is characterized, in part, by the recovery of painful and terrifying memories capable of being progressively maintained in consciousness, and is associated with depression in the working through phase of the experience. As these memories are reorganized in secondary process mentation, the analysand's compulsive pursuit of illusions of narcissistic perfection for the self-representation is diminished.

The profound disturbances in Mr. M's and Mr. Q's relationships with their parents contributed to a significant vulnerability of their self-representations to dedifferentiation.[4] It seems

---

[4] The emphasis of this presentation is on development rather than maturation. However, it is worth remembering Hartmann's (1950b) emphasis on the influence of maturation of autonomous ego functions on ego development. He stated: ''The presence of such factors . . . the timing of the appearance of

reasonable to hypothesize that throughout Mr. M's first 18 months of life he was exposed to a chronic, traumatic, developmental process wherein his active seeking of gratification in general, and empathic responsiveness and affirmation in particular, were responded to significantly with cold unavailability and/or angry and sadistic rejection. In response he withdrew and sustained himself through a variety of self-stimulating modes. This process was probably associated with a premature and fragile integration of his self-representation. In addition, in elaboration of Freud's (1923, p. 29) hypothesis concerning the ubiquitous defensive nature of identification, Mr. M's sadism and cold detached demeanor can be conceived to derive, in part, from his mother's cold, angry and sadistic nature. Moreover, his alcoholic father was rarely available and was prone to violent outbursts.

In contrast, Mr. Q was exposed to a traumatic developmental process characterized by inconsistency. His mother was unempathically overstimulating or unavailable for his phase-appropriate attempts at fusion and eliciting affirmation. Her maternal inconsistency may have contributed to the fluidity of the regressive potential that was characteristic of the integration of his self-representation. In addition, Mr. M painfully perceived his father's manipulative and dishonest nature. This disappointment deprived him of an opportunity to idealize his father and left him angry, anxious, defiantly self-destructive and perpetually seeking illusions of perfection in others and for himself.

Mr. M, like McDougall's (1980) "anti-analysand," was not aware of, or interested in, his own inner world. Instead, his interest and sublimatory potential were directed at manipulating

---

grasping, of walking, of the motor aspect of speech . . . in all aspects of the child's behavior makes them essential elements in the development of his self experience'' (p. 121). In this regard, Weil (1978) noted that ''if variations . . . [such as] special sensitivities, maturational delays and lags in achievement . . . occur in the beginning of life, they primarily effect ego structuring, and anxiety and aggression potentials'' (p. 488). With regard to the "*perceptual apparatus*," she stated, ''I would stress that the experience of mothering in itself depends on the perceptual constellation and interplay of each individual child with his individual mother'' (p. 468).

the environment to be gratifying rather than applied to those ego functions more typical of creative work in general, and analysis in particular.

It is probable that a loving "optimally available" maternal object during the first two years of life facilitates internalizations characterized by a self-representation that progressively maintains its integrity in the face of angry introjects. In addition, such a self-representation feeling loved and affirmed by the internalized presence of increasingly complex and well integrated parental internalizations can begin to play with derivatives of these internalizations. This play in fantasy and with toys is associated with delay, and is reflective of a developing capacity for sublimation. In that regard, Mahler et al. (1975) noted that "the growing individuation associated with the diminishing rapprochement struggle" (p. 101) was characterized by "the development of language, . . . the beginnings of superego . . . and progress in the ability to express wishes and fantasies through symbolic play" (p. 101).

Freud (1933) hypothesized that "self-observation" (p. 66) was one of three fundamental functions of the superego. I am suggesting that the self-observing function of the ego necessary for successful analytic work derives, in part, from an identification with a "loving and beloved superego" (Schafer, 1960) introject and, in that sense, represents a "change of function" (Hartmann, 1939b, p. 25) characteristic of more optimal ego and superego development. Unfortunately, Mr. M's object world was characterized by terrifying introjects, which were predominantly primary process elaborations of the ego of a differentiating toddler prematurely forced to be self-sufficient. If Mr. M played at all, it was probably limited to repetitive expressions of aggressive drive derivatives. His ego had the capacity to fantasize sensual pleasures but little potential for fantasy in the service of adaptive delay when faced with a frustrating object. Similarly, his identifications with preoedipal and oedipal superego introjects remained almost solely combative "identifications with the aggressor."

Freud's (1920a) psychoanalytic concept of trauma conceived of an ego overwhelmed by excessive internal and/or external stimuli. Infant research, particularly the findings of Sander (1964, 1976) and Stern (1974), implies that the infant is born with a preprogrammed set of needs for maternal responsiveness and temporally determined set of behaviors for initiating and sustaining a reciprocally gratifying and developmentally facilitating relationship with the maternal object. When the maternal object is unable to respond optimally, the resulting reciprocity is traumatic rather than nurturant. In examining the influence of early factors on Mr. M's and Mr. Q's analyzability, I am suggesting that their entire developmental process can be considered traumatic, i.e., they were exposed to *process*[5] trauma. Instead of the mother figure facilitating the progressive integration and affirmation of the infant's experience, she more often contributed a disturbing influence that traumatically interfered with her offsprings' personality development, leaving them fixated in rigidly maintained adaptive modes. Other analyzable subjects have been more fortunate. Their early development may have been quite satisfactory and only disrupted by subsequent *shock trauma*. I have suggested that the latter may be associated with a better prognosis. However, there is often a history of both process and shock traumas.

The influences of early development have a fundamental impact on the development of a therapeutic alliance so essential to a fulfilling analytic experience. With narcissistic personality disorders I have noted that at the beginning of an analysis the

[5] When discussing psychic trauma it is important to note that for Freud (1920a) trauma represented an acute economic crisis in which the ego's stimulus barrier is overwhelmed. Kris (1956) characterized such acute crises as "shock" traumas (p. 73) and distinguished "strain trauma" (p. 73) to refer to "the effect of long lasting situations, which may cause traumatic effects by the accumulation of frustrating tensions" (p. 73). The concepts of "cumulative trauma" (Kahn, 1963) and "process trauma" are synonymous with Kris' original conception of strain trauma.

collaborative alliance is usually enmeshed in an idealizing trans-ference. Meissner (1981) has elaborated Mehlman's (1976) con-tribution and delineated distinctions between a narcissistic alliance, a narcissistic misalliance, and a therapeutic alliance. The "nar-cissistic alliance requires . . . basic trust . . . the therapeutic al-liance . . . requires a more . . . evolved form of trust" (p. 181). Patients similar to McDougall's (1980) "anti-analysands" de-velop a narcissistic misalliance "in which they cooperate with the external requirements of analysis but withhold themselves from a commitment to the analytic process" (p. 203). In "nar-cissistic patients" the "misalliance is based on magical expec-tations" (p. 203), rather than on an active identificatory process. These distinctions are particularly helpful in evaluating the de-velopment of the analytic process and in assessing questions of analyzability.

Mr. M's and Mr. Q's therapeutic experiences with this an-alyst, as well as the latter's past analytic efforts, can be char-acterized by the predominance of a narcissistic misalliance. In spite of Mr. Q's tenacious struggle to obtain insight, which af-forded him some moments of self-awareness, this occurred within the context of a narcissistic misalliance maintained in his inter-minable quest for a magical analytic cure. In addition to his transient paranoid psychotic regressions, Mr. Q seemed to ex-perience as disorganizing any attempts at analytic collaboration characteristic of a therapeutic alliance based on "secondary trust" (Mehlman, 1976, p. 23). He appeared to regard the analyst's separate existence as a threat to the integration of his self-rep-resentation, and was compelled to complete or emend most of the analyst's statements in order to make them his own. In spite of his need to cling to the external idealized analytic object, he remained rigidly walled off from a more salutary introjection of the analyst as a trustable collaborator.

Mr. Q's mistrust was fundamentally derived from experi-ences of his mother's inconsistent ministrations and unavailabil-ity. These early developmental influences were reinforced by his father's illegal business transactions and infidelity. Mr. Q always believed that his father was attempting to manipulate him into doing what he desired. When he was sent away from home to boarding school or camp he felt that his parents wanted to be rid of him to pursue their own pleasures, although his father told him it was for his "own good." Mr. Q. felt abandoned and clung to the wish to make the world respond to him as he imagined his mother did when she was overvaluing and adulating him as her first-born son. As a consequence, he is alternately anxious, manipulative, enraged and depressed when he perceives his own limits and those of his object world.

I have suggested that flexibility of response to narcissistic injury is a complex characteristic of the ego that can facilitate the mourning experience typical of analytic work with these patients. Although Mr. M and Mr. Q were resilient, they were quite inflexible in response to narcissistic injury. To definitively accept a limit not only evoked "feelings of catastrophic annihilation" (Reich, 1960, p. 225); it was associated with paranoid decompensation.

Better early development provides enough basic trust to develop a narcissistic alliance, rather than misalliance, within the context of an idealizing transference. Later, shock and process traumas, such as those experienced by Mr. Z or by McDougall's (1980) Sabine whose parents died during her sixth year of life, interfere with the development of secondary trust. However, sensitive work with such patients' narcissistic defenses can ultimately facilitate the development of a therapeutic alliance.

Before attempting a discussion of diagnosis it is important to emphasize the obvious; all diagnoses are incomplete designations attempting to highlight data representing only an aspect of a human being. Moreover, most diagnoses are psychiatric rather than psychoanalytic, although some descriptive diagnoses are more psychoanalytic because they are enriched by metapsychological formulations. For example, Kohut's (1971) and McDougall's (1980) diagnoses are particularly psychoanalytic because they derive from data on the analytic process: Kohut's diagnosis of the narcissistic personality disorder derives from a description of unique transference constellations and their associated countertransference configurations, while McDougall's conception of the "anti-analysand" is intended to alert the analyst to a particular defensive configuration manifest in an analytic process associated with a dismal prognosis.

Mr. M could be given a number of diagnostic labels, all associated with a poor or guarded prognosis: narcissistic personality (Kernberg, 1970a), narcissistic behavior disorder (Kohut, 1977), or a subgroup of psychotic personality (Frosch, 1970). McDougall (1980) might consider him a sicker variety of the "anti-analysand." Mr. Q would fall within Kernberg's (1975) third group of narcissistic personalities who "function overtly on a borderline level and present nonspecific manifestations of ego weakness" (p. 34). Kohut and Wolf (1978) might consider him as suffering from a *"fragmenting self"* (p. 418).

Kohut (1960, 1977) and McDougall (1980) have commented on the diagnostic dilemma posed by individuals such as Mr. M. Of Scheber's "father's pathology" Kohut (1960) asked:

> What is this pathology? *We have no accepted diagnostic category,* but I believe he represented, not a severe kind of psychoneurosis but a special kind of psychotic character structure in which reality testing remains broadly intact so long as it is in the service of the psychosis, of the central idee fixe. It is probably *a kind of healed over psychosis.* . . . His fanatical activities belong to *a hidden narcissistic delusional system* [p. 306; italics added].

McDougall (1980) noted that although the "anti-analysand" disavows involvement in an analytic process he "cling[s] tenaciously to his analytic adventure [object]" (p. 246). Of this kind of resistance she noted that "Freud considered this defense mechanism [repudiation from consciousness] as predominant in psychotic structures'' (p. 244).

Mr. M and Mr. Q represent a subgroup of narcissistic personality disorders who are not overtly psychotic but who constantly avoid deepening involvement in an analytic process because they fear psychotic disorganization. I find the term ''borderline'' unsatisfactory for these patients because there are analyzable subjects who have borderline features and even transient psychotic regressions. In a similar vein, Menaker (1953) suggested that in selected individuals masochism ''serve[s] as a defense against psychosis'' (p. 220). I have suggested that the diagnosis of narcissistic personality disorder has two components, the dynamic complemented by a structural consideration. These patients' dynamics are characterized by their tenacious pursuit of illusions of narcissistic perfection for their self-representations. These pursuits are structured in a latent psychotic integration that *invariably* becomes manifest if analysis of these defenses *is attempted*. Their regressions are characterized by disturbances of the reality testing and judgment functions of their egos, serious acting out and/or disorganization. A reality-oriented, affirming psychotherapy that facilitates mutative internalizations is indicated, rather than analysis. Many of these patients require an interminable tie to the therapist, which is of varying intensity.

In contrast to the narcissistic personality disorder with latent psychotic integration, one group of patients can be delineated who have a particularly favorable prognosis. These are analysands whose character organization is heavily invested in narcissistic defenses that are primarily a regressive response to oedipal or postoedipal conflict. These patients often have considerable sublimatory potential and islands of good object relations. Their difficulties in object relations arise in the intensity of their response to disappointments in selected objects with whom they are attempting to be more intimately involved. There is often an associated penchant for defiant (Freud, 1917) conflicts with authority figures. Mahler, Pine, and Bergman (1975) have noted that "the infantile neurosis may have its obligatory precursor, if not its first manifestations, in the rapprochement crisis" (p. 227), and this is particularly so for narcissistic personality disorders. All narcissistic defenses are based on self-object, self-, and object images with roots in the first two years of life. The patients being considered here, however, have experienced reasonable preoedipal, and often oedipal, development and its associated structuralizations, but these have been traumatized by oedipal or postoedipal narcissistic injuries. (In this regard, Mahler's concept of "on the way toward object constancy" might be broadened to "on the way toward structuralizations.") The superego development of these patients has been traumatically disrupted and remains vulnerable to regressive dedifferentiation and externalization. A history of warm, reasonably empathic early-life experience associated with subsequent disruption secondary to enforced separations, divorce, parental illness, failure, or death may portend a more favorable prognosis.

The disappearance of the large nuclear family, family disruption secondary to a holocaust, military service, the increasing incidence of divorce, as well as the decline of the church and other social institutions as viable repositories for narcissistic investment, may contribute to the increased incidence of narcissistic personality disorders in general and to that of those with a quite good prognosis in particular.

Part II

EXAMPLES WITHIN THE CLASSIFICATION

6

Levin and Kitty: Neurotic Narcissistic Personality and Normal Suppliant Personality Disorders

Happy families are all alike; every
unhappy family is unhappy in its own way.
　　　　　　　　—Tolstoy, *Anna Karenina*

Tolstoy's *Anna Karenina* can be viewed as a compilation of exquisite life portraits of individuals whose destinies are importantly, if not definitively, molded by the quality of parenting they have received. A case could be made that this novel represents an attempt by Tolstoy to analyze narcissistic investments that were interfering with his own ability to form realistic object relationships and achieve a happy family. Whatever the truth of his motivations, it is certain that *Anna Karenina* presents a number of characters who have experienced early object loss and/ or parents who were themselves preoccupied by the pursuit of narcissistic perfection for their self-representations. These traumatic disappointments have interfered with the development of the characters' psychic structures, resulting in quests

161

for illusions of narcissistic perfection for their own self-representations (usually without the modulation of well-developed ego ideals and superegos). These addictive pursuits have sapped their energies and contributed to their unhappiness.

All human beings perceive various threats during their development to the integrity of their self-representations. Formative experiences of helplessness and frustration, as well as more definitive perceptions of separateness and experiences of being left alone, are associated with disorganizing affects and thoughts that are experienced as threats to the self-representation. Defensive internalizations, which result in structural development, are ubiquitous responses to such normal trauma.

Human beings who develop the capacity for happiness have usually had admirable parents who were "optimally available" (Mahler, 1971, p. 410), particularly during crucial developmental events. Such an experience of parenting results in the well-integrated primary identifications that are the foundations both of psychic structure and of important secondary identifications that contribute to the further development of the ego, ego ideal, and superego. These structuralizations provide the developing ego with systems to modulate its own struggle against pursuits of narcissistic perfection, as well as with narcissistically invested parental representations and psychic structures that provide illusions of protection and security. With such a family background, a child may still be the overvalued repository of the narcissistically invested fantasies of hard-working, loving, respected parents; even so, the result can be normal structural development and the integration of narcissism in one or another mode with associated capacity for a rich, full, object-related life.

Tolstoy's genius for describing human behavior provides, in *Anna Karenina*, specific examples of a variety of integrations of narcissism, ranging from those that cover the spectrum from neurotic to normal frequently found in members of happy families to those that are seriously pathological. Our discussion will focus on four factors that influenced the integration of the narcissistic investments in each character: (1) traumatic developmental injuries; (2) narcissistic characterological defenses based on the interplay of the ego endowment and identificatory opportunities available (these defenses protect against remembering and integrating profoundly painful and disorganizing formative experience, as well as against recapitulating the formative trauma); (3) narcissistic injuries in adult life; and (4) narcissistic regressions and defensive responses to these injuries.

Levin and Princess Kitty Shcherbatsky are characters whose integration of narcissism develops in a manner that enables them to love each other and create a happy family. They are individuals ultimately able to respond to the exigencies of life with progressive growth. Despite regressive and defensive responses to narcissistic injuries they prove flexible enough to return to reality and to progress to more intimate involvement with others. Levin does "not remember his own mother" who died, as did his father, when he was a child. The trauma of losing his mother and father leave him identified with parents who have died and deprived him of the optimal developmental opportunity to idealize and identify with warm, related, respectable parents in a progressively realistic manner.

These identificatory processes and their associated differentiations are the building blocks of psychic structure. Children fortunate to have such develop-

mental opportunity can delegate their narcissism first
to representations of idealized parents and then to
their ego ideals. Such development, and the associated
identifications and differentiations, offers a better
prognosis for a subject's ability to enjoy loving and nurturing. He will not have to relate to his objects
primarily as vehicles to restore narcissistic perfection
to his self-representation.

Children who lose their parents often remain more
intensely fixated on identificatory modes heavily invested with various forms of narcissistic perfection. They
may strive to maintain the original narcissistic perfection for their self-representations; this process
helps them avoid a spectrum of painful and potentially
disorganizing affects (rage, disappointment, and anxiety) and provides the only viable repository for their
narcissistic strivings. These children often develop into
adults who remain fixated on the pursuit of narcissistic perfection for their self-representations and who do
not have much left for other people or a family.

Why Levin did not become a typical narcissistic
personality disorder is a difficult question. In addition
to a satisfying first two years of life, he had a warm,
consistent mother surrogate whose presence reduced
the traumatic impact of his early loss. In addition there
was a family legacy; generations of Levins who had
lived on and managed the land were idealized and employed as identifications for his ego ideal.

Levin's development was characterized by a struggle between defensive narcissistic investments and a
hunger for related involvement. His rage at and
disappointment in his mother for dying contributed to
a defensive fixation on an idealized view of her and on
the fantasy of the perfect family he might have had, had
his parents lived. These losses and the resultant fixa-

tions, typical of patients clinically considered narcissistic personality disorders, made him vulnerable to seeking qualities of perfection for himself and for his external objects in order to undo his sense of loss. This traumatically disappointing loss, experienced as a sense of "want" (A. Reich, 1953), or void, stimulated defensive, narcissistically invested identificatory activities designed to repair his ego ideal. As an adolescent, Levin had been a fine athlete. Through skating, he had attempted to find perfection in his body. The content of skating provides identificatory opportunities for investing both masculine and feminine self-representations with narcissistic perfection. For Levin, on a conscious level, skating was experienced as an activity which affirmed his masculine physical prowess. It assuaged the anxiety derived primarily from an idenfication with his dead father and perhaps secondarily from oedipal guilt (see chapter 3). On a more repressed level, the grace of skating restored a sense of feminine perfection to his self-representation. This satisfied his deep-seated identification with his dead mother, providing a sense of her presence within him and dulling the pain of her loss. The attraction to both masculine and feminine content for one's perfectionistic strivings—the hermaphroditic orientation—is a ubiquitous human experience, but it is quite commonly accentuated in patients considered narcissistic personality disorders.

As a child, Levin had adopted and idealized the Shcherbatsky family in an attempt to undo his sense of loss and that of inner defect derived from it; as an adult, he falls in love with Kitty. He perceives her as without defect, perfect.

Kitty was so perfect in every respect that she was a

creature far above everything earthly; and he was a creature so low and so earthly that it could not even be conceived that other people and she herself could regard him as worthy of her [1878, p. 26].[1]

If he can win Kitty's love, her perfection will undo his inner sense of loss and worthlessness. Her valence as a narcissistic object derives in part from her association with her family. If he can win her he can be part of her family.

All the members of that family, especially the feminine half, were pictured by him, as it were, wrapped in a mysterious poetical veil, and he not only perceived no defects whatever in them, but behind the poetical veil that shrouded them he assumed the existence of the loftiest sentiments and every possible perfection [p. 25].

That perfection will be part of his self-representation and create the illusion of undoing the vulnerability and loss he experienced when his parents died.

Levin scarcely remembered his mother. His conception of her was for him a sacred memory, and his future wife was bound to be in his imagination a repetition of that exquisite, holy ideal of a woman that his mother had been [p. 101].

In the in-love state, the subject, like Levin, over-values the object and feels a passive submissiveness in relationship to it. The subject incorporates a representation of the idealized object and feels elated by virtue of this association. At moments when a sub-

[1]All subsequent references to *Anna Karenina* will cite page numbers only.

ject is in-love, his mode of narcissistic investment is primarily in the object. Such a subject is obsessed with the pursuit of the idealized object and is panicked at the prospect of its loss. The true attitude toward the object is ambivalent, but its conscious component is adulating idealization.

The state of mind associated with the term "in-love" can be seen more clearly by contrasting it with that associated with the term "loving." "Loving" implies a more active state of mind than being "in-love." It is associated with more defined representations. In addition a significantly greater emphasis on synthetic judgments of the ego is found than in an in-love state. The subject respects the object of his love, with whom he shares ideals, and is able and willing to endure frustration for that object. Such frustration may be gratifying both by virtue of the synchrony the subject gains with his ego ideal and superego in the process of giving and by virtue of associated processes of empathic identification. The loved object can be mourned because of its relative representational separateness from the subject's self-representation and because of its less ambivalent investment. The idealized object of the in-love state cannot be mourned as easily because it is ambivalently invested and because the subject feels that the object's loss threatens his survival.

Kitty, eighteen years old and very beautiful, is the youngest of three daughters. She is her parents' precious narcissistic object. While Levin is in-love with her, she falls in-love with Vronsky. Kitty seems to be attempting to fulfill her mother's wishful dreams: "When Vronsky appeared on the scene, she was still more delighted, confirmed in her opinion that Kitty was to make not simply a good but a brilliant match. . . . Nothing better could be wished for" (p. 48).

Kitty rejects Levin's proposal of marriage, and for

him the rejection is a narcissistic injury. He has been told he cannot have what he feels is most important to him. This adult narcissistic injury associatively recapitulates the primal trauma of his childhood, the death of his mother. Kitty's rejection of Levin for another man lends a triadic quality to this adult injury. The normal primal narcissistic injury of the loss of symbiotic perfection associated with the processes of separation-individuation was traumatically accentuated for Levin by his mother's death in the midst of crucial developmental differentiations (probably during the rapprochement crisis). As normal development proceeds the dyad becomes a triad. No matter how special and overvalued a child is to his mother, she usually sleeps with another man. This oedipal rejection is a two-fold narcissistic injury. First, mother sleeps with another man, thus rejecting the boy; second, his competitor is an adult, and, by comparison, the child is confronted with the immaturity of his body which is experienced as an inadequacy, an imperfection. Thus, for Levin, his rejection by Kitty probably reawakened memories of both preoedipal and oedipal narcissistic injuries.

Levin's admirable response to this injury is a reflection of the strength of his ego. Although he attempts numerous defenses, he remains capable of trying to understand the insult. Most important, he preserves the ability to wish for love again and ultimately to forgive and love the person who has hurt him. Within minutes of his rejection, he sees his rival for the first time, and is able to look at him.

There are people who, on meeting a successful rival, no matter in what, are at once disposed to turn their backs on everything good in him, and to see only what is bad. There are people, on the other hand, who

desire above all to find in that lucky rival the qualities by which he has outstripped them, and seek
with a throbbing ache at heart only what is good.
Levin belonged to the second class. But he had no
difficulty in finding what was good and attractive in
Vronsky. It was apparent at the first glance [p. 55].

He does not have to destroy the rejecting object or his
rival. Only a very rare individual can experience a rejection of great magnitude without some defensive response. One that maximizes sustained contact with the
object and minimizes distortions of reality offers
greater adaptational potential than one that encourages withdrawal from and denigration of the object.

Levin's rage, however, has to be expressed in some
manner. It is self-directed. This mode of response,
which might be considered masochistic, usually reflects a defense against the expression of rage at idealized objects (that is, for Levin against his parents who
had died).

"Yes, there is something in me repulsive and
repellent. . . .And I don't get on with other people.
Pride, they say. No, I have no pride. If I had pride, I
would not have put myself in such a position." And he
pictured to himself Vronsky, happy, good-natured,
clever, and self-possessed, certainly never placed in
the awful position in which he had been that evening.
"Yes, she was bound to choose him. So it had to be,
and I cannot complain of anyone or anything. I am
myself to blame. What right had I to imagine she
would care to join her life to mine? Who am I and
what am I? A nobody, not wanted by anyone, or of
use to anybody" [p. 90].

The blame for his loss is all his; he cannot be angry at
them. These defenses against rage and the acute sense
of loss only temporarily assuage the pain, and his disappointment weighs on him as he journeys home. A patient in a similar situation described his chronic pain
in response to a rejection by a profoundly important
person as "a continual noise in the back of my head."
Levin attempts to ward off the "noise" of his memories
by withdrawing into himself and proclaiming his
resolve to avoid future injury.

> He began to see what had happened to him in quite a
> different light. He felt that he was himself, and did
> not want to be anyone else. All he wanted now was to
> be better than before. First, he resolved that from
> that day he would give up hoping for any extraordi-
> nary happiness, such as marriage might have given
> him, and consequently would not so disparage what
> he really had. Second, he would never again let him-
> self give way to disgusting passion, the memory of
> which had so tortured him when he had been making
> up his mind to make a proposal [pp. 98–99].

Yet for Levin the fantasy of love, marriage, and a
family was "the chief affair of life, on which its whole
happiness turned" (p. 101). The interminable un-
mourned losses of early childhood will be assuaged by
creating the ideal family he never had. As the pain of
his current loss diminishes, his optimism fuels hopes
of future happiness: "He felt that, however strange it
might be, he had not parted from his daydreams, and
he could not live without them. Whether with her or
with another, still it would be" (p. 101).

Since important rejections experienced as narcissistic injuries often recapitulate early life trauma, they

heal slowly and leave their scar. Thus, when Levin hears of Kitty's rejection by Vronsky, he is pleased at what he hears, though he would be "ashamed to admit it": "He was pleased that there was still hope, and still more pleased that she who had made him suffer so much was now suffering" (p. 176).

As time passes, his rage at her and his pleasure in her suffering diminish and the "intoxication of the news" (p. 180) that Kitty is not married gradually begins to work on him. However, his fear of another narcissistic injury and his defenses against the painful and angry feelings associated with the memories of her rejection interfere with his enjoying and pursuing his "intoxication." The conflict between his wish for ecstasy and his fear of pain is apparent in this later conversation with Dolly, Kitty's sister:

> "You know I proposed and I was refused," said Levin, and all the tenderness he had been feeling for Kitty a minute before was replaced by a feeling of anger for the slight he had suffered. . . .
> "Yes, to choose between me and Vronsky," thought Levin, and the dead thing that had come to life within him died again, and only weighed on his heart and set it aching. . . .
> "Darya Aleksandrovna [Dolly]," he said, "that's how one chooses a new dress, or some purchase or other, not love. The choice had been made, and so much the better. . . . And there can be no repeating it."
> "Ah, pride, pride!" said Darya Aleksandrovna. . . .
> "But whether I am right or wrong, that pride you so despise makes any thought of Katerina Aleksandrovna out of the question for me—you understand, utterly out of the question" [pp. 285–286].

Levin's wish to avoid further pain fuels an idealized interest in the apparent happiness of his serfs Ivan
Parmenov and his wife: "In the expressions of both
faces was to be seen vigorous, young, freshly awakened
love" (p. 290). Levin is vulnerable to the narcissistic investment of his serfs' lives and elaborates the defensive
process of his idealization in fantasy:

> Often Levin admired this life, often he had a sense
> of envy of the men who led it; but today for the first
> time, especially under the influence of what he had
> seen in the attitude of Ivan Parmenov toward his young
> wife, the idea presented itself definitely to his mind
> that it was in his power to exchange the dreary, ar-
> tificial, idle, and individualistic life he was leading for
> this laborious, pure, and delightful life. . . .
> "Well, what am I going to do? How am I to do it?"
> he said to himself, trying to express to himself all the
> thoughts and feelings he had passed through in that
> brief night. All the thoughts and feelings he had
> passed through fell into three separate trains of
> thought. One was the renunciation of his old life, of
> his utterly useless education. This renunciation gave
> him satisfaction, and was easy and simple. Another
> series of thoughts and mental images related to the
> life he longed to live now. The simplicity, the purity,
> the sanity of this life he felt clearly, and he was con-
> vinced he would find it in the content, the peace, and
> the dignity, of the lack of which he was so miserably
> conscious. But a third series of ideas turned upon the
> question of how to effect this transition from the old
> life to the new. And there nothing took clear shape for
> him. "Have a wife? Have work and the necessity of
> work? Leave Pokrovskoe? Buy land? Become a mem-
> ber of a peasant community? Marry a peasant girl?
> How am I to do it?" he asked himself again, and

could not find an answer. "I haven't slept all night, though, and I can't think it out clearly," he said to himself. "I'll work it out later. One thing's certain, this night has decided my fate. All my old dreams of married life were absurd, not the real thing," he told himself [pp. 291–293].

The illusion of a life without the pain of narcissistic injury he has experienced motivates his wish to believe he can transmute his identity. He longs to believe that in the "pure" life of a peasant he can find love. His sense of reality intrudes on this process, but in the pleasure of the fantasied narcissistically invested identificatory transmutation, he tells his critical faculties, "I'll work it out later." Levin catches sight of Kitty the next morning and his defensive fantasies are shattered.

Everything that had been stirring Levin during that sleepless night, all the resolutions he had made, all vanished at once. He recalled with horror his dreams of marrying a peasant girl. Only there, in the carriage that had crossed over to the other side of the road and was rapidly disappearing, only there could he find the solution to the riddle of his life, which had weighed so agonizingly upon him of late [p. 293].

The nidus of "the riddle of his life" is the death of his parents, particularly the loss of his mother during the rapprochement process, and he has sought Kitty as a narcissistically invested solution. He feels winning her will undo his inner sense of discord and set things right in his life, yet he continues to struggle. He wants to go and see her but feels he cannot do so:

Levin himself had felt, on seeing Kitty, that he had never ceased to love her; but he could not go over to the Oblonskys', knowing she was there. The fact that he had proposed and that she had refused had placed an insuperable barrier between her and him. "I can't ask her to be my wife merely because she can't be the wife of the man she wanted to marry," he said to himself. The thought of this made him cold and hostile toward her. "I will not be able to speak to her without a feeling of reproach" [p. 341].

His awareness of the rival highlights the oedipal aspect of his adult injury and his struggle to overcome his defensive response to it. His conflict revolves around his wish for love and his simultaneous and contradictory wish to avoid the painful feelings associated with memories of his narcissistic injury. His abandoned fantasy of an idealized, pure love was based on the illusion that both wishes could be satisfied. If they could, he would never be hurt, frustrated, or rejected. These are ubiquitous human fears derived from the perception of limits: the limits of separateness, of mother's imperfections, of the presence of competitors for her attention, and of the demands of socialization in general. In Levin's case, as in the cases of many patients considered narcissistic personality disorders, the fear of frustrating limits is more intensely felt. His mother's death has accentuated Levin's potential to believe in the matricidal potential of his rage. Frustration, rage, and object loss are equated, and they motivate Levin to seek narcissistic solutions. Levin longs for the narcissistically invested nurturing love he experienced in his first year of life; he is terrified by the prospect that if he finds it he may lose it again, as he did when his mother died and when

Kitty rejected him. He vacillates between his longing for Kitty and his wish to avoid pain, as he struggles with the realization that to love means to be vulnerable to the pain implicit in the fact that the object of his love, Kitty, is fallible and has her own spectrum of longings that are not a mirror image of his. She is separate, she will frustrate him, may leave him or die. For the moment Levin's fear of being vulnerable supersedes his excitement at the possibility of winning Kitty's love.

Levin's involvement with his peasant associates exposes him to the vulnerability of other human relationships. He loves his peasant friends but hates their ignorance and their backward ways. Rather than face the painful feelings implicit in living with these differences, he proposes to try to change them by devising an ideal system of agriculture that will transmute them and their life into a frustration-free utopia. He will write a book on the subject. The defensive grandiosity of this effort is evident in his daydreams in which he sees his work as being "not merely to effect a revolution in political economy, but to annihilate that science entirely and to lay the foundations of a new science of the relationship of the people to the soil" (p. 363). His pursuit of these matters allows him to avoid thinking of Kitty most of the time, allows him to avoid integrating painful perceptions. His avoidance of her is an expression of his anger and fear. The illusion of achieving a painless nirvana reveals the defensive narcissistically invested nature of these intellectual activities.

In spite of the gloominess of nature around him, he felt peculiarly elated. The talks he had been having with the peasants in the further village had shown that they were beginning to get used to their new position. The old servant to whose hut he had gone to get dry evidently approved of Levin's plan. . . .

"I need only continue stubbornly on toward my aim, and I will attain my end," thought Levin; "and it's something to work and take trouble for. This is not a matter of myself individually, the question of the public welfare enters into it. The whole system of culture, the chief element in the condition of the people, must be completely transformed. Instead of poverty, general prosperity and content; instead of hostility, harmony and unity of interest. In short, a bloodless revolution, but a revolution of the greatest magnitude, beginning in the little circle of our district, then the province, then Russia, then the whole world. Because a just idea cannot but be fruitful. Yes, it's an aim worth working for. And it's being me, Kostya Levin, who went to a ball in a black tie, and was refused by the Shcherbatskaya girl, and who was intrinsically such a pitiful, worthless creature—that proves nothing; I feel sure Franklin felt just as worthless, and he too had no faith in himself when summing himself up" [p. 364].

The book will not only protect him from having to integrate his rage and disappointment at the peasants for being their imperfect selves, it will transform him from a rejected "pitiful worthless creature" to a great man, a "Franklin." His narcissistically invested product, the book, will transmute his self-representation by imbuing it with attributes of narcissistic perfection. The book is perfect, the book is his product, therefore he is perfect. In addition the perfect system of the book creates a world that protects him from having to experience painful and conflicting feelings toward people in general, and particularly toward those he loves. Although he perceives the nature of the serf, the rage and disappointment connected with the perception of these and other frustrations continue to fuel his fantasied pursuit of a painless ideal.

At the height of his elation in his perfect solution, Tolstoy confronts him with the ultimate human vulnerability, death: "The question of how to live had hardly begun to grow a little clearer to him when a new, insoluble question presented itself—death" (p. 369). His brother Nikolai is dying. He struggles to avoid this fact.

> His thoughts were of all sorts of things, but the end of all his thoughts was the same—death. Death, the inevitable end of us all, for the first time presented itself to him with irresistible force. And death, which was here in this beloved brother, groaning,. . . was not so remote as it had hitherto seemed to him. It was in himself too; he felt that. If not today, tomorrow, if not tomorrow, in thirty years, wasn't it all the same! And what was this inevitable death—he did not know, had never thought about it, and, what was more, had not the power, had not the courage to think about it [pp. 368–369].

Levin is alone with his perception of Nikolai's morbidity. He knows what to do, but in his loneliness, he lacks the courage to communicate intimately.

> Levin felt himself to blame, and could not set things right. He felt that if they had both not kept up appearances but had spoken from the heart—that is to say, had said just what they were thinking and feeling—they would simply have looked into each others'

faces, and Konstantin could only have said, "You're
dying, you're dying." And Nikolai could only have
answered, "I know I'm dying, but I'm afraid, I'm
afraid, I'm afraid!" And they could have said nothing
more if they had said only what was in their hearts.
But life like that was impossible, and so Konstantin
tried to do what he had been trying to do all his life
and never could learn to do, though, as far as he
could observe, many people knew so well how to do
it, and without it there was no living at all. He tried
to say what he was not thinking, but he felt continually that it had a ring of falsehood, that his brother
detected him in it, and was exasperated at it [p. 370].

He perceives the imminence of death, and to avoid
its impact he throws himself, with vengeance, into his
work where a vestige of the possibility of controlling
frustration seems to exist.

Levin said what he had genuinely been thinking of
late. He saw nothing but death or the advance toward
death in everything. But his cherished scheme only
engrossed him all the more. Life had to be got
through somehow till death did come. Darkness had
fallen upon everything for him; but just because of
this darkness he felt that the one guiding clue in the
darkness was his work, and he clutched it and clung
to it with all his strength [p. 372].

In his work he tenaciously clings to the illusion that the
inevitable vulnerabilities of life can be avoided.

Kitty falls in-love with Vronsky, her ideal man. If
she can win him she will be fulfilled. By gratifying her
mother's narcissistically invested fantasies she will be

her mother's successful narcissistic object. At eighteen, she feels at the crossroads of the life she was raised to live. Tolstoy captures the intensity, the life-felt imperative, associated with such narcissistically invested events: "Kitty was feeling a sensation akin to that of a young man before a battle. Her heart throbbed violently, and she could not fix her thoughts on anything. . . . She felt that this evening, when they would meet each other for the first time, would be a turning point in her life" (p. 51).

Her in-love state and its characteristic narcissistic overvaluation are evident in her thoughts of "brilliant happiness" in a future with Vronsky, but her fantasy is shattered by her perception of Vronsky's infatuation with Anna. She feels "crushed" and her heart aches "with horrible despair" (p. 88). She attempts to deny her perception but cannot. She, like Levin, has the ability to look at and admire the person who has defeated her: "Kitty admired her more than ever and more and more acute was her suffering" (p. 89).

In response to her injury, Kitty becomes depressed and remains ill for months. In hopes of a "cure" her family takes her to a German spa, where she meets Varenka. Tolstoy describes a depressed young woman with a moral masochistic character integration:

Of Mademoiselle Varenka it could be said that she had passed her first youth, but that she seemed a creature without youth; she might have been taken for nineteen or for thirty. If her features were examined separately, she was good-looking rather than plain, in spite of the sickly hue of her face. She would have had a good figure, too, if it had not been for her extreme thinness, and the size of her head, which was too large for her medium height. But she was not likely to be attractive to men. She was like a fine flower already past its bloom and without fragrance, though the petals were still unwithered....

She always seemed absorbed in work about which there could be no doubt, and so it seemed she could not take interest in anything outside it [pp. 227–228].

Kitty is "inexplicably attracted" to her. This attraction is motivated by the same defensive longing that motivates Levin's identification with his peasant neighbors: the wish to avoid a repetition of painful narcissistic injury.

It was just this contrast with her own position that was for Kitty the great attraction of Mademoiselle Varenka. Kitty felt that in her, in her manner of life, she would find an example of what she was now so painfully seeking: interest in life, a dignity in life— apart from the worldly relations of girls with men, which so revolted her, and appeared to her now as a shameful hawking about of goods in search of a purchaser. The more attentively Kitty watched her unknown friend, the more convinced she was that this girl was the perfect creature she imagined her to be [p. 228].

In such "perfection" she imagines she will find safety from the pain of humiliating rejection. Kitty's defensive identification is total; she is not attempting to identify with a trait of Varenka's, but to be Varenka.

Kitty did not merely imitate Varenka in her conduct, but unconsciously imitated her in her manner of walking, of talking, of blinking her eyes. But later on, the princess noticed that apart from this adoration, some kind of serious spiritual change was taking place in her daughter [p. 237].

Varenka displays the moral masochist's almost total inability to tolerate admiration. In response to a compliment regarding her good deeds, she replies: "I don't remember, I don't think I did anything" (p. 231). On being told that her singing talent is "extraordinary," Varenka answers simply: "I am glad if it gives you pleasure" (p. 233). Kitty's experience of pain has been caused by her pursuit of narcissistic victory, and now she is attracted to Varenka for what she misperceives as her "power" in seemingly not being seduced by praises.

> Kitty looked with pride at her friend. She was enchanted by her talent, and her voice and her face, but most of all by her manner, by the way Varenka obviously thought nothing of her singing and was quite unmoved by their praises. She seemed only to be asking: "Am I to sing again, or is that enough?"
>
> "If it had been me," thought Kitty, "how proud I would have been! How delighted I would have been to see that crowd under the windows! But she's utterly unmoved by it. Her only motive is to avoid refusing and to please Mama. What is there in her? What is it that gives her the power to disregard everything, to be calm independently of everything? How I should like to know it and to learn it from her!" thought Kitty, gazing into her serene face [p. 233].

Kitty does not understand the punitive quality of Varenka's conscience, her low sense of self-esteem (what S. Levin [1970] refers to as "negative entitlement"), and her resulting masochistic character integration.

Kitty sees Varenka's self-absorption as a virtue and not as the massive inhibition of appropriate self-oriented pleasure that it is. Fortunately Kitty's own intrinsically positive sense of self-worth reasserts itself and her attraction for a defensive identification with the masochistic Varenka loses its lustre.

Kitty's attraction raises the question of the relationship between masochism and narcissism. Recently, Cooper (1977) and Stolorow (1975a and b) have elaborated a relationship between masochistic and narcissistic phenomena. Stolorow (1975b) conceives of masochistic activities as functioning to maintain the stability of the self-representation and thus as serving a "narcissistic function" (p. 442). Although explicitly functional, this definition is implicitly dynamic, for it presents these activities as defensively motivated responses to the ego's perceptions of external reality or the internal representational world—perceptions that threaten the cohesiveness of the self-representation.

The terms *narcissism* and *masochism*, as used here, denote contents of identificatory processes. These identificatory processes, mediated by the integrative and synthetic functions of the ego, maintain the stability of the self-representation. The narcissistic injuries experienced by Levin and Kitty threatened to overwhelm them with affects painful enough to be disorganizing to their egos. In defense, Levin pursued activities that promised to protect him from a recapitulation of painful injury by changing his self- and object-representational world and by imbuing his self-representation with illusions of narcissistic perfection. Kitty's defensive masochistic identification was motivated by a similar longing for safety from the pain of a narcissistic injury experienced in adult life. Why does one person choose a predominantly narcissistic and another a predominantly masochistic mode to defend against the helplessness implicit in any narcissistic injury?

Masochists feel helpless and hopeless about any possibility of undoing a rejection that has been profoundly injurious to their self-esteem. They feel unlovable. Varenka's early life sheds light on the genetics of her character organization.

> Madame Stahl, of whom some people said that she had worried her husband to death, while others said it was he who had made her wretched by his immoral behavior, had always been a woman of weak health and hysterical temperament. When, after her separation from her husband , she gave birth to her only child, the child had died almost immediately, and the family of Madame Stahl, knowing her sensibility,and fearing the news would kill her, had substituted another child, a baby born the same night and in the same house in Petersburg, the daughter of the chief cook of the palace. This was Varenka. Madame Stahl learned later on that Varenka was not her own child, but she continued bringing her up, especially because very soon afterwards Varenka had not a relation of her own living [p. 232].

Deserted by her own mother, from infancy on, Varenka had been "told" by the attitudes of the adult world that it was her role in life to assuage her adopted mother's depression. These attitudes were internalized and became part of her self-representation. She was deprived of any semblance of a "gleam" in her mother's eye. Based on her life experience, it was hopeless for her to feel any possibility of being loved for herself. Her value to her object world was as someone who assuaged the pain of others. In return she could expect safety from the rejection and rage of the object. She and the object would remain intact and together. Such a masochistic view of self is often complemented by a suppliant attitude toward the object.

Kitty, as the youngest child and her father's favorite, was bathed in parental admiration and overvaluation. Her mother thought nothing of spending large sums of money to prepare her dramatic entrance at a ball. Her parents' attitudes and wishes encouraged her sense of self-worth and entitlement, and her pursuit of narcissistic gratifications. From her earliest years she felt of value. Her rejection by Vronsky momentarily made her feel a worthless failure, and her own rejection of Levin (a fine man, her father's choice over Vronsky, and a friend of her dead brother) compounded the injury by making her feel a fool. Enraged at herself, she felt helpless and hopeless concerning any possibility of reversing her circumstances. Her passive sense of helpless hopelessness contributed to the choice of a masochistic defensive mode.

Levin, after some transient self-flagellating fantasies, felt less the fool, hungry for a family and *capable* of actively undoing the frustrating limits of reality, albeit in a displaced sphere. This illusion of the possibility of effecting change *actively* contributes to the choice of narcissistically invested defensive activity.

Many factors influence the choice of a symptom, character organization, or defensive response. The perspective being stressed here is the subject's attitude of self and its relationship to the qualtity of parenting. Pursuit of a narcissistic solution is organized around a self-perception that contributes to the subject's feeling he can undo the injury. It is constructed from an internalized affective nidus of the maternal smile and his ability to elicit it. A masochistic solution is constructed from internalized memory traces of rage-filled maternal dissatisfaction and of the subject's inability to reverse it. Cooper (1977) has emphasized that narcissistic and masochistic responses are ubiquitous. Internalized parental attitudes contribute affective components to the subject's identifications, which are secondarily reinforced by ego endowments also including gender anatomy,[2] cultural attitudes, and sociocultural opportunities.

Time, circumstances, and enough healthy ego enable Levin to forgive Kitty and propose once again. She accepts and all that is required is her parent's approval. Waiting fills him with the dread typically associated with helpless anticipation of narcissistic injury.

When Kitty had gone and Levin was left alone, he felt such uneasiness without her and such an impatient longing to get as quickly, as quickly as possible, to tomorrow morning, when he would see her again and be plighted to her forever, that he felt afraid, as though of death, of those fourteen hours that he had to get through without her [p. 419].

He has won his prized, narcissistically invested object, and her possession holds out the illusion of perfect hap-

[2] It is possible that the masculine gender with its penchant for activity, as organized around its phallic identity (Michels, 1973), contributes an additional factor to this choice and makes it a more common mode in men.

piness. Yet he is terrified by the separation, afraid "as though of death." She represents the prized object, union with whom holds out the illusion of recapturing feelings of perfection associated with the original satiated self-object duality; the imminence of union, happiness, promises loss of identity. "Happiness is only in loving and wishing her wishes, thinking her thoughts, that is to say, not freedon at all—that's happiness!" (p. 467). It also, however, recaptures the associated primordial affective experience of his mother's death and the feelings of disorganizing helplessness stimulated by that primal object loss. His temporary separation from Kitty had filled him with the terror of loss by death of the object.

Patients considered narcissistic personality disorders are subject to intense separation anxiety and often experience separation as equivalent to object loss (see pp. 57–59). During early stages of development, separations are associated with simultaneous and transient dedifferentiation of the tenuously established self- and object representations. Adult patients considered narcissistic personality disorders frequently elaborate and experience these feelings as the ultimate dedifferentiation of the self-representation—death.

Levin experienced real object loss at the height of the separation-individuation process. Real object loss in childhood is not an infrequent finding in narcissistic personality disorders. The disturbance in maternal relatedness and empathic responsiveness typically experienced by narcissistic personality disorders as infants is associated with "cathectic fluency" (Jacobson, 1954, p. 114) and representational dedifferentiation perceived as akin to object loss.

Upon confirmation of the betrothal, Levin is infused

with a hypomanic elation that results from his self-representation's being inbued with the illusion of narcissistic perfection. Kitty, his perfect narcissistic object, is the vehicle for this illusionary transformation. In such a state the subject's ego misjudges its capabilities; anything seems possible:

> Levin...felt perfectly lifted out of the conditions of material life. He had eaten nothing for a whole day, he had not slept for two nights, had spent several hours undressed in the frozen air, and felt not simply fresher and stronger than ever, but utterly independent of his body; he moved without effort of his muscles, and felt as if he could do anything. He was convinced he could fly upward or lift the corner of the house, if need be [pp. 423–424].

At the same time, because winning Kitty has restored a sense of the original narcissistic perfection to his self-representation, Levin loses interest in other narcissistically invested fantasies—that is, in his perfect agricultural system. His perception of the system's limits does not "in the least annoy him"; he sees the "whole business" as "of little value" (p. 421).

We can see in Levin, as his happiness approaches, a "joyful terror" (p. 425). This terror, another important affective component of the in-love state, is due in part to the subject's perception of vulnerability and is related to the previously mentioned anxiety over object loss through death. The feeling is more intense in patients referred to as narcissistic personality disorders. The subject's feeling he has found the perfect object and won her fill him with a sense of omnipotence and completeness. His terror, of course, derives from his awareness that his sense of perfect happiness is contingent on the presence of the object.

Levin and Kitty marry, and the bond is forged in their sharing Levin's brother's death. Her presence makes possible what was too painful alone a year earlier. Now, united with Kitty, Levin can face Nikolai's morbidity, and can love and communicate with him in spite of it.

> Terrible as it was to Levin to put his arms around that terrible body, to take hold of that under the blanket of which he preferred to know nothing, under his wife's influence he made his resolute face that she knew so well, and putting his arms into the bed, he took hold of the body.... While he was turning him over, conscious of the huge emaciated arms about his neck, Kitty swiftly and noiselessly turned the pillow, fluffed it up, and settled in it the sick man's head, smoothing back his hair, which was sticking again to his moist brow.
>
> The sick man kept his brother's hand in his own. Levin felt that he meant to do something with his hand and was pulling it somewhere. Levin yielded with a sinking heart: yes, he drew it to his mouth and kissed it. Levin, shaking with sobs and unable to articulate a word, went out of the room [pp. 520–521].

His love of Kitty and of his as yet unborn children make tolerable the impact of death, the profound anonymity and transience of existence. "Loving," in the individual and humanistic sense, provides for Levin an involvement with living that makes the ever-present imminence of death less oppressive.

The sight of his brother and the nearness of death revived in Levin that sense of horror in the face of the

insoluble enigma, together with the nearness and
inevitability of death, that had come upon him that
autumn evening when his brother had come to him.
This feeling was now even stronger than before; even
less than before did he feel capable of apprehending
the meaning of death, and its inevitability rose up before him more terrible than ever. But now, thanks to
his wife's presence, that feeling did not reduce him to
despair. In spite of death, he felt the need for life and
love. He felt that love saved him from despair, had
become still stronger and purer. The one mystery of
death, still unsolved, had scarcely passed before his
eyes, when another mystery had arisen, as insoluble,
calling to love and to life [p. 503].

Love saves him from dread and despair, but brings new
vulnerabilities, and new terror associated with them—
the pain of the parent. Levin empathizes with his son,
and the process is associated with a reawakening of the
overwhelmingly disorganizing experiences of his childhood loss. He is confronted with the awareness that he
has sired a child who is potentially vulnerable to
similar profound disappointments.

What he felt toward this little creature was utterly
unlike what he had expected. There was nothing
cheerful and joyous in the feeling; on the contrary, it
was a new torture of apprehension. It was the
consciousness of a new sphere of liability to pain.
And this sense was so painful at first, the apprehension lest this helpless creature should suffer was so
intense, that it prevented him from noticing the
strange thrill of senseless joy and even pride that he
had felt went the baby sneezed [p. 748].

The experience of a more-than-average expectable quotient of phase-specific disappointments leaves patients considered narcissistic personality disorders more vulnerable to this kind of torture. This contributes to their propensity to attempt to avoid intimate, committed relationships in general and the bearing and nurturing of children in particular.

On a more unconscious level, the birth of Levin's son shatters his dyadic relationship with Kitty with its illusion of the perfection of symbiotic bliss. This potentially narcissistically gratifying male son impounds Levin's senses with an increased awareness of his separateness. His terror signals that he can no longer be a child connected to an all gratifying object perceived as narcissistically perfect; rather he is a parent his son will need to narcissistically invest.

To love and have a family, Levin must better integrate his state of separateness and the paradox of the murderous rage he feels toward those dearest to him. He is enraged at them, because their existence destroys the illusion of finding perfect unity.

Levin becomes accustomed to the terror and pleasures of family life and work, but despite this happiness, he is profoundly aware of his finiteness: "In infinite time, in infinite matter, in infinite space, is formed a bubble-organism, and that bubble lasts a while and bursts, and that bubble is I" (p. 822). This perception motivates him to struggle with the question of how to live his life in the face of such finiteness. He reads the great philosophers and theologians, but quickly tires of their narcissistic overvaluation of thought.

> He had been stricken with horror, not so much of death, as of life, without any knowledge of whence, and why, and how, and what it was. The organism, its decay, the indestructibility of matter, the law of the

conservation of energy, evolution, were the words that usurped the place of his old belief. These words and ideas associated with them were very useful for intellectual purposes. But for life they yielded nothing, and Levin felt suddenly like a man who has changed his warm fur cloak for a muslin garment, and, going for the first time into the frost, is immediately convinced, not by reason, but by his whole nature that he is as good as naked, and that he must inevitably perish miserably [pp. 818–819].

Finally he sees that *for him* loving and working and doing good within his family and his community bring him a sense of well-being. His mode of life results in an intersystemic harmony between his ego, self-representation, ego ideal, and superego. In this sense of synchrony, he finds a satisfying meaning to life. When he allows this to happen and no longer evaluates his actions in relationship to some scheme of personal narcissistic perfection, he finds that he can experience present reality in a fuller, more meaningful way:

In former days—almost from childhood, and increasingly up to full manhood—when he had tried to do anything that would be good for all, for humanity, for Russia, for his own village, he had noticed that the idea of it had always been pleasant, but the work itself had always been clumsy, that then he had never been fully convinced of its absolute necessity, and that the work that had begun by seeming so great had grown less and less, till it vanished into nothing [p. 823].

After his marriage he progressively begins to feel differently:

To live the same family life as his father and forefathers — that is, in the same condition of culture — and so bring up his children, was incontestably necessary. It was as necessary as eating when one was hungry. And to do this, just as it was necessary to cook dinner, it was necessary to keep the Pokrovskoe farmed in such a manner that it would yield profit. Just as incontestably as it was necessary to repay a debt it was necessary to keep the property in such condition that his son, when he received it as a heritage, would say thank you to his father as Levin had said thank you to his grandfather for all he'd built and planted. And to do this, it was necessary to look after the land himself, not to lease it, and to breed cattle, manure the fields, and plant timber.

It was impossible not to look after the affairs of Sergey Ivanovich, of his sister, of the peasants who came to him for advice and were accustomed to do so — as impossible as to fling down a child one is carrying in one's arms. It was necessary to look after the comfort of his sister-in-law and her children, and of his wife and baby, and it was impossible not to spend with them at least a short time each day.

And all this, together with shooting and his new beekeeping, filled up the whole of Levin's life, which had no meaning at all for him, when he began to think [pp. 823–824].

Levin has struggled to find an illusionary narcissistic perfection in his work and his wife that would protect him against a recapitulation of his formative disorganizing disappointments. As he integrates the inevitablity of disappointment and death, he is able to be more realistically involved in life and to love.

He finds personal meaning and fulfillment, as well

as happiness, within his family by shifting from efforts to recapture narcissistic perfection for his self-representation (by acquiring the perfect wife, child, or agricultural system) to an attempt to live in synchrony with his ideals (of love and loving in the mode of his forefathers). He accepts the realistic human limits of his self-representation, but commits himself to gaining some semblance of synchrony with his ego ideal.

> "I shall go on in the same way, losing my temper with Ivan the coachman, falling into angry discussions, expressing my opinions tactlessly; there will still be the same wall between the holy of holies of my soul and other people, even my wife; I shall still go on blaming her for my own terror, and being sorry for it, . . . but my life now, my whole life apart from anything that can happen to me, every minute of it is no longer meaningless, as it was before, but it has an unquestionable meaning of the goodness which I have the power to put into it" [p. 851].

In this relationship to his ego ideal, he maintains, as Freud (1914) has pointed out, a relationship to his original narcissistic perfection derived from primal self-object experiences delegated to his ego ideal.

In spite of the object losses of his early childhood, Levin can be considered a neurotic with mixed modes of narcissistic investment. His primary investment was in idealized objects—Kitty and her family. In response to an adult narcissistic injury, he regressed. He temporarily withdrew from efforts to win an idealized object in order to create a world within which there would be no frustration. As the creator of that world, he would be a great man like Benjamin Franklin—that is, he would restore a sense of narcissistic perfection to his self-representation.

Levin can be considered neurotic because he has an intact superego and an ego ideal which are composed of abstract and humanistic ideals of loving. His major defense is repression of both rage and sexual desires. He is "neurotic" rather than "normal" because his conflicts over rage and sexuality lend a strict quality to his superego. He is excessively hard on himself and somewhat inhibited in the pursuit and enjoyment of personal success and exhibitionistic, sensual, or sexual pleasures. He is probably predisposed to this strictness by the intensification of his ambivalence that resulted from the traumatic loss of his mother during rapprochement. However, his ego and his neurotic character integration facilitate his struggle between the pursuit of illusion and object relatedness.

Kitty can be considered a normal suppliant personality disorder. She has an intact superego and ego ideal and is more able to enjoy herself while remaining loving and related. She was indulged as a child by loving parents who loved each other and were respected by their children in a progressively realistic manner. She first chose Vronsky because he represented a perfect object choice (A. Reich, 1953) that she fantasied would totally fulfill her. Her choice of Levin was more realistic and less idealized. She narcissistically invested those ego functions associated with being a woman, daughter, wife, and mother that won her the admiration and approval of her narcissistically invested structures (ego ideal) and objects (God, parents, Vronsky, and Levin).

7

Stiva: An Entitled Hedonist

People unable to have happy family lives often have experienced serious disappointment in one or both parents—either the death of a parent during early childhood and/or the quality of a parent's less-than-optimal relatedness. For a toddler such disappointment results in narcissistic investments in self- and object representations, investments which contribute to and complement traumatic developmental interference within ego-ideal and superego structuralization. Disappointments occurring in subsequent phases of development often add further impediments to structural development and may result in regressive dedifferentiation of tenuously established structuralizations.

The integration of narcissism in six characters unable to find happiness in married life will be explored to demonstrate that such unhappiness is often related to entitled, rigid, and tenacious pursuits of perfection for the self-representation. That a number of these characters meet tragic destinies underlines the self-destructive component frequently found in such character disorders.

In discussing Levin, we noted the difficult question, why does one person develop a neurotic character organization which permits relatively full, pleasing object relations while another does not? Like Levin the six characters who had significant difficulty in finding happiness in relationships all had formative experiences that closely approximate the genetics of patients typically considered narcissistic personality disorders. What differentiates all of them from Levin is their adult response to narcissistic injury. None of them was able to grow in response to a traumatic insult to his particular quest for perfection. All remained rigidly fixed on the pursuit of affectively pleasing illusions of perfection. What changed was the content of the pursuit whenever a particular avenue of gratification was frustrated.

Prince Stepan Arkadyevich Oblonsky, Stiva, is a typical entitled hedonist. He is a thirty-four-year-old man struggling to avoid the narcissistic injuries of aging and of no longer being the adulated first-born son. He married Dolly, Darya Aleksandrovna, Kitty's sister, because it was a comfortable "good match," and because she had a propensity to adulate, overvalue, and indulge him. The birth of their children has deprived him of her total adulation. He is jealous of his son as a competitor and loves him less than the little girl, his "favorite" (p. 11). He enjoys her adulation and is seductive with her.

We see his pursuit of perfection for his self-representation via two narcissistically invested activities: love affairs and perfect meals. In both activities he attempts to recapture the lost sense of specialness he associates with the gleam in his mother's eye—a formative overvaluing experience. His addiction to this perfection-rendering smile interferes with his ability to smile at, nurture, and love his own children.

The ubiquitous frustrations of involved adult life, especially with his family in Moscow, are experienced as depressing, oppressive reminders that he is no longer "His Majesty the Baby":

He reached a point when he positively began to be worrying himself over his wife's ill-humor and reproaches, over his children's health and education, and the petty details of his official work; even the fact of being in debt worried him. But he had only to go and stay a little while in Petersburg, in the circle there in which he moved, where people lived—really lived—instead of vegetating as in Moscow, and all such ideas vanished and melted away at once, like wax before the fire [pp. 757–758].

His pursuit of perfection in Petersburg soothes the insults of reality and diminishes his potential to be enraged at his family for existing.

In a conversation between Stiva and Levin, Tolstoy captures nicely the nature of the narcissistic pursuit for the perfect woman:

Stepan Arkadyevich's eyes sparkled merrily. "You don't agree, I know, that one can be fond of fresh rolls when one has had one's rations of bread —to your mind it's a crime; but I don't count life as life without love," he said, taking Levin's question in his own way. "What am I to do? I'm made that way. And really, one does so little harm to anyone, and gives oneself so much pleasure..."

"What! Is there something new, then?" queried Levin.

"Yes, my boy, there is! There, do you see, you

know the Ossian type of woman...Women such as one sees in dreams...Well, these women are sometimes to be met in reality...and these women are terrible. Woman, you know, is such a subject that however much you study it, it's always perfectly fresh."

"Well, then, it would be better not to study it."

"No. Some mathematician has said that enjoyment lies in the search for truth, not in finding it" [pp. 172–173].

In response to the depression-motivated quest for the perfect woman, the entitled hedonist will explain, justify, and attempt to externalize his guilt. For Stiva, pursuit is more important than the real object. The pursuit is motivated by the fantasy of finding the perfect object; once found and conquered, the real object cannot assuage for long Stiva's perception of disappointing reality.

When Dolly catches Stiva in an affair with their children's French governess, Stiva does not consciously experience any guilt; his only wish is to put things back in order so he can return to his pursuit of perfect pleasure. After three nights with an angry, disapproving wife, threatening to leave him, he awakens to a reminder of her alienation. He attempts to regress into sleep in quest of a narcissistically invested dream of perfect sensual experience.

"Yes, yes, how was it, now?" he thought, going over his dream. "Now, how was it? To be sure! Alabin was giving a dinner at Darmstadt; no, not Darmstadt, but something American. Yes, but then, Darmstadt was in America. Yes, Alabin was giving a dinner on glass tables, and the tables sang *Il mio tesoro*—not *Il mio tesoro*, though, but something better, and there were some sort of little decanters on the table, and there were women, too," he remembered [p. 4].

In the preparation of such perfect meals Stiva is a gourmet. Smiles are reciprocally exchanged by those who enjoy the meal. He is admired when he selects the perfect wine to complement a particular sauce. The meal is perfect; he feels perfect in having created it and in having symbolically united with it, incorporatively, in its consumption. Through his knowledge and the power of his wealth, Stiva is able to create and orchestrate the perfect meal. He recaptures a sense of the original narcissistic perfection for his self-representation by being able to make the perfect maternal object (the meal) responsive to him.

These meals are enjoyed at private clubs, where the servants lavish attention that reinforces the wished-for illusion that Stiva is perfect

One would have thought that out of two dozen delicacies one might find something to one's taste, but Stepan Arkadyevich asked for something special, and one of the liveried waiters standing by immediately brought what was required [p. 718].

Stiva's relationship to the "liveried waiters" demonstrates the often-encountered, overdetermined nature of narcissistically invested activities. While ingestion of the meal represents an oral incorporative union with the maternal object, the event is experienced within a narcissistically inverted oedipal context: The meal (mother) is suppliantly served by a male (the submissive conquered father).

We can see in Stiva the deliberate nature of his

pursuits and their defensive relationship to the frustrations of life.

> There was not a single cross or worried-looking face. All seemed to have left their cares and anxieties in the porter's room with their hats, and were all deliberately getting ready to enjoy the material blessings of life [p. 718].

The non-pejorative identification of this defensive relationship is a central analytic task with patients considered narcissistic personality disorders. The pursuit of pleasurable activities as a defense against depression is an aspect of many, if not all, addictions. If the subject is addicted to drugs, there is often a regressive denial of the realistic implications of his actions. Although such actions truly endanger his life, he will usually refuse to accept this when the therapist points it out. Patients like Stiva do things that interfere with their enjoyment of a fuller life, but are not objectively harmful in any life-threatening sense. Labeling their activities harmful or implying they are hurting someone else (their wife or their children) will often interfere with productive analytic work and result in the analysands' attempts at seduction, manipulation, or defiance of the analyst.

Stiva felt entitled to pursue an elixir for his ennui in the smiles of "Ossian" women. His sense of entitlement intruded on his capacity for empathic responsiveness to his wife's fate: "What am I to do? I'm made that way. And really, one does so little harm to anyone, and gives oneself so much pleasure" (p. 172).

Stiva did have a capacity for empathic responsiveness when his illusory sense of perfection in his self-representation was not threatened. The analytic task with such a subject would not be to judge or caution but rather to help the analysand understand the defensive meaning of his behavior and to help him begin to perceive that he is missing something, that the addictive nature of his life deprives him of the pleasures of loving and nurturing. Such analysands often struggle to repress their own judgment of themselves as bad or degenerate or lecherous, but their addiction deprives them of the pleasures of positive self-esteem associated with what Erikson (1950, p. 226) termed "generativity."

When Stiva's narcissistic defensive outlets are not immediately available, he feels no conscious inner sense of guilt. His chief concern is dealing with his disapproving wife.

He did not succeed in assuming an expression suitable to the position in which he was placed by his wife's discovery of his guilt. Instead of acting hurt, denying, defending himself, begging forgiveness, instead of remaining indifferent, (anything would have been better than what he did do), his face utterly involuntarily (reflex action of the brain, reflected Stepan Arkadyevich, who was fond of physiology)— utterly involuntarily assumed its habitual, good-humored, and therefore foolish smile.

This foolish smile he could not forgive himself. Catching sight of that smile, Dolly shuddered as though in physical pain, broke out with her characteristic passion into a flood of cruel words, and rushed out of the room. Since then she had refused to see her husband.

"It's that idiotic smile that's to blame for it all," thought Stepan Arkadyevich [p. 5].

He (self-as-agent) is not to blame; some reflex action of his brain (self-as-object) controls his action. This rationalization helps him avoid any sense of responsibility; to avoid the perception of Dolly's "physical pain" and his responsibility for it he blames it on his brain. Stiva justifies his entitled pursuit of pleasure by rationalizing it is "just the way he is."

Stiva does not choose political philosophies or friends. He is attracted to people and ideas that sanction his behavior, thereby sustaining the externalization of his critical conscience. Their presence and ideas assuage his ever-present potential to perceive his wife's pain, his responsibility in having caused it, and the excruciating guilt that follows.

The externalization of superego function is a frequent characteristic of narcissistic personality disorders and complements their ego attitudes of entitlement. Its interpretation is another important task in analytic work with such patients. These patients like to believe that life is a game, and they often refer to it in ways that imply painful feelings are not real. It is important, after a good working alliance has been established, to help a patient like Stiva explore his denial of painful feelings. Such analysands struggle not only to avoid a sense of guilt for the pain they cause others, but also to avoid their ever-present subliminal awarenes of their own disturbing inner life.

Stiva wanted it both ways. Not only did he want the comfort and pleasure of family life and the advantages of his wife's wealth, he also wished the freedom to pursue illusions of perfection whether or not this pursuit violated his marriage vows. Narcissistic personality disorders defensively wish the analyst to judge them. Then they can fight with the analyst rather than face the impossibility of having it both ways. As they integrate their own pain and the pain of others, it becomes progressively more difficult to manipulate others in quest of the momentary relief of defensive, narcissistically invested activities. This process is associated with rage and depression as they integrate the inevitable limits of their lives.

It is interesting to ponder Stiva's smile. It may represent a sadistic pleasure in hurting Dolly. Perhaps he was struggling against experiencing murderous rage at her for not being a perfect need-satisfying narcissistic object and for not allowing and not facilitating his pursuit of perfection for his self-representation.

Diagnostically Stiva could be considered a well-functioning narcissistic personality disorder with a significant potential for depression and regression if the characterological integration of his narcissistically invested pursuits is significantly threatened.

When Stiva married Dolly he *momentarily* felt that her beauty, her adulation and indulgence of him, as well as her family's money and social position, had allowed him to create a nirvana in which a sense of perfection for his self-representation could be attained and maintained. In addition he hoped his sister Anna's husband, Aleksey Aleksandrovich, would facilitate his professional advancement. The arrival of children (which forever shattered any possibility of gratifying his wish to be one and only to his wife), the progressive limits of her physical beauty, and his own awareness of the limits of his own body and mind all "conspired" to threaten the integration of his quest for perfection. The resulting painful affects (rage, anxiety, and depression) stimulated his narcissistically regressive quest for the perfect woman and the perfect meal.

Stiva was active in pursuing a passive position. His narcissistically invested ego functions were organized in the pursuit of a passive position in relationship to a wished-for flawless need-satisfying environment.

All narcissistic personality disorders are dependent on their external world to some degree. They all relate to that external world as a potential source of the admiration upon which they feel the integrity of their ego organization depends. However, potentially more disturbed narcissistic personality disorders relate to the external world with an entitled attitude reflective of their expectation that the world should gratify them just because they wish it. This attitude influences their ego development. Like Stiva they do little to attain their narcissistically invested gratifications other than smile and wish for them. When these are not forthcoming, they feel free to manipulate their object world to elicit them.

Narcissistic personality disorders who may be more easily helped in analysis have developed narcissistically invested ego functions and interests that are pursued actively in the hope of restoring a sense of narcissistic perfection to their self-representation. Although they relate to the world, in part, to elicit smiling admiration, they are more self-contained.

8

Dolly: A Depressed Neurotic Suppliant Personality Disorder

Darya Aleksandrovna, Dolly, is a typical example of the kind of feminine integration of narcissism that Women's Liberation abhors. For Dolly, her husband Stiva and her children are narcissistically invested possessions (objects). She narcissistically invests the ego functions associated with her identity as a beautiful woman, housewife, and mother. The smiling admiration she receives for her beauty and possessions and for her performance of activities associated with her identity represent the substance of her narcissistic integration. In these smiles she momentarily recaptures a sense of narcissistic perfection for her self-representation.

Stiva's infidelity shatters her system. She longs for her husband's love, or for the love of another adult male. She stays with Stiva after he has hurt her because she is afraid and weak.

She should leave him, but she was conscious that this was impossible; it was impossible because she could not get out of the habit of regarding him as her husband and loving him. Besides this, she realized that if even here in her own house she could hardly manage to look after her five children properly, they would be still worse off where she was going with them all.

Seeing her husband, . . . she tried to give a severe and determined expression, [but she] betrayed bewilderment and suffering [p. 13].

She had been raised to find purpose and a sense of completeness in union with a man. She finds it inconceivable that she could survive alone: "Dolly was crushed by her sorrow, utterly swallowed up by it" (p. 72). Such attitudes of self, still prevalent among women but more typical in the nineteenth century, interfere with Dolly's ability to see her own worth and strength more realistically and potentiate her self-destructive suppliant attachment to a weak little boy of a man who in fact gains his sustenance from her family's wealth. Her weakness contributes to her indulgence of Stiva, an indulgence and lack of appropriate limit setting that probably also characterized his mother's attitude toward him. She comes in touch with these issues as she considers her friend Anna's affair with Vronsky.

"And they attack Anna. What for? Am I any better? . . . I ought then to have cast off my husband and have been loved the real way. And is it any better as it is? I don't respect him. He's necessary to me," she thought about her husband, "and I put up with him. Is that any better? At that time I could still have been admired, I had beauty left me."

She thought that even now it was not too late; and she thought of Sergey Ivanovich, who was always particularly attentive to her, of Stiva's good-hearted friend Turovtsyn, who had helped her nurse

her children through scarlet fever, and was in love
with her. And there was someone else, a quite young
man who—her husband had told her as a joke—
thought her more beautiful than either of her sisters.
And the most passionate and impossible romances
rose before Darya Aleksandrovna's imagination. "Anna did quite right, and certainly I shall never reproach her for it. She is happy, she makes another
person happy, and she's not broken down as I am, but
most likely just as she always was—bright, clever,
open to every impression," thought Darya Aleksandrovna, and a sly smile curved her lips, for, as she
pondered on Anna's love affair, Darya Aleksandrovna
constructed on parallel lines an almost identical love
affair for herself, with an imaginary composite
figure, the ideal man who was in love with her. She,
like Anna, confessed the whole affair to her husband.
And the amazement and perplexity of Stepan Arkadyevich at this avowal made her smile [pp. 635–636].

Lack of autonomy and dread of standing alone in a
world of real and imagined dangers and vulnerabilities
make Stiva seem "necessary." Dolly feels less special
and entitled than Anna. In addition, her more integrated superego makes it too difficult for her to act
on her fantasy of leaving Stiva.

These factors contribute to her sense of dependency and vulnerability, keeping her tied to an unhappy
marriage, and her narcissism, deprived of gratification
through the love of an adult, finds expression in her
love of her children: "Had it not been for them, she
would have been left alone to brood over her husband
who did not love her . . . she was happy in them, and
proud of them" (p. 277). She narcissistically invests in
them to avoid the narcissistic injury of Stiva's infidelity

and the narcissistic vulnerability of being single, a vulnerability more intensely felt because of her incomplete autonomy. Because she perceives her aging and the diminution of her physical attributes, she feels imperfect as a narcissistic object. Her felt imperfection stimulates anxiety in response to anticipated rejection by another adult male; fear of a humiliating rejection inhibits any quest for narcissistic perfection in the manner of Anna. Instead she invests in her children as narcissistic objects. Their perfection is experienced as her own by a process of narcissistic identification. Their beauty assures her admiring glances and the admiration of her peers.

> Darya Aleksandrovna had done her hair, and dressed with care and excitement. In the old days she had dressed for her own sake to look pretty and be admired. Later on, as she got older, dressing up became more and more distasteful to her. She saw that she was losing her good looks. But now she began to feel pleasure and interest in dressing up again. Now she did not dress for her own sake, not for the sake of her own beauty, but simply so that as the mother of those exquisite creatures she might not spoil the general effect. And looking at herself for the last time in the mirror, she was satisfied with herself. She looked nice. Not nice as she would have wished to look nice in the old days at a ball, but nice for the object she now had in view [p. 278].

Deprived of the sensual pleasures of an adult heterosexual relationship, Dolly indirectly seeks them in her children.

> Darya Aleksandrovna, who had always liked bathing

herself, and believed it to be very good for the children, enjoyed nothing so much as bathing with all the children. To go over all those fat little legs, pulling on their stockings, to take in her arms and dip those little naked bodies, and to hear their screams of delight and alarm, to see the breathless faces with wide-open, scared, and happy eyes of all her splashing cherubs, was a great pleasure to her [p. 280].

There is something in Dolly that enjoys the child-like qualities of Stiva. It is probable that Dolly identifies with Stiva's sense of entitlement, that it reawakens a disavowed aspect of herself. This repressed identification would provide various gratifications that would interfere with her ability to set limits for both her children and Stiva. A feeling that she could not do without them would only reinforce this tendency.

Dolly could be diagnosed a suppliant personality disorder with a neurotic character integration. Her narcissistic investments are in her objects, Stiva and her children. She is inhibited from more assertively pursuing narcissistic gratification for her self-representation by her sexual identity, the roles afforded by her society, and by their internalized representations in her ego ideal and superego. These inhibit her activity, her more appropriate expression of anger, and contribute a masochistic, self-sacrificing quality to her character organization.

Dolly and Kitty are sisters who have experienced similar, although certainly not identical, genetics. It is reasonable to ask why one finds significant happiness in her life while the other does not. Such a question, never easy to answer in any case, is even more so here since these are fictional characters whose life histories thus have a somewhat two-dimensional quality. One obvious factor that remains unclear, for example, is the influence of their sibling order on their parents' attitudes toward them. It may be that Kitty, as the youngest, was more overvalued and that this contributed to her greater sense of specialness. Nor can we know what role luck played in the exigencies of their lives. The serendipity of her rejection by Vronsky certainly allows Kitty to experience an injury to her sense of specialness that facilitates the development of a more realistic view of herself and a more realistic choice of object in the fortunately present Levin.

9

Vronsky: A Phallic-Narcissistic Character in Regression

Vronsky, a young, unmarried cavalry captain, devotes his life to success in his military career. His narcissism is invested in those activities that fulfill his identity as a military man. His appearance is stereotypically phallic. He pursues perfection in his body and the horses he owns, rides, and races. To the degree he feels he has captured perfection in his appearance or in that of his horse he momentarily feels that perfection as an attribute of his self-representation. Perfection is also sought through continued competition for promotion. The narcissistic personality disorder can never rest; the stakes keep going up. At the age of twenty-five Vronsky could feel narcissistically fulfilled as a captain; at thirty-five, he must be a colonel.

Tolstoy introduces Vronsky to the reader two years after he has experienced a setback to his military aspirations:

Ambition was the oldest dream of his youth and childhood, a dream which he did not confess even to himself, though it was so strong that now this passion was even doing battle with his love. His first steps in the world and in the service had been successful, but two years before he had made a great mistake. Anxious to show his independence and to advance, he had refused a post that had been offered him, hoping that this refusal would heighten his value; but it turned out that he had been too bold, and he was passed over. And having, whether he liked it or not, taken the position of an independent man, he carried it off with great tact and good sense, behaving as though he bore no grudge against anyone, did not regard himself as injured in any way, and cared for nothing but to be left alone, since he was enjoying himself. In reality he had ceased to enjoy himself as long ago as the year before, when he went away to Moscow. He felt that this independent attitude of a man who might have done anything but cared to do nothing was already beginning to pall, that many people were beginning to think that he was not really capable of anything but being a straightforward, good-natured fellow [p. 324].

Vronsky's entitled, self-imposed style of defiance contributes to his failure. He struggles to avoid perceiving the pain of his setback as a humiliating defeat. He is bored and mildly depressed by having no prospect of success. The stage is set for a regressive in-love state. We noted that Stiva was "fixated" at a passive in-love state; his primary mode of seeking perfection was in winning the smiling adulation of a perfect woman. Vronsky, in contrast, seeks perfection more actively through his own narcissistically invested phallic attributes and accomplishments. Only when he feels it impossible to attain narcissistic perfection for his self-representation by phallic modes does he become vulnerable to a regression to the passive in-love state. The possession of Vronsky's narcissistically invested object by another man lends an overt triadic phallic-oedipal quality to his in-love state.

The in-love state here is regressive because it derives from a fixation at a period when perfection was perceived as possible only through the union of the incomplete, or narcissistically deflated, self with the idealized external object. Vronsky's phallic modes are built in part on identifications with narcissistically invested attributes derived from a later, more individuated period. Successful attainment is associated with internalized representations of the smiling self and object, in addition to external smiling approval. Successful functioning in the phallic mode more frequently results in a greater degree of autonomy than do activities based on fixations to modes dependent upon the response of the external object.

Vronsky's genetics are very similar to those described by Wilhelm Reich (1933), Kernberg (1970a), Kohut (1971), and others. His father, a manipulating "wheeler dealer," was virtually absent from his life, so that Vronsky was deprived of a paternal object who could serve as a model for the processes of internalization and idealization crucial to ego and superego development. His mother is the type of woman frequently described as "narcissistic." Her narcissism has always been invested in her physical appearance which she has used to attract the male adulation necessary to undo her sense of narcissistic want. Vronsky learned early in life that to gain his mother's smiling attention, her brand of love, he must be her perfect phallic object. (His education in a military school, the Corps of Pages, lent content to his mother's demands for phallic performance.) As an adult, in his thirties, he suppliantly pays her homage, ritualistically seeking her smiling approval.

> His mother, a dried-up old lady with black eyes and ringlets, screwed up her eyes, scanning her son, and smiled slightly with her thin lips. Getting up from the seat and handing her maid a bag, she gave her little wrinkled hand to her son to kiss, and, lifting his head from her hand, kissed him on the cheek [p. 67].

The extractive quality of his mother's relatedness has left Vronsky with an intensely ambivalent attitude toward her and women like her. Success wins their smiling approval and is associated with feelings of elation; however, his perception that he is loved not for himself, but rather for his performance, fills him with hate and although his rage is repressed, its derivatives are consciously experienced.

> He did not in his heart respect his mother, and without acknowledging it to himself, he did not love her, though in accordance with the ideas of the set in which he lived, and with his own education, he could not have conceived of any behavior to his mother not in the highest degree respectful and obedient, and the more externally obedient and respectful his behavior, the less in his heart he respected and loved her [p. 66].

We might speculate that although Vronsky consciously strove for success his rage may have contributed to his failure. For him failure would be equated with loss of his mother's attention and love, while a fear of his humiliating helplessness to change her might have contributed to the defensive independence that resulted in his being passed over.

Her lack of concern for his feelings and her investment of him as a narcissistic object is emphasized by
her response to his affair with Anna.

Vronsky's mother, on hearing of his liaison, was
at first pleased by it, because nothing to her mind
gave such a finishing touch to a brilliant young man
as an affair in the highest society; she was pleased,
too, that Madame Karenina, who had so taken her
fancy, and had talked so much of her son, was, after
all, just like all the other pretty and well-bred women
—at least according to the Countess Vronskaya's
ideas. But she had heard of late that her son had
refused a position offered him of great importance to
his career, simply in order to remain in the regiment,
where he could constantly see Madame Karenina.
She learned that important people were displeased
with him because of this, and she changed her opinion. She was vexed, too, that from all she could learn
of this liaison it was not that brilliant, graceful,
worldly liaison which she would have welcomed, but
a sort of Werther-like desperate passion, so she was
told, which might well lead him into something
foolish [p. 185].

It is not uncommon for men with mothers like his
to seek more related love from other men. This love
may or may not be sexualized, but it is often deeper
because it is less ambivalent. Vronsky is gratified in
this way by his friendship with Yashvin. Their friendship is motivated by a number of factors. Yashvin's
rigid pursuit of a limited spectrum of phallic-narcissistic activities makes him attractive to Vronsky as a
most admirable phallic-narcissistic object.

Vronsky liked him both for his exceptional physical strength, which he showed for the most part by being able to drink like a fish, and do without sleep without being in the slightest degree affected by it; and for his great strength of character, which he showed in his relations with his comrades and superior officers, commanding both fear and respect, and also at cards, when he would play for tens of thousands and, regardless of how much he might have drunk, always with such skill and control that he was considered the best player at the English Club [pp. 187–188].

Yashvin's rigid preference for men and his overt defiant denigration of women make it unlikely that he will hurt Vronsky by leaving him for a woman's attention as his father had. Vronsky might lose money to his friend and Vronsky might have to lend Yashvin money, but Vronsky knows his friend will always be there; he will not disappear, as Vronsky's father had. Most important, however, is Vronsky's feeling that Yashvin truly likes him and cares about him.

Vronsky respected and liked Yashvin particularly because he felt that Yashvin liked him, not for his name and his money, but for himself. And of all men he was the only one to whom Vronsky would have liked to speak of his love. He felt that Yashvin, in spite of his apparent contempt for every sort of feeling, was the only man who could, so he thought, comprehend the intense passion which now filled his whole life. Moreover, he felt certain that Yashvin took no delight in gossip and scandal, and interpreted his feeling properly [p. 188].

He feels that in this relationship he can be himself and

share his feelings: a striking contrast to what he has experienced with his parents.

In male patients considered narcissistic personality disorders one often observes that a male friendship or homosexual love affair serves the dual purpose of attempting to undo the injuries resulting from the primal relationship to both the father and the mother.

Although Vronsky was unaware of his ambivalence and repressed rage, as motivating forces in his life, the rage and the images associated with it probably had roots that were under primary repression. Anna Freud (1968) has emphasized this factor and its relationship to characterological defensive activity in such subjects. Vronsky's rage was probably derived in part from his mother's lack of "optimal availability" during his first years of life. His responses to such deprivation would be disorganizing in an affective and physiological sense. Since they would not be associated with secondary process elaboration, would not be truly under the influence of the ego as a more developed structure, they would be, therefore, in a state of primary repression. In Vronsky's case a characterological attitude to mother has developed that is primarily nonverbal and motoric with phallic attributes added associatively.

Consciously Vronsky feels humiliated by his competitive setback—his failure as his mother's phallic-narcissistic object. He struggles to avoid experiencing the pain of his humiliating inability to reverse this situation. Simultaneously he hungers to discharge both his lust for adulation and his increasingly intense, although unconscious, rage at the adulator. His failure increases the strength of this rage as a motivational force in his life. He cannot succeed in the difficult setting of male competition in the work world. Competition in play—gambling and racing—progressively bores him. Time has made his failure harder to deny and he becomes increasingly susceptible to displaced male competition, expressed in his infatuated pursuit of another man's wife, Anna. In this pursuit he may assuage his painful envy of his peer's more realistic success:

> The friend of his childhood, a man of the same set, of the same coterie, his comrade in the Corps of Pages, Serpukhovsky, who had left school with him and had been his rival in class, in gymnastics, in their scrapes and their dreams of glory, had come back a few days before from Central Asia, where he had gained two steps up in rank, and an order rarely bestowed upon generals so young.
>
> As soon as he arrived in Petersburg, people began to talk about him as a newly risen star of the first magnitude. A classmate of Vronsky's and of the same age, he was a general and was expecting a command which might have influence on the course of political events... "And with her love, I cannot feel envious of Serpukhovsky" [p. 325].

In addition to mitigating his envy his affair stimulates the admiring attention of individuals who bestow success.

> His affair with Madame Karenina, by creating so much sensation and attracting general attention, had given him a fresh distinction which soothed his gnawing worm of ambition for a while [p. 324].

In patients considered narcissistic personality disorders, one typically perceives the intermingling of preoedipal and oedipal determinants in the subject's motivation. Vronsky is a fine example of this phenomenon. Vronsky's behavior attempted to (1) win his mother's smiling attention, her love, (2) express his rage at her for demanding performance for that love, (3) win her love by beating a male competitor, a pre-oedipal and oedipal elaboration of the theme, and (4) win his father's attention, through that of other men, and undo his life-long experience of disappointment at his father's lack of interest in him, a preoedipal and negative oedipal experience.

Vronsky's failure in his quest to restore illusions of perfection for his self-representation in military pursuits predisposes him to be vulnerable to an in-love state. If he cannot be the perfect phallic-narcissistic object at work, he can be such to Anna, an object he perceives as perfect. In winning Anna and her smiling attention, his perfection is reaffirmed. Winning her smiling attention revivifies memories of his mother's approval of his perfect phallic exhibitionism (W. Reich, 1933; Kohut, 1966, 1971). On a deeper level, winning her alters his self-representation by a process of internalization that recaptures a sense of self-object duality.

Vronsky falls in-love with Anna, the idealized, adulated object; he is passive, in "slavish adoration" (p. 107), and feels "reverential ecstasy" (p. 109). She becomes the entire meaning of his life:

> He felt that all his forces, hitherto dissipated, wasted, were concentrated on one thing, and bent with fearful energy on one blissful goal. And he was happy at it. He knew only that he had told her the truth, that he had come where she was, and all the happiness of his life, the only meaning in life for him, now lay in seeing and hearing her [p. 111].

Without her love he feels there is no value in life. "They

haven't an idea of what happiness is; they don't know that without our love, for us there is neither happiness nor unhappiness—no life at all" (p. 195).

Tolstoy captures the feelings of helplessness and the representational and "cathectic fluency" (Jacobson, 1954, p. 114) of the in-love state, in his description of Vronsky's response to Anna's suffering: "In her presence he had no will of his own: without knowing the grounds of her distress, he already felt the same distress unconsciously passing over him" (pp. 332–333).

Vronsky's in-love state has a number of motivational aspects. First, it recaptures a sense of narcissistic perfection for his self-representation related to preoedipal and oedipal issues. Second, it discharges his unconscious rage at his mother and his father. Third, it gratifies self-destructive urges that are themselves multiply determined.

An incorporative identification with Anna as the preoedipal idealized object recaptures a sense of narcissistic perfection for his self-representation. He feels entitled to pursue and possess her: "He could recognize in no one but himself an indubitable right to love her" (p. 112). Those ego attributes, functions, and activities that entice and attract her are narcissistically invested aspects of his self-representation, and their successful performance recaptures an elated sense of perfection for that representation. He feels himself "His Majesty the Baby" (Freud, 1914): "Vronsky saw nothing and no one. He felt himself a king" (p. 311).

The elation associated with the narcissistic victory of making "an impression on Anna" protects Vronsky from recapturing memories of painful and disorganizing preoedipal experiences of his mother's self-involved unavailability. This sexualized preoedipal experience influenced his oedipal complex. As a young boy he did not possess the equipment to satisfy his mother, while his father and other men did. The victory of winning Anna, another man's wife, transiently undoes the narcissistic injury of oedipal defeat.

Vronsky's relationship with his father — whom "he scarcely remembers" — including both his preoedipal relationship and his negative oedipal constellation, plays an important role in his involvement with Anna. It was even harder to get his father's than it was his mother's attention. It is probable that his father resented him for existing, first in his mother's body, and then as a competitor for her attention. Paternal "mirroring" and admiring attention are important facilitators of development, particularly important to oedipal phase internalizations and the development of gender identity, as well as to that of the ego ideal and superego. Deprivation of a responsive paternal presence has significantly contributed to Vronsky's longing for the admiring attention of men. His competitive involvements with men create an illusion of his father's presence; the fantasied resolution of these competitive skirmishes assuages a myriad of developmental disappointments. His relationships with comrades such as Yashvin soothe the narcissistic injury of his father's rejection, desertion, and death.

Anna's husband, Aleksey Aleksandrovich, treats Vronsky with cold indifference stimulating repressed traumatic memories of his father's self-involvement.

Aleksey Aleksandrovich looked at Vronsky with displeasure, vaguely recalling who this was. Vronsky's composure and self-confidence here struck, like a scythe against a stone, upon the cold self-confidence of Aleksey Aleksandrovich.

"Count Vronsky," said Anna.

"Ah! We are acquainted, I believe," said Aleksey Aleksandrovich indifferently, giving his hand [p. 113].

He could not make his father, nor can he make Anna's husband, *love* him, but through his pursuit of Anna he will make her husband *notice* him. In the future he may not be loved but he will not be treated with cold indifference. To be noticed, regardless of the affect, gratifies the narcissistic ambition to be looked at; it recaptures an omnipotent sense of perfection for the self-representation derived from the subject's sense of having been able to control his mother's attention and the resulting sense of presence and union with the object.

The negative oedipal motive has primacy over any potential of Vronsky's to love Anna. It contributes to his attraction for her and is an important factor in the relationship's destruction. When Anna's husband gives her an ultimatum, Vronsky's preoccupation with a narcissistically gratifying fantasied involvement with Aleksey Aleksandrovich intrudes on his capacity for empathic relatedness to Anna.

Again, just as at the first moment of hearing of her break with her husband, Vronsky, on reading the letter, was unconsciously carried away by the natural feeling aroused in him by his own relation to the betrayed husband. Now while he held his letter in his hands, he could not help picturing the challenge, which he would most likely find at home today or tomorrow, and the duel itself, in which, with the same cold and haughty expression that his face was assuming at this moment he would await the injured husband's shot, after having himself fired into the air....

Having read the letter, he raised his eyes to her, and there was no determination in them. She saw at once that he had been thinking about it before by himself. She knew that whatever he might say to her, he would not say all he thought. And she knew that her last hope had failed her. This was not what she had been expecting [p. 334].

The humiliating defeat of his oedipal competitor is reversed by Aleksey Aleksandrovich's revision of the competitive rules. Vronsky anticipates a challenge and a duel; instead Aleksandrovich's response undercuts the foundations of Vronsky's competitive involvement, leaving him in the narcissistic personality disorder's most dreaded state: humiliated and helpless to reverse humiliation.

"This is my position: you can trample me in the mud, make me the laughingstock of the world, I will not abandon her, and I will never utter a word of reproach to you," Aleksey Aleksandrovich went on. "My duty is clearly marked for me; I should be with her, and I will be. If she wishes to see you, I will let you know, but now I suppose it would be better for you to go away.". . .

After the conversation with Aleksey Aleksandrovich, Vronsky went out onto the steps of the Karenin house and stood still, with difficulty remembering where he was and where he should walk or drive. He felt disgraced, humiliated, guilty, and deprived of all possibility of washing away his humiliation. He felt thrust out of the beaten track along which he had so proudly and lightly walked till then. All the habits and rules of his life that had seemed so firm had turned out suddenly false and inapplicable. The be-

trayed husband, who had figured till that time as a
pitiful creature, an incidental and somewhat ludicrous obstacle to his happiness, had suddenly been
summoned by herself, elevated to an awe-inspiring
pinnacle, and on the pinnacle that husband had
shown himself not malignant, not false or ludicrous,
but kind and straightforward and dignified. Vronsky
could not but feel this, and the parts were suddenly
reversed. Vronsky felt Karenin's elevation and his
own abasement, Karenin's rightness, his own wrong-
doing [pp. 436–437].

To undo the excruciatingly disorganizing sense of
humiliating helplessness and to restore a narcissistic
equilibrium to his character organization, Vronsky attempts suicide (see pp. 72–74). Vronsky feels mortified,
destroyed by Anna's husband. A split in his self-representation allows his self-as-agent to impose destruction
on his self-as-object. At such a moment a subject
believes the narcissistically invested self-as-agent to be
immortal. At the last moment, Vronsky's sense of reality overrides this breach in his self-representation and
he delivers a nonlethal injury to his chest wall.

Unconscious rage at women in general, and at Anna in particular, was another important motivator of
Vronsky's behavior. Wilhelm Reich (1933) first identified this factor and elaborated its genesis:

On the basis of a phallic mother-identification a phallic-narcissistic character usually develops, whose
narcissism and sadism is directed especially toward
women (vengeance on the strict mother). . . . This attitude is the character defense against the deeply repressed original love of the mother which could not
continue in the face of her frustrating influence [pp.
152–153].

The rage is mobilized in response to this frustration. Reich described its expression in sadistic and other sexual perversions and in the character attitudes and behavior of these male patients toward women. Kernberg (1970a) emphasizes the importance of this rage, defining it more specifically as "oral rage" (p. 52) in response to "cold hostile" mothers (p. 59).

Disappointment and repressed murderous rage in response to maternal unrelatedness stimulate both Vronsky's *narcissistic* investments designed to win attention from women and his unconscious *sadistic* attitudes toward women. Tolstoy captures both these factors in the seduction of Anna.

> He felt what a murderer must feel when he sees the body he has robbed of life. That body, robbed by him of life, was their love, the first stage of their love.... But in spite of all the murderer's horror before the body of his victim, he must hack it to pieces, hide the body, must use what he has gained by his murder.
>
> And with fury, as it were with passion, the murderer falls on the body and drags it and hacks at it; so he covered her face and shoulders with kisses [pp. 158–159].

Vronsky's and Anna's involvement develops as a defense against integrating life's limits; their rage-filled insistence on having things their way drives them to the brink of death. They resolve to separate and attempt to recapture their previous lives, but Vronsky's passion "infects" Anna and she is "conquered." Tolstoy's portrait of this intense in-love state suggests the deeply repressed homosexual component of Vronsky's narcissistic object choice.

Anna's hair has been cut short during her illness.

Vronsky responds to this: "I hardly know you with this short hair. You've grown so lovely like a little boy" (p. 456). He loves her in a nurturing, adulating manner, as his mother must have loved him at isolated, preindividuated moments.

Freud (1905) has described the homosexual's narcissistic object choice.

> ...the future inverts, in the earliest years of their childhood, pass through a phase of very intense but short-lived fixation to a woman (usually their mother), and after leaving this behind, they identify themselves with a woman and take *themselves* as their sexual object. That is to say, they proceed from a narcissistic basis and look for a young man who resembles themselves and whom *they* may love as their mother loved *them* [p. 145].

Freud captured the inconsistent, intense, overvaluing nature of the maternal influence on the genesis of this narcissistic fixation in his description of the child's "very intense but short-lived" relationship to his mother. The narcissistic fixation defends against the loss of that intensity. By becoming the perfect narcissistic objects, narcissistic personality disorders hope to regain it.

A final determinant of his in-love state is Vronsky's self-destructive urge. Vronsky is unable to tolerate the pleasure and positive self-esteem he has experienced in Kitty's infatuation with him.

> "What is so exquisite is that not a word has been said by me or by her, but we understand each other so well in this unseen language of looks and tones that this evening more clearly than ever she told me she

loves me. And how secretly, simply, and most of all, how trustfully! I feel myself better, purer. I feel that I have a heart, and that there is a great deal of good in me. Those sweet, loving eyes" [p. 163].

An "unconscious need for punishment," a sense of guilt and defect, prevent Vronsky from allowing himself the purification and cleansing internalizations that being in-love with Kitty would bring him.

This need for punishment derives from his superego's judgment of his murderous oral, anal, and phallic-oedipal feelings toward his mother and father. Murderous feelings are a ubiquitous response in narcissistic personality disorders to frustrating, humiliating narcissistic injuries imposed by parents at any phase of development. The same quality of parenting often permeates all phases and is itself the humiliating injury. Vronsky felt guilty about his murderous rage at his parents' desertion of him, while at the same time his sense of oedipal guilt was intensified by his implied partial oedipal victory.

Vronsky's self-destructive path seems unalterable:

This child's presence called up both in Vronsky and in Anna a feeling akin to the feeling of a sailor who sees by the compass that the direction in which he is swiftly moving is far from the right one, but that to arrest his motion is not in his power, that every instant is carrying him further and further away, and that to admit to himself his deviation from the right direction is the same as admitting his certain ruin [p. 197].

Vronsky's inability to admit his mistake and, in so doing, to impose a narcissistic injury on himself by ac-

knowledging an imperfection is the other major determinant of his self-destructive behavior. To acknowledge
this would require that he relinquish his sense of entitlement, accept the inevitability of limits, and give up
the fantasy of total control of his destiny.

Once Vronsky and Anna have come together after a
great deal of turmoil, the illusionary and transient nature of their narcissistic fulfillment emerges.

> Vronsky, meanwhile, in spite of the complete
> realization of what he had so long desired, was not
> perfectly happy. He soon felt that the realization of
> his desires gave him no more than a grain of sand of
> the mountain of happiness he had expected. It showed
> him the mistake men make in picturing to them-
> selves happiness as the realization of their desires.
> For a time after joining his life to hers, and putting
> on civilian dress, he had felt all the delight of
> freedom in general, of which he had known nothing
> before, and of freedom in his love—and he was con-
> tent, but not for long. He was soon aware that there
> was springing up in his heart a desire for desires—
> ennui [p. 488].

After he has won the prized, narcissistically invested
object, the victory and the attention associated with it
diminish. The narcissistic personality disorder
"desires" new affirmations of perfection for his self-
representation. The "mass of desires" (p. 489) that de-
mand satisfaction now invest painting and his prospective identity as an artist, and Vronsky fantasies finding
perfection in this role. Vronsky, however, is not an artist; he is merely a technician. He remains so because
he is trapped in his need for the smiling approval of the
external world.

He appreciated all kinds, and could have felt inspired by any of them; but he had no conception of the possibility of knowing nothing at all of any school of painting, and of being inspired directly by what is within the soul, without caring whether what is painted will belong to any recognized school. Since he knew nothing of this, and drew his inspiration, not directly from life, but indirectly from life embodied in art, his inspiration came very quickly and easily, and as quickly and easily came his success in painting something very similar to the sort of painting he was trying to imitate.

More than any other style he liked the French—graceful and effective—and in that style he began to paint Anna's portrait in Italian costume, and the portrait seemed to him, and to everyone who saw it, extremely successful [p. 489].

Vronsky can gain a degree of success in his role as artist but he lacks an inner feeling of the potential for attaining perfection in his artistic creation. He has no internal sense that his work is perfect. Tolstoy contrasts Vronsky with the true artist Mikhailov:

He began to look at his picture with his own full artist vision, and was soon in that mood of conviction of the perfectibility, and so of the significance, of his picture—a conviction essential to the intensest fervor, excluding all other interests—in which alone he could work [p. 500].

This inner sense allows Mikhailov to withdraw from external approval and become intensely invested in the creative effort. To be truly creative, the artist must transiently suspend attachment to the external object's approving smile. Such self-involvement implies an ability to face the possible narcissistic injury of failure—an ability essential to the creative experience. The inner "conviction of perfectibility," which assuages the pain of possible failure, is probably based, in part, on an internalization of a preoedipal, adulating maternal object representation.

As Vronsky becomes aware of his lack of genius, his interest in painting wanes. Whatever is associated with perfection is perceived as beautiful. When that association is lost, denigration ensues.

The relationship between Anna and Vronsky declines and dies because Anna is no longer the perfect narcissistic object and winning her has lost its valence as a longed-for narcissistic victory. This process of disenchantment with the possessed narcissistically invested object is a typical response in patients considered narcissistic personality disorders. A panoply of resentments fuel the subject's descent from his in-love state. The narcissistically invested object is perceived as having, and potentially offering, something the subject wants and feels is necessary for his survival. Hence there is always an underlying envy of the fantasied perfection of the object. At the same time, the object is subliminally resented because she is perceived as potentially withholding. In sicker subjects, the frustrating object can be elaborated as malevolently, spitefully, and pleasurably withholding. Because the object must frustrate the subject, she is resented. She is resented for having her own interests and for being involved with others. These resentments of her other involvements are intensified by the birth of siblings and are particularly focused in the triadic oedipal constellation.

The narcissistically invested object once possessed

often becomes the dependent object. Vronsky particularly resents Anna's dependency. They are now outside "smiling" society. Anna is now a degraded object, subject to ridicule in society. Now instead of eliciting envious smiling attention for Vronsky, Anna brings him the jeering contempt of his contemporaries. Rather than sympathizing with Anna, Vronsky's primary response is humiliation, a humiliation intensified by oppressive thoughts of Anna's husband.

> "My daughter is by law not my daughter but Karenin's. I cannot bear this deception!". . .
> "One day a son may be born, my son, and he will be legally a Karenin; he will not be the heir of my name or of my property, and however happy we may be in our home life and however many children we may have, there will be no real tie between us. They will be Karenins. You can understand the bitterness and horror of this position! I have tried to speak of this to Anna. It irritates her" [p. 655].

For Levin, narcissistic perfection is significantly invested in his ego ideal. There it is invested in idealized and real imagos of his forefathers engaged in farming and family life, as well as in the abstraction of a "spiritual" life. His efforts are devoted to an attempt to live up to these abstract and internalized ideals. His sense of well-being depends upon an internalized feeling of synchrony with those ideals. Vronsky is much more concerned with how he appears to external others. No matter how happy he is in his real family life, if he *looks* like a fool to others, particularly to men, the ensuing feeling of humiliation taints and destroys any possibility of inner happiness and well-being. Vronsky's sense of well-being is more dependent upon the smiling affirmation of the external object.

Anna responds to the loss of her idealized position with a combination of defiant rage, paranoid jealousy, and compliance. Vronsky experiences her compliance as a controlling limit to his freedom to pursue perfection elsewhere, in racing and politics.

> Vronsky appreciated this desire not only to please but to serve him, which had become the sole aim of her existence, but at the same time he wearied of the loving snares in which she tried to hold him fast. As time went on, and he saw himself more and more often entangled in these meshes, he had an ever-growing desire, not so much to escape from them, as to try whether they hindered his freedom. . . . "I can give up anything for her, but not my independence," he thought [pp. 672–673].

Vronsky's sense of her degraded state is intensified by her undignified controlling nature. His sensitivity to her extractive narcissistic investment of him motivates him to defiantly proclaim his independence. Her behavior toward him and her investment of him recapitulate his mother's investment in him, and he flees her like an individuating toddler running from an engulfing maternal object. A patient, Mr. C, elaborated such a conflict in a dream as a terrifying "Manta Ray" coming to engulf him with her "flapping wings" as he struggled to stay afloat while she threatened to "drag him under."

In the process of fleeing her, Vronsky discovers a new activity in which to pursue narcissistically invested illusions:

> Vronsky had come to the elections partly because he was bored in the country and wanted to show Anna

his right to independence.... But he had not in the least expected that the election would so interest him, so keenly excite him, and that he would be so good at this kind of thing.... And now at his own table, celebrating Nevedovsky's election, he was experiencing an agreeable sense of triumph over the success of his candidate. The election itself had so fascinated him that, if he could succeed in getting married during the next three years, he began to think of standing himself—much as after winning a race ridden by a jockey, he had longed to ride a race himself [p. 692].

Anna's rage and Vronsky's guilt bind them together and ultimately destroy these "lover-combatants." Anna's perception of her fallen position fuels her controlling compliance which contributes to Vronsky's pursuits of perfection elsewhere. This further intensifies her perception of loss. A neurotic circle that is to strangle them is irreparably closed. He cannot face, perceive, and articulate the issue. He cannot say, "I am not in love with you anymore because you are conquered, degraded, and humiliated." He feels tied to her because he has destroyed her and she feels enmeshed with him, because he and his loving attention seem to her the only means of restoring illusions of perfection to her self-representation.

10

Anna: A Stereotypical Female Narcissistic Personality Disorder

Anna Karenina, Stiva's sister, is a very beautiful, elegant, grace-ful woman in her early thirties. Like Vronsky's mother, she narcissistically invests her physical beauty. This wins smiling admiration from others as well as from herself. In these smiles she recaptures a sense of narcissistic perfection. Anna's narcis-sistic investment of her physical beauty is a traditional and typical characteristic of most women (as well as of many men). The mode is most intense during adolescence and early adulthood. Traditionally, as beauty wanes, women like Anna or Countess Vronskaya become depressed. Others like Dolly and Kitty adapt and narcissistically invest children and functions related to the identity of mother and wife. Children or husband may be invested as narcissistic objects. For a woman to happily follow this developmental route she must be able to relinquish the wish to be the central admired overvalued object and obtain gratification through an identification with her own objects. For such a situation to work these modes have to be in

235

synchrony with the subject's ego ideal and the woman must be appreciated by her husband and social group. Anna and Countess Vronskaya are unable to achieve the transition from their investment of themselves to an investment of objects. Their objects remain vehicles for their own aggrandizement.

From a diagnostic perspective, many more women than men narcissistically invest their self-representations during adolescence as a phase-appropriate developmental event.[1] For women to achieve a traditional feminine position in a family, their narcissistic investments must be in their objects (children and husband) to some significant degree. Like Kitty and Dolly, such women are suppliant personality disorders with normal or neurotic integrations.

Anna has difficulty relinquishing her wish to be desired and adulated. She wishes to be the central object of admiration, the focus of attention:

Anna read and understood; but it was distasteful to her to read, that is, to follow the reflection of other people's lives. She had too great a desire to live herself. If she read that the heroine of the novel was nursing a sick man, she longed to move with noiseless steps about the room of a sick man; if she read of

[1]Present-day life offers challenging adaptational possibilities for women and men to alternatingly invest themselves and their objects at different moments and stages of development. For example, during youth (Kenniston, 1973), one may pursue narcissistic perfection in quest of vocational success and then, during the late twenties or thirties, enjoy a family with its narcissistic and object-loving involvements. Such a person could be considered a narcissistic personality disorder during youth by virtue of the primary mode of narcissistic investment in his self-representation. During adulthood, there could be a more balanced distribution of investments in both self- and object representations.

a member of Parliament making a speech, she longed to be delivering the speech; if she read of how Lady Mary had ridden after the hounds, and had provoked her sister-in-law, and had surprised everyone by her boldness, she too wished to be doing the same [pp. 106–107].

Her husband, Aleksey Aleksandrovich, a successful bureaucrat, obsessively pursues perfection for his self-representation in his work. This narcissistic personality disorder has invested those ego functions that fuel his pursuit of power. He has invested in "merit badge" accoutrements that represented the attainment of power, among which he includes Anna. She is a beautiful possession to complement his appearance and support his professional efforts. Anna experiences this as a stifling deprivation:

"He's right!" she said; "of course, he's always right; he's a Christian, he's generous! Yes, vile, base creature! And no one understands it except me, and no one ever will; and I can't explain it. They say he's so religious, so high-principled, so upright, so clever; but they don't see what I've seen. They don't know how he had crushed my life for eight years, crushed everything that was living in me. He has not once given thought that I'm a live woman who must have love. They don't know how at every step he's humiliated me, and been just as pleased with himself" [p. 309].

For Anna, not to be loved, to be ignored, is experienced as a humiliating mortification.

In addition to being self-involved and ignoring Anna, Aleksey is defensively disdainful of her, jeering and

sarcastic in his demonstration of affectionate attention.

> "Yes, as you see, your tender spouse, as devoted as
> the first year after marriage, burned with impatience
> to see you," he said in his deliberate, high-pitched
> voice, and in that tone which he almost always took
> with her, a tone of jeering at anyone who should say
> in earnest what he said [pp. 110–111].

She is *enraged* at him for his humiliating disdain,
and for his inability to want, need, and adulate her.
Simultaneously she is excited by Vronsky's infatuation
with her, and by the narcissistic gratification implicit
in his reverential smile. She struggles to defend against
the resulting painful intersystemic conflict (between
her "grandiose self" which seeks smiling adulation and
her superego which reminds her she is married and
tells her it is dangerous to be an adultress). Her narcissistic rage at her husband, expressed in her denigration of him, wins.

> "All the same, he's a good man; truthful, good-
> hearted, and remarkable in his own line," Anna said
> to herself, going back to her room, as though she
> were defending him to someone who had attacked
> him and said that one could not love him. "But why is
> it his ears stick out so strangely? Or has he had his
> hair cut?" [p. 119].

Aleksey is not able to make himself vulnerable and
deeply feel a need for Anna. When she is unfaithful he
cannot insist on his feelings for her and fight for her.
Instead his focus is the effect her behavior will have on
his public image and on their son.

"Anna, for God's sake don't speak like that," he said gently. "Perhaps I am mistaken, but believe me, what I say, I say as much for myself as for you. I am your husband, and I love you."

For an instant her face fell, and the sardonic gleam in her eyes died away; but the word "love" threw her into revolt again. She thought: "Love? Can he love? If he hadn't heard there was such a thing as love, he would never have used the word. He doesn't even know what love is."

"Aleksey Aleksandrovich, really I don't understand," she said. "Define what it is you find—"

"Excuse me, let me say all I have to say. I love you. But I am not speaking of myself; the most important persons in this matter are our son and yourself. It may very well be, I repeat, that my words seem to you utterly unnecessary and out of place; it may be that they are called forth by my mistaken impression. In that case, I beg you to forgive me. But if you are conscious yourself of even the smallest foundation for them, then I beg you to think a little, and if your heart prompts you to speak out to me. . ." [pp. 156–157].

Sometime later, her narcissistic rage and his narcissistic and obsessional defensiveness are more extreme.

"I hear you, but I am thinking of him. I love him, I am his mistress; I can't bear you; I'm afraid of you, and I hate you. . . . You can do what you like to me."

And dropping back into the corner of the carriage, she broke into sobs, hiding her face in her hands. Aleksey Aleksandrovich did not stir, and kept looking straight before him. But his whole face suddenly bore the solemn rigidity of the dead, and his

expression did not change during the whole time of
the drive home. On reaching the house, he turned his
head to her, still with the same expression.

"Very well! But I expect a strict observance of
the external forms of propriety till such time"—his
voice shook—"as I may take measures to protect my
honor and communicate them to you" [p. 225].

Her narcissistic rage derives from her sense of
entitlement. She feels she must be central to survive.
Simultaneously she feels entitled to pursue her goal.
She is enraged at anyone who frustrates her wish to be
adulated and experiences in a self-centered manner
Aleksey's defensive disdain of the adulation she longs
for. She conceives of her form of narcissistic investment and its associated in-love state as the real type of
love. She disdains the passions of Aleksey's life and is
enraged at his defenses because they frustrate hers.

In the early years of her marriage the intoxication of having won a wealthy, successful man satisfies
her narcissistic equilibrium. Although he does not adulate and admire her, she and others can admire her
achievement and the inanimate objects associated with
it. The exhibitionistic activities associated with these
achievements assuage the insult of her husband's self-
involvement. Within a year, she is pregnant and gives
birth to a son, Seryozha. In a phase-appropriate manner, he can temporarily be invested in as an object to
love and adulate. As he grows into latency, his phase-
appropriate idealization of his mother diminishes as
does her narcissistic investment of him.

And her son, like her husband, aroused in Anna a
feeling akin to disappointment. She had imagined
him better than he was in reality. She had to let

herself descend to reality to enjoy him as he really was [p. 114].

Anna wants more. She wants the intensely gratifying experience of being adulated and revered. Her disappointment with her husband and son set the stage for her affair with Vronsky. As did Vronsky's object choice, Anna's narcissistic search for gratification through being admired reveals homosexual aspects. Her first infatuation is associated with Vronsky's mother's admiration.

"Good-by, darling," answered the Countess. "Let me have a kiss of your pretty face. I speak plainly, at my age, and I tell you simply that I've lost my heart to you."
Stereotyped as the phrase was, Madame Karenina obviously believed it and was delighted by it. She flushed, bent down slightly, and put her cheek to the countess's lips, drew herself up again, and with the same smile fluttering between her lips and her eyes, she gave her hand to Vronsky [p. 69].

Vronsky falls completely under the spell of an in-love state with Anna. He looks at her face with "reverential ecstasy" (p. 109) and pursues her with a "slavish adoration" (p. 107). This gratifies Anna's deep sense of "narcissistic want." Tolstoy expresses the intensity of her feelings descriptively and metaphorically:

At that moment the wind, as if surmounting all obstacles, sent the snow flying from the carriage roofs, and clanked some sheet of iron it had torn off, while the hoarse whistle of the engine roared in front, plaintively and gloomily. All the awfulness of the storm seemed to her more splendid now. He had said what her soul longed to hear, though she feared it with her reason. She made no answer, and in her face he saw conflict [p. 109]

Her confict derives from the fact that Anna is more related and has a more intact superego that does Vronsky's mother. Countess Vronskaya is comfortable with many affairs. She, like Stiva, can move easily from admirer to admirer: men, women, and children are alternately exchanged and related to for the extraction of their smiling admiration. Once an object's smile is extracted, the object becomes less valuable; it is conquered and can be discarded.

There is a spectrum of callousness in the quality of subjects' extractiveness that can often be correlated with the degree and quality of their mothers' hostility toward them. On the sicker extreme, the subject sadistically, manipulatively, and disdainfully elicits an admiring smile. On the healthier extreme the narcissistic personality disorder subtly and with tenderness evokes an approving response. In all cases, however, the smiling response, rather than the object, is primary. Anna's guilt and the greater ambivalence of her attachment result in more intense conflict. This derives from the discordance caused by the prospect of intense narcissistic gratification contrasted with the prohibitions of her superego, its associated object representations, and their externalized social representatives. Anna, like many narcissistic personality disorders, has an intrasystemic superego conflict. On the one hand, there are internalizations that forbid infidelity. Simultaneously other internalizations encourage it. There is a corresponding intrasystemic conflict in Anna's ego. Her self-representation as agent organized in relationship to the "reality principle" (Freud, 1911a, p. 226) struggles to "assimilate" (Waelder, 1936, p. 48) the self-representation as agent organized in relationship to the "pleasure principle" (Freud, 1911a, p. 219) and structured to feel entitled.

Tolstoy portrays Anna's attempts to resolve her conflict in a dream:

> She dreamed that both were her husbands at once, that both were lavishing caresses on her. Aleksey Aleksandrovich was weeping, kissing her hands, and saying, "How good it is now!" and Aleksey Vronsky was there too, and he too was her husband. And she was amazed that it had once seemed impossible to her, was explaining to them, laughing, that this was so much simpler, and that now both of them were happy and contented [pp. 159–160].

This dream portrays a common technical issue in the analytic management of narcissistic personality disorders. Anna wished to avoid conflict. She wished to simplify life. She had a superego and felt guilty. She hated her husband and longed for the pleasure of Vronsky's adulation, but she perceived and empathized with Aleksandrovich's pain. The dream solved her conflict by omnipotently decreeing her right to polygamy. The analyst's task with narcissistic personality disorders is to accept the nature of their narcissistic strivings; simultaneously he must help the analysand to accept that life and relationships are complex rather than simple, that choice and, therefore, frustration and pain are inevitable.

Narcissistic personality disorders often come to analysis hoping to find, through narcissistically invested analytic insight, the key to unlock the door to a pure pleasure, a frustration-free nirvana where no conflict exists. They do not want to choose between two imperfect possibilities. They wish to solve, that is to remove, a conflict. It is the analyst's task to help them resolve it, to help them integrate the inevitability of tension and relative dissatisfaction in their adult lives. The analysand gradually integrates an understanding that the illusory wish for one or another form of a tensionless, pure pleasure state is a defense. It defends against the disorganizing perceptions of the traumas or of the traumatically disappointing nature of the early-life experiences. These early frustrations were experienced as humiliations the subject was helpless to undo. Frustrations of adult life are associatively linked to and threaten to revivify affectively laden memory traces of painful early-life experiences. The illusion of narcissistic perfection seems the only route away from pain. Insight and its secondary process elaboration can facilitate the understanding and acceptance that adult frustrations are not life-threatening, as they were felt to be in childhood. They do not have to be fled from and defended against.

Anna's husband's frustration of her sense of entitlement stimulates her rage. When this sense is frustrated by a reality she is not able to change, she becomes depressed.

> "Do you see, I love. . . equally, I think, but both more than myself — two beings, Seryozha [her son] and [Vronsky]. . ."
>
> "It is only those two beings that I love, and one excludes the other. I can't have them together, and that's the only thing I want. And since I can't have that, I don't care about the rest. I don't care about anything, anything" [p. 669].

Anna and Vronsky consummate their love affair by breaking with society. Anna leaves her husband and abandons her son. Vronsky resigns his army commission and they leave Russia for Italy. Anna's lustre begins to diminish after she is possessed by Vronsky who then seeks narcissistic fulfillment in other activities. Because of who she was, characterologically, and where and what she was, temporally (nineteenth century) and socially (aristocracy), she has cut herself off from other sources of restoring a sense of narcissistic perfection to her self-representation. She becomes a dependent woman with no means of gaining narcissistic gratification other than through the admiration of overvalued phallic-narcissistic male objects. By virtue of her dependent state, Anna's character organization undergoes a metamorphosis from narcissistic to suppliant personality disorder. Previously, she had felt capable of affirming the perfection of her self-representation; now she feels degraded and defective. Her only possibility of regaining a sense of perfection is through the perfection of her phallic-narcissistic object, as Annie Reich (1953) has described. She feels she needs Vronsky's love to be complete, to undo her sense of "narcissistic want." This being the case, she feels totally tied to Vronsky.

Her complete ownership of him was a continual joy to her. His presence was always sweet to her. All the traits of his character, which she learned to know better and better, were unutterably precious to her. His appearance, changed by his civilian dress, was as fascinating to her as though she were some young girl in love. In everything he said, thought, did, she saw something particularly noble and elevated. Her adoration of him alarmed her; she sought and could not

find in him anything not beautiful. She dared not
show him her feeling of her own inferiority beside
him. It seemed to her that, knowing this, he might
sooner cease to love her; and she dreaded nothing
now so much as losing his love [p. 487].

She does not feel, as a woman, capable of pursuing
perfection in an autonomous ego interest. Her liaison
with Vronsky has devalued her idealizable valence for
other men of her class; she is forever branded "a fallen
woman." Vronsky is her only potential for fulfillment.
This contributes to her perception of his perfection and
her inferiority. She cannot, however, fail to perceive
the diminished ardor of his passion. Despite his tenderness, she is enraged at him for no longer revering her:
"Even the rare moments of tenderness that came from
time to time did not soothe her; in his tenderness now
she saw a shade of complacency, of self-confidence,
which had not been of old and which exasperated her
[pp. 769–770].
    At a moment of painful truth, she perceives the
real narcissistic nature of the majority of his investment in her.

"What was it he sought in me? Not love so much as
the satisfaction of vanity." She remembered his
words, the expression of his face, which recalled an
abject setter-dog, in the early days of their love affair. And everything now confirmed this. "Yes, there
was the triumph of success in him. Of course there
was love too, but the chief element was the pride of
success" [pp. 792–793].

Because she is the defeated party in narcissistically invested combat, she is unable to perceive that she has

invested Vronsky in a very similar manner.

Anna pursues a variety of tactics to assuage the pain of her perception of the loss of their in-love state (a conglomerate of anxiety, disappointment, rage, sense of loss, and depression). First, she tenuously and manipulatively attempts to control Vronsky's activities by guilt. Next, she pursues a tack commonly seen in shrewd dependent people: she manipulatively feeds his narcissism.

> He told her about the election, and Anna knew how by adroit questions to bring him to what gave him most pleasure—his own success. She told him of everything that interested him at home; and all that she told him was of the most cheerful description [p. 697].

She engages in defensive, tentative attempts to seduce other men.

> She had unconsciously the whole evening done her utmost to arouse in Levin a feeling of love—as of late she had fallen into doing with all young men—and she knew she had attained her aim, as far as was possible in one evening, with a married and honorable man [p. 733].

Her activities can be viewed as an exercise of her narcissistically invested character armor. Anna's ability to extract another's smiling attention momentarily assuages her sense of painful helplessness to win Vronsky's undivided smiling attention.

This is the core motive of all narcissistic investments: the struggle to support denial of the perception of the subject's inability to maintain the total, infinite and undivided attention of (and connection to) mother. Because this perception corresponds with the more definitive establishment of the representational world, it can be broadly correlated with the emergence of narcissistic investments. The processes of separation-individuation are life-long and probably never complete. They are fluid in the developmental sense that they have progressive and regressive aspects. The first defensive narcissistic investments can be correlated with the subject's first perceptions of vulnerability. Subsequent vulnerabilities at later moments in development are associated with a potential for defensive narcissistic investments designed to create the illusion of undoing the threatening perception of vulnerability. As development proceeds the perception of death emphasizes the profoundness of vulnerability. To the degree one integrates one's finiteness, one has individuated and can relinquish the use of narcissistically invested illusions. This is an interminable struggle. The acceptance of and commitment to that struggle is a goal of all analyses, but is particularly important in analytic work with narcissistic personality disorders.

Anna's sense of reality and her deep ambivalent attachment to Vronsky limit the success of her defenses. As soon as Levin is out of the room, she ceases to think of him: "One thought, and one only, pursued her in different forms, and refused to be shaken off. 'If I have so much effect on others, on this man who loves his home and his wife, why is it *he* is so cold to me?'" (p. 733).

Suicide emerges as the only defensive escape from the pain she is experiencing. It is motivated by a number of related factors. The most elemental injury for the narcissistic personality disorder is to not be noticed. This recaptures primal experiences of separateness which were transitorily experienced as an object loss and, because the momentarily unavailable object was felt to be a necessary part of the self, as a life-threatening insult. Anna's experience of this *enraging humiliation* is revealed in a dream: "she, as she always did in this nightmare (it was what made it so horrible), felt that this peasant was taking no notice of her" (p. 782). Suicide holds out the illusion of turning passive humiliation into active mastery. First, it will allow her to escape the painful feelings associated with the humiliation of her rejected state. Second, it is a retaliation and expression of her rage. Vronsky will suffer. Third and probably most important, it recaptures the hope of restoring his loving attention.

And death rose clearly and vividly before her mind as the sole means of bringing back love for her in his heart, of punishing him and of gaining the victory in that strife which the evil spirit in possession of her heart was waging with him [p. 781].

The tragedy of Anna (and of many narcissistic personality disorders) is that the quest for a perfect existence destroys her real life.

11

Aleksey Aleksandrovich: Narcissistic Investment in Bureaucratic Power

Aleksey Aleksandrovich, Anna's husband, is a success. From a traditional diagnostic perspective, he would be considered a well-functioning obsessional character. Within the classification proposed in this work, Aleksey is a narcissistic personality disorder with an obsessional neurotic integration.

> Precisely at five o'clock, before the bronze Peter the First clock had struck the fifth stroke, Aleksey Aleksandrovich came in. . . . Every minute of Karenin's life was portioned out and filled. And to make time to get through all that lay before him every day, he adhered to the strictest punctuality. "Without haste, without rest" was his motto [p. 116].

When we meet Aleksey his narcissism is primarily invested in his political career and in the ego functions associated with gaining power and advancement through winning the approval of his superiors. His sense of well-being derives from that accomplishment. He gains smiling attention by being thorough and con-

scientious in his work and by being particularly well-
informed. He feels it imperative that he be informed
about everything that anyone important might ask him.

> She knew, too, that he was really interested in books
> dealing with politics, philosophy, and theology, that
> art was utterly foreign to his nature; but, in spite of
> this, or rather, in consequence of it, Aleksey Alek-
> sandrovich never missed anything in the world of
> art, but made it his duty to read everything. She
> knew that in politics, in philosophy, in theology he
> often had doubts, and made investigations; but on
> questions of art and poetry, and, above all, of music,
> of which he was totally devoid of understanding, he
> had the most distinct and decided opinions. He was
> fond of talking about Shakespeare, Raphael, Beetho-
> ven, of the significance of new schools of poetry and
> music, all of which were classified by him with very
> logical consistency [pp. 118–119].

Aleksandrovich needs to know everything to feel
safe. At the moment he demonstrates that his knowledge is "perfect," a sense of original narcissistic perfection is recaptured; he is smiled at either by himself or by
a respected object. His narcissistic gratifications derive
from a number of modes of winning smiling approval.
He performs for his superiors in a somewhat obsequi-
ous manner. He takes great pride in the grandeur of his
official position and in his uniform which exhibit concrete proof of his power for all subordinates to admire.
To them and to himself he demonstrates his power.
These processes make him feel good, grand, and safe.

Anna knows that his quest for knowledge and his
superior's good will is driven by an ambition for power
and the illusions of security associated with it.

She watched his progress toward the pavilion, she saw him now responding condescendingly to an ingratiating bow, now exchanging friendly, nonchalant greetings with his equals, now assiduously trying to catch the eye of some great one of this world, and tipping his big round hat that squeezed the tips of his ears. All these ways of his she knew, and all were hateful to her. "Nothing but ambition, nothing but the desire to get ahead, that's all there is in his soul," she thought; "as for these lofty ideals, love of culture, religion, they are only so many tools for advancing" [p. 219].

Anna's rage permits her to penetrate his rationalizations and to perceive that the idealized qualities of his objects—"the great ones"—are based on their positions of power and their ability to bestow approval. Her rage derives from his rejection of her as someone worth idealizing. His rejection of her evolves from the essentially homosexual nature of Aleksey Aleksandrovich's idealized investments in objects. He denigrates women and subtly ridicules Anna. For him, women in general and Anna in particular are viewed as animate possessions whose narcissistic valence derives from their ability to complement and aggrandize his narcissistic investments and strivings. They are not supposed to pursue their own independent narcissistic interests and identity. Their fulfillment should derive from their contribution to and association with the male subject. He feels entitled to this kind of a wife. He feels this is the way it should be.

The discordance in his marriage derives from a lack of synchrony in his and Anna's narcissistic strivings. They both wished to be the central overvalued narcissistic object. Anna is bored by his work. Before she meets Vronsky, she tolerates her husband.

> "Come, what do they say about the new act I got passed
> in the council?"
>   Anna had heard nothing of this act, and she felt
> conscience-stricken at having been able so readily to
> forget what was to him of such importance [p. 118].

The quality of Aleksey's involvement with Anna is highlighted in his annoyed response to his grudging perception of her involvement with Vronsky. He is jolted at
the prospect of her "separate" pursuit of narcissistic
gratification.

> For the first time he pictured vividly to himself her
> personal life, her ideas, her desires, and the idea that
> she could and should have a *separate* life of her own
> seemed to him so alarming that he made haste to dis-
> pel it [p. 153].

Deriving from his devalued view of women, his experience of the need to spend time and mental energy
on matrimonial discord is a stupid waste of his energies. From Anna, he feels entitled to service, not
frustration. He feels his energies should be employed
pursuing "great work," not in intimate communication
with women. His work will win him the admiring glances of his male superiors.

> "And the worst of it all," thought he, "is that just
> now, at the very moment when my great work is ap-
> proaching completion" (he was thinking of the proj-
> ect he was bringing forward at the time), "when I
> stand in need of all my mental peace and all my ener-
> gies, just now this stupid worry should fall on me.". . .

Thinking over what he would say, he somewhat regretted that he should have to use his time and mental powers for domestic consumption with so little to show for it [p. 153].

In Aleksey's childhood, we see again the factor of early object loss in the genesis of his narcissistic investments:

Aleksey Aleksandrovich grew up an orphan. There were two brothers. They did not remember their father, and their mother died when Aleksey Aleksandrovich was ten years old. The property was a small one. Their uncle Karenin, a government official of high standing, at one time a favorite of the late emperor, had brought them up.

On completing his high school and university courses with honors, Aleksey Aleksandrovich had, with his uncle's aid, immediately started in a prominent position in the service, and from that time forward he had devoted himself exclusively to political ambition [p. 532].

Aleksey's investment in a government career derives from a compensatory identification with his uncle. As has been mentioned, it is not an uncommon finding that male narcissistic personality disorders have experienced significant disappointment in their fathers. When that disappointment is the father's early death, the child finds himself with a task of mourning that his ego may not be prepared to accomplish. This difficulty may be further compounded by the unavailability of other adults who are ill-equipped or uninclined to facilitate, encourage, and support a mourning experience (Wolfenstein, 1966, 1969). Simultaneously, the child finds himself identified with a dead man. In Aleksey's case this identification was reinforced by his mother's death. These traumatic events provoked a narcissistic regression that reactivated dormant narcissistically invested self-representations that in turn interacted with his ego endowment and his identificatory opportunity with his uncle. The defensive nature of this narcissistically invested identification is emphasized by the almost total involvement of his energies in pursuit of his ever illusive goals.

Narcissistic investments defend against perceptions of vulnerability. I have correlated the fact that these defenses are more extreme in patients considered narcissistic personality disorders with their relatively traumatic formative experiences. It is of interest that Tolstoy and a number of his characters experienced early object loss—a concrete example of the ultimate human vulnerability, a vulnerability we all seek to defend against perceiving. The first sustained perception of vulnerability of the self is associated with its tenuous establishment. "Hatching" (Mahler, Pine, and Bergman, 1975) from the symbiosis of self-object duality is experienced as an object loss or more correctly as a "self-object" loss.

All toddlers' egos are unprepared to mourn this fantasied loss and its associated vulnerabilities. In Aleksey's and Levin's lives, this difficult developmental experience was compounded by the real nature of the loss; both found themselves identified with a dead man. A profound sense of vulnerability derives from this identification. The anxiety associated with this sense of self is often reinforced by the fear of retaliation by the dead father (an oedipal elaboration of the loss). Both Aleksandrovich and Levin were fortunate in having respectable surrogate objects that contributed building blocks to facilitate ongoing ego-ideal and superego structuralizations, resulting in more neurotic integrations to their character organizations. Vronsky experienced a different kind of loss: his father deserted the family and was degraded by his mother. Thus Vronsky's father, experienced as weak and degraded, was not idealizable, exacerbating Vronsky's more serious disorder of ego-ideal and superego structuralization, the kind more commonly encountered in the typical narcissistic personality disorder.

All three men, however, by virtue of their losses were vulnerable to intense efforts to restore a sense of narcissistic perfection to their self-representations. Defensive narcissistic investments provide terrified subjects with illusions that the self-representation is once again endowed with a narcissistic perfection derived from memory traces of self-object experiences. These assuage the ego's more correct, but disorganizing, perceptions. The more traumatic the percept, and the more passively overwhelming the experience of the subject's ego, the more tenaciously sought are his narcissistic investments.

Aleksey's perception of his wife's infidelity is momentarily disorganizing. It violates his logical, isolated, ordered adaptation and profoundly confronts him with vulnerability: the essence of the human situation in general and of involvement in particular.

> He felt that he was standing face to face with something illogical and irrational, and did not know what was to be done. Aleksey Aleksandrovich was standing face to face with life, with the possibility of his wife's loving someone other than himself, and this seemed to him very irrational and incomprehensible because it was life itself. All his life Aleksey Aleksandrovich

had lived and worked in official spheres, dealing
with the reflection of life. And every time he had
stumbled against life itself he had shrunk away from
it. Now he experienced a feeling akin to that of a man
who, while calmly crossing a bridge over a precipice,
should suddenly discover that the bridge is broken,
and that there is a chasm below. That chasm was life
itself, the bridge that artificial life in which Aleksey
Aleksandrovich had lived. For the first time the question presented itself to him of the possibility of his
wife's loving someone else, and he was horrified at it
[p. 151–152].

It is of interest to note Tolstoy's choice of
metaphors to describe Aleksey's relationship to his object world. He is isolated by "character armor," likened
to a bridge isolating him from the involvements and
vulnerabilities of his life. His wife's infidelity momentarily shatters his defensive organization. Levin, in contrast, is better able to face the narcissistic injury of being rejected by Kitty. He is capable of dealing with
more of the pain of humiliating defeat and although he
mobilizes narcissistically invested defenses, they are
less rigid and less pervasive than either Vronsky's or
Aleksey's. This allows the trauma to function as a
stimulus for growth and to facilitate his ultimate ability to face the terror of his involvement with Kitty, Nikolai, and his children. The relative flexibility of his
ego's narcissistic investments and his greater capacity
to tolerate narcissistic injury result in a character
organization that allows him to "involuntarily cut more
and more deeply into the soil like a plow" (p. 823). He is
able to become more involved with life.

Aleksey responds with catastrophic terror and becomes defensively involved with his work. This defen-

sive involvement in his narcissistically invested activities helps him avoid thinking of Anna and Vronsky: "Aleksey Aleksandrovich needed mental exercise to drown the thoughts of his wife...and Vronsky" (p. 220).

Despite his defensive efforts, "in the bottom of his heart" Aleksey knows "beyond all doubt" that he is a deceived husband, and he is "profoundly miserable about it" (p. 214). He responds to his excruciating pain with a defense common to patients considered narcissistic personality disorders and well-described by Kernberg (1970a): denigration and emotional erasing of the object.

> "No honor, no heart, no religion; a corrupt woman. I always knew it and always saw it, though I tried to deceive myself to spare her," he said to himself. And it actually seemed to him that he always had seen it: he recalled incidents of their past life, in which he had never seen anything wrong before—now these incidents proved clearly that she had always been a corrupt woman. "I made a mistake in linking my life to hers; but there was nothing reprehensible in my mistake, and so I cannot be unhappy. It's not I that am to blame," he told himself, "but she. But I have nothing to do with her. She does not exist for me" [p. 295].

To avoid any sense of loss he focuses on that aspect of the experience that applies to the preservation of his narcissistic investments.

> "My aim is simply to safeguard my reputation, which is essential for the uninterrupted pursuit of my public duties." Official duties, which had always been of great consequence in Aleksey Aleksandrovich's

eyes, seemed of special importance to his mind at
this moment [p. 297].

The narcissistic, self-involved nature of Aleksey's
involvement with Anna is emphasized in his response
to her visit to Moscow: "Yes, my solitude is over. You
wouldn't believe how embarrassing" (he laid stress on
the word 'embarrassing') "it is to dine alone" (p. 116). He
has not missed her; he has been embarrassed to have
his servants see him eating without a wife to complement the illusion of a happy family eating dinner together. The tenacity of his narcissistic orientation intrudes on the couple's ability to grow from their experience. Instead of the trauma ultimately serving a
growth-promoting function, it eventually results in
more profound defensive activity.

Anna becomes ill. Her husband is able to pity and
forgive her. This limited experience of love provides
him, "not merely relief of his own sufferings, but also. . .
a spiritual peace he had never experienced before. . . .
What had seemed insoluble while he was judging,
blaming, and hating had become clear and simple when
he forgave and loved" (p. 440). However, his vulnerability to the opinion of others soon intrudes on his peace
of mind.

He felt that besides the blessed spiritual force controlling his soul, there was another, a brutal force, as
powerful, or more powerful, which controlled his
life, and that this force would not allow him that
humble peace he longed for. He felt that everyone
was looking at him with questioning amazement [p.
441].

This potential to respond—defensively—rather than

lovingly, to be more sensitive to "everyone looking" rather than to what Anna was feeling contributes to her renewed involvement with Vronsky.

His narcissistic investment in "official" and "social" activities leaves Aleksey without love and friendship when he is faced with the intense pain of his loss.

> His despair was even intensified by the consciousness that he was utterly alone in his sorrow. In all Petersburg there was not a human being to whom he could express what he was feeling, who would feel for him, not as a high official, not as a member of society, but simply as a suffering man; indeed, he had not such a friend in the whole world [p. 532].

In Aleksey's case this despair provokes further defensive activity under the facilitating guidance of Countess Lydia Ivanovna. Today, such a person might find himself in an analyst's office. The suffering might be mobilized in the service of self-scrutiny that might ultimately motivate a modern-day Aleksey to analytically pursue the question, "What is it about me that contributed to my being in my present condition?"

In the Countess's presence Aleksey focuses on his narcissistic injury:

> "I am crushed, I am annihilated, I am no longer a man! . . .
> "It's not the loss of what no longer is, it's not that," pursued Aleksey Aleksandrovich . "I do not grieve for that. But I cannot help feeling humiliated before other people for the position I am placed in. It is wrong, but I can't help it, I can't help it" [pp. 534–535].

It is a premise of this book that narcissistic investment originates as a coping device of the toddler's ego to undo its sense of passive helplessness in the "face" of frustration. Defensive internalizations accomplish the task by restoring a sense of narcissistic perfection (derived from perceptions of self-object oneness) to the self-representation. When habitual narcissistic modes fail, secondary modes become available. When his primary modes fail, Aleksey resorts to masochistic defenses. (It is important to emphasize a distinction between a descriptive and structural use of terms. Aleksey's behavior is descriptively masochistic.) Aleksey imposes suffering on himself by the manner in which he tolerates Anna's infidelity: "'Whosoever shall smite thee on thy right cheek, turn to him the other also; and if any man take away thy coat, let him have thy cloak also,' thought Aleksey Aleksandrovich" (p. 453). Yet in his experience of himself he admired the grandeur of his suffering: "There was bitterness, there was shame in his heart, but with bitterness and shame he felt joy and emotion at the greatness of his own humility" (p. 454). The behavior is narcissistic if the subject is pleasurably admiring himself. Structurally, it is narcissistic if by association the "greatness" restores an illusion of narcissistic perfection to his self-representation.

In response to Aleksey's feelings of emasculated humiliation, Countess Ivanovna invokes another explanation that offers him a second, slightly different masochistic defense against the injury to his self-esteem. It is not Aleksey alone but Aleksey transformed by an internalization of the idealized object, Christ, the greatest of all sufferers, that is responsible for the splendor of his forgiveness.

"Not you it was that performed that noble act of forgiveness, at which I and everone was moved to rapture, but He, working within your heart," said Countess Lydia Ivanovna, raising her eyes ecstatically, "and so you cannot be ashamed of your act" [p. 535].

This defensive activity is, however, imperfect:

He was thinking every instant that Christ was in his heart, and that in signing official papers he was doing His will. But for Aleksey Aleksandrovich it was a necessity to think that way; it was such a necessity for him in his humiliation to have at least some elevation, however imaginary, from which, looked down upon by all, he could look down on others, that he clung to his mock salvation as if it were genuine [p. 537].

To escape the disorganizing effect of humiliation and to stave off a more intense depressive response some means of restoring his self-esteem was imperative. As long as the defenses consist of narcissistically invested pursuits, no true mourning occurs; Aleksey did not deal with the profoundly painful issue of a love object lost.

Aleksey's experience of real object loss in childhood predisposed him to a more rigid pursuit of perfection for the self-representation as a life-style and to narcissistic defensive responses to significant disappointments and losses in adult life. His preference for this defensive mode is highlighted in diagnosing Aleksey a neurotically integrated narcissistic personality disorder rather than an obsessional character.

12

Sergey Ivanovich: Narcissistic Investment in Thinking

Sergey Ivanovich Koznyshev is Levin's older half brother. His narcissism is totally involved in his intellectual functions and their products. He derives a sense of well-being from the successful functioning of these narcissistic investments. People are related to primarily to reflect the fantasied magnificence of his thoughts. Tolstoy describes him as "so used to intellectual activity that he liked to put into concise and eloquent shape the ideas that occurred to him, and liked to have someone listen to him" (p. 253).

Koznyshev ponders weighty, abstract, intellectual questions, such as, "Is there a line drawn between psychological and physiological phenomena in man?" (p. 27). However, he avoids more important "questions concerning the meaning of life and death to himself" (p. 28). Many questions are asked, but none is experienced personally. His intellect is not employed to deepen his involvement in life. Rather it is exhibited as a product to win the object's admiration. Levin observes that not only does Sergey avoid the personal implication of questions, but he also misses their true humanistic implications.

> Levin was confirmed in this generalization by observing that his brother did not take questions affecting the public welfare or the question of the immortality of the soul any more to heart than he did chess problems, or the ingenious construction of a new machine [p. 253].

Sergey Ivanovich represents a narcissistic personality disorder whose ego is organized around narcissistically invested ego functions of thinking, speaking, and writing. These are life-long modes central to his experience and rigidly integrated in a neurotic obsessional organization. Compare this to Levin's employment of similar activities as a transient defense in response to a narcissistic injury of his adult life. (The comparison is similar to that between Varenka as a masochistic character and Kitty as an employer of masochistic defenses.) Levin became excessively involved in the fantasy of writing the great book on agriculture as a narcissistically invested defensive activity to assuage the pain of Kitty's rejection and to protect against its repetition. It was a transient defensive activity in a healthier individual in response to a trauma of his adult life. His ability to more squarely face the insult, as well as his capacity and wish for intimacy, allowed the defensive activity to subside in preference for the love of another adult. Sergey's investment is life-long and defends against a quality of perceived potential rejection. As long as he is brilliant he feels safe from rejection. The object reflects his brilliance, while his energies are invested in a self-loving, self-involved pursuit of his fantasied genius.

Tolstoy contrasts Levin's involvement with Sergey's isolation: "Sergey used to say that he knew and liked the peasantry" (p. 251). This is the statement of a man apart looking down on a lesser category of mortals, a man quite different from Levin:

If he had been asked whether he liked or didn't like the peasants (he) would have been absolutely at a loss as to what to reply. He liked and did not like the peasants, just as he liked and did not like men in general. Of course, being a good-hearted man, he liked men more than he disliked them, and so too with the peasants. But like or dislike the common people as something apart he could not, not only because he lived with them, and all his interests were bound up with theirs, but also because he regarded himself as a part of them, did not see any special qualities or failings distinguishing himself from the common people and could not contrast himself with them. Moreover, although he had lived so long in the closest relations with the peasants, . . . he had no definite views of the peasantry, and would have been as much at a loss to answer the question whether he knew the common people as the question whether he liked them. For him to say he knew the peasantry would have been the same as to say he knew men. He was continually watching and getting to know people of all sorts, and among them peasants, whom he regarded as good and interesting people, and he was continually discovering new traits, altering his former views of them and forming new ones. With Sergey Ivanovich it was quite the contrary. Just as he liked and praised a country life in comparison with the life he did not like, so too he liked the peasantry in contradistinction to the class of men he did not like, and so too he knew the peasantry as something distinct from and opposed to men generally [p. 252].

Levin is involved with all men in his human and imperfect way. He attempts to know them and judge them as individuals, not as classes apart, above or below himself. For Levin too many words diminsh "the beauty" (p. 255) of what he sees. Too much talk interferes with the experience.

Sergey's self-involvement demands that all eyes be focused on his narcissistic perfection. He is forty and a bachelor: there has been room for no one person in his life. His love has been his thoughts; his children, the product of those thoughts. This bachelor enters a transient in-love state with his antithesis, the masochist Varenka. It seems that she will be content to smile at Sergey and reflect his "greatness" for a lifetime. This appeals to and excites him. However, the feelings make him anxious and judgmental:

> All at once he heard, not far from the edge of the wood, the sound of Varenka's contralto voice calling Grisha, and a smile of delight passed over Sergey Ivanovich's face. Conscious of this smile, he shook his head disapprovingly at his own condition [p. 588].

He seems to regard feelings associated with being in-love as something beneath him. He struggles to logically examine his feelings and Varenka, dissecting each of her attributes:

> "If I were choosing by considerations of suitability alone, I could not have found anything better."
> However many women and girls he thought of whom he knew, he could not think of a girl who

united to such a degree all, positively all, the qualities he would wish to see in his wife. She had all the
charm and freshness of youth, but she was not a
child; and if she loved him, she loved him consciously
as a woman ought to love; that was one thing.
Another point: she was not only far from being
worldly, but had an unmistakable distaste for worldly society, and at the same time she knew the world,
and had all the ways of a woman of the best society,
which were absolutely essential to Sergey Ivanovich's conception of the woman who was to share
his life. Third: she was religious, and not like a child,
unconsciously religious and good, as Kitty, for example, was, but her life was founded on religious principles. Even in trifling matters, Sergey Ivanovich
found in her all that he wanted in his wife: she was
poor and alone in the world, so she would not bring
with her a mass of relations and their influence into
her husband's house, as he saw now in Kitty's case.
She would owe everything to her husband, which
was what he had always desired too for his future
family life. And this girl, who united all these qualities, loved him. He was a modest man, but he could
not help seeing it. And he loved her [p. 589].

He concludes that she is perfect in much the same way
that one invests in a stock. Her perfection derives from
the fact that all her good points will allow her to complement his existence and bring him no frustration.
She will be the all good, totally gratifying mate, his
mirror image, the other half of his hermaphroditic self.

Thinking that she possesses this perfection, he can
allow himself to feel. "His heart throbbed joyously. A
tender feeling came over him" (p. 590). He thinks of saying to her:

"When I was very young, I set before myself the ideal of the woman I loved.... I have lived a long life, and now for the first time I have met what I sought—in you. I love you, and offer you my hand."....

Varenka saw that he wanted to speak; she guessed of what, and felt faint with joy and panic. They had walked so far away that no one could hear them now, but still he did not begin to speak. It would have been better for Varenka to be silent. After a silence it would have been easier for them to say what they wanted to say than after talking about mushrooms. But against her own will, as it were accidentally, Varenka said: "So you found nothing? In the middle of the wood there are always fewer, though." Sergey Ivanovich sighed and made no answer. He was annoyed that she had spoken about the mushrooms [pp. 590–591].

He is annoyed by her speaking out of synchrony with his feelings or mood. Sergey wants "mirroring" (Kohut, 1968). Varenka's anxiety and the question it stimulates establish her as a separate person, therefore an inevitably frustrating person. If she has a separate existence, discordance, frustration, annoyance, and rage will inevitably ensue. Her separateness and her potential criticism make a relationship with her an impossibility.

And as soon as these words were uttered, both he and she felt that it was over, that what was to have been said would not be said; and their emotion, which had up to then been continually growing more intense, began to subside [p. 591].

Sergey withdraws into his work. He completes his great work, *Sketch of a Survey of the Principles and*

Forms of Government in Europe and Russia, a labor of six years' love. During these six years of self-involved rapturous toil, he has elaborated a narcissistically invested fantasied ability to stir the smiling admiration of the world with his book. In so doing, he will undo his father's death which he experienced as a selfish desertion of him. Like Vronsky, this loss deprived him of phase-appropriate paternal "mirroring."

> Sergey Ivanovich had expected that on its appearance his book would be sure to make a serious impression on society, and if it did not cause a revolution in social science it would, at any rate, make a great stir in the scientific world [p. 801].

World destruction fantasies are associated with paranoid schizophrenia. Such fantasies are often provoked by a paranoid response to a narcissistic injury. Sergey's grandiose dream might be termed a *world attention fantasy:* a typical fantasy in patients considered narcissistic personality disorders.

Instead of attention, however, there follows the ultimate narcissistic injury, three months of silence. The world becomes his lost object; silence recapitulates the loss.

> Only in the *Northern Beetle,* in a comic article on the singer Drabanti, who had lost his voice, was there a contemptuous allusion to Koznyshev's book, suggesting that the book had been long ago seen through by everyone, and was a subject of general ridicule [p. 802].

When finally one serious review of the book appears, it is quite critical. Sergey begins to defend against the pain of this humiliation by rationalization.

> The critic had undoubtedly put an interpre-
> tation upon the book which could not possibly be
> put on it. But he had selected quotations so adroit-
> ly that for people who had not read the book
> (and obviously scarcely anyone had read it) it
> seemed absolutely clear that the whole book was
> nothing but a medley of high-flown phrases, not
> even — as suggested by marks of interrogation —
> used appropriately, and that the author of the
> book was a person absolutely without knowledge
> of the subject. And all this was so wittily done that
> Sergey Ivanovich would not have disowned such wit
> himself. But that was just what was so terrible
> [p. 802].

Because of the critical quality of the review he cannot
protect against it by reason alone. He regresses to a
quasi-paranoid defense, projective identification. This
is a not uncommon defense in narcissistic personality
disorders defending against narcissistic injuries felt to
be life-threatening. The criticism is overwhelming and
life-threatening because it challenges the very foundations of his character organization. What Sergey experiences as his perfect attention-obtaining product, the
critic considers no more than inappropriate "high-
flown phrases."

Sergey feels that the critic has insulted his intelli-
gence, the cement of his self-representation. He must
avoid thinking about the substance of the criticism to
protect himself from a disorganizing experience of
fragmentation of his self-representation. He projec-
tively assumes that the critic is criticizing him because
he had criticized the critic.

In spite of the scrupulous conscientiousness with which Sergey Ivanovich verified the correctness of the critic's arguments, he did not for a minute stop to ponder over the faults and mistakes that were ridiculed; but unconsciously he began immediately trying to recall every detail of his meeting and conversation with the author of the article.

"Didn't I offend him in some way?" Sergey Ivanovich wondered.

And remembering that when they met he had corrected the young man about something he had said that betrayed ignorance, Sergey Ivanovich found the clue to explain the article.

This article was followed by a deadly silence [p. 802].

The public's silence is experienced as "deadly" because Sergey feels that if he is not admired he is separate (the object is lost) and will die. He projects his conflict onto the critic; then he feels superior. He feels attacked by the critic for the very reason he would attack the critic—as hurt and angry at him for being superior to him and exposing his imperfect intellect. Sergey believes the critic's attack of his work is a retaliation.

What makes this defense so difficult is that the subject really believes, in a quasi-delusional manner, that the object *is* attacking him for personal reasons. With a more disturbed variety of patients considered narcissistic personality disorders the projective mechanisms can take on a truly delusional nature and disrupt a therapeutic alliance. The experience of narcissistic injury in the transference can provoke such a defense, and the ability to successfully analyze it has profound prognostic implications. Its analysis implies that

the subject has the potential of integrating the narcissistic injury of separation in the transference. The
resulting and progressive individuation should be associated with the subject's ability to experience narcissistic injuries and the painful affects associated
with them without dedifferentiation of his self-representation.

Sergey's defenses work. He finds another arena to
invest in and within which to strive for narcissistic
perfection.

> And the more he worked in this cause, the more in-
> contestable it seemed to him that it was a cause des-
> tined to assume vast dimensions, to create an epoch
> in Russian history.
>
> He threw himself heart and soul into the service
> of this great cause, and forgot to think about his
> book [p. 804].

He temporarily relinquishes the fantasy of attaining perfection for his self-representation by a
parthenogenic creative effort. Instead he delegates perfection to a cause outside himself, associated with his
*mother*land. By association with and incorporative internalization of this external perfection of "other" he
fantasies regaining the original narcissistic perfection.
This is analogous to the shift that Kohut (1966)
describes in terms of the toddler's first seeking narcissistic perfection in his "grandiose self" and then, in response to perceptions of limits of the self, seeking it in
the "ideal parent imago."

Sergey's shift in mode of investment would change
his diagnostic label from neurotic narcissistic personality disorder to a neurotic suppliant personality disorder. Unfortunately because of his rigidity neither mode

is associated with much freedom to love another. This state emphasizes the important distinction made by Kohut (1971) between object relatedness and object love. Sergey is related to many objects in his various pursuits of narcissistic perfection for himself. These relationships are superficial and basically extractive. There is no tangible ability to enjoy another human being and the pleasures of sharing, giving, and nurturing.

Part III

NARCISSISM AND THE LIFE CYCLE

13

The Vicissitudes of Narcissism

The perception of separateness, the loss of the "original narcissistic perfection," with its painful awareness of the self-representation's vulnerability is the first sustained narcissistic injury of the life cycle. Prior to the establishment of a relatively stable self-representation, the "practicing" (Mahler, Pine, and Bergman, 1975, pp. 65–76) toddler has moments during his "love affair with the world" in which he feels that narcissistic perfection is part of his emerging and unstable self-representation. These alternate with disorganizing experiences of an overwhelming sense of vulnerability. The presence of an available, reasonably responsive parental object functions to help the toddler reestablish his sense of emotional equilibrium. Furer has referred to some of the toddler's typically observed reconstitutive behavior toward that object as "emotional refueling" (Mahler, Pine, and Bergman, 1975, pp. 69–70). In the course of this process, it is probable that a state of "cathectic fluency" (Jacobson, 1954, p. 114) exists in which the toddler has the sense of being part of the narcissistic perfection of the parental object. Once a more stable self-representation is available, other reparative modes develop.

These normal developmental events are traumatic in the sense that they shatter the practicing toddler's delusions of grandeur. Freud regarded the toddler's delegation of his primary narcissistic perfection to his ego ideal as a ubiquitous defensive attempt to assuage the mortification of these developmental events. Kohut's (1971) concepts "grandiose self" and "idealized parent imago," divested of their association with his earlier (1966) "idealizing libido" and his later (1977) concept "bipolar self," can clarify this development if viewed as representational precursors of a more depersonified hierarchically organized ego ideal. The development of such an affect-modulating structure takes time. It is often not completed until late adolescence or early adulthood and, like any other structure, is vulnerable to regressive dedifferentiation.

Excessive disappointments in oneself or one's objects can result in fundamental disorders in structural development as well as in excessive attempts to restore a sense of narcissistic perfection to the self-representation and/or to find a viable object to serve as a repository for narcissistic investments. When such disappointments occur very early in life, a subject's life cycle may have the quality of repetitive reparative quests, in one or another form, for the original narcissistic perfection. Disappointments occurring at any later stage in the life cycle, at the oedipal stage, during adolescence, or in middle age, can provoke regressive efforts to restore a sense of narcissistic perfection to the self-representation or to find the perfect object. Erikson's (1950) epigenetic schema of psychosocial development is particularly helpful in exploring the vicissitudes of man's attempts to avoid perceiving the limits of the self-representation. Narcissistic injuries are influenced by the qualities of the object world in general and hence by the opportunities for gratification available in a society during the various stages of life. Central to the perspective of epigenetic development is that earlier events shape and influence responses to subsequent experiences. Because processes of separation-individuation are a ubiquitously experienced primal narcissistic injury, all human beings are subject to dedifferentiating narcissistic regression. The greater the degree of fixation of the primary narcissistic injury, separation-individuation, the greater the subject's predisposition to narcissistically invested regressions in response to the narcissistic injuries and adaptive challenges of adult life.

Although biological endowment may shape and influence these events in a profound manner, this presentation emphasizes that the greater the disappointment in one's primal objects, the greater the potential for excessive narcissistic investment in one's character defense organization. These primal disappointments are associated with painful feelings of disorganizing anxiety, loneliness, and rage. There is greater vulnerability to the inevitable narcissistic injuries that characterize various critical stages of the life cycle. They are experienced as object losses—that is, as losses of objects that are likely to be narcissistically invested, internalized, and integrated in a progressively more depersonified manner. Patients typically considered narcissistic personality disorders long for the lost nirvana of the preindividuated era more intensely. This longing is associated with disorders in object constancy. The preindividuated memory-experiences of moments of gratification are isolated and maintained as an all-good idealized object to protect the subject from a correspondingly isolated representation of a terrifying bad object.

The subjet yearns for reunion with the all-gratifying narcissistically invested object, only to experience any frustration deriving from the limits of the object as evocative
of intense rage, disorganizing disappointment, and/or
denigration of the object. The "all-good" object is "lost."

THE EARLY STAGES

During Erikson's first stage, "basic trust versus basic mistrust," a subject's development of a basically trusting attitude toward its primary object is implicitly associated
with a greater ability to tolerate the loss of narcissistic
perfection in the self-representation. Erikson (1950), like
Freud, understood the incompleteness of this mourning
process — "even under the most favorable circumstances
. . . a universal nostalgia for a paradise forfeited" (p. 250).
Optimally available parenting, as we have discussed it,
contributes profoundly to the sense of basic trust, to the
development of stable self- and object representations, to
the phase-appropriate mourning of one's original narcissistic perfection, and to its delegation to object representations of idealized parents. Less optimal parenting is associated with a greater tendency to basic mistrust, disorders in self- and object constancy, an associated penchant
for more intense and rigidly maintained splitting and
more intense efforts to restore a sense of original narcissistic perfection to the self-representation. One factor
may have more significance at a particular developmental phase. The empathically attuned and available mother
is of primary importance to the neonate, while the idealized parent is of greater importance to the oedipal child.
    Erikson's second stage of psychosocial develop-
ment is "shame and doubt versus autonomy." Autonomy builds on basic trust and develops optimally in an
ambience created by empathically responsive parents
who enjoy phase-appropriate nurturing responses. The

individuating child's ability to elicit consistent smiling maternal responses is one of the central characteristics of a favorable rapprochement phase in the separation-individuation processes. The progressive internalization of this ambience contributes to the fabric of the ego within which autonomy flowers. The inner-glow experience of the gleam in the parents' eyes provides an important component of a developing autonomous self-representation in synchrony with its idealized object representations and ultimately with its depersonified ego ideal. Conversely shame and doubt develop in response to less-than-optimally-available, particularly hostile, critical, rejecting parental responses that are experienced as mortifying humiliations.

Erikson was acutely aware of the object's influence on the developing child's sense of shame and doubt. "He who is ashamed... would like to destroy the eyes of the world" (1950, pp. 252–253). An individuating child's ego is not equipped to integrate the painful perception of a parent who is disinterested, self-involved, excessively critical, or murderously enraged at him (consciously or unconsciously) for existing. Typically the child blames himself for his inability to consistently elicit parental availability. The result is a progressively internalized sense of doubt in the ability to elicit a gratifying response. This ambience fosters the individuating child's sense of the loss of original narcissistic perfection as derived from an inner defect in himself rather than as an inevitable part of life. Because, for such a child, limits are more often harshly imposed, they are more frequently experienced as derived from the harshness of the object rather than as inevitable. The humiliating affect of shame requires the presence of an object perceived as in some way unempathic—critical, harsh, denigrating, etc. For these reasons the ubiquitous tendency to anthropomorphize narcissistic injuries is more frequently pursued by typical narcissistic personality disorders. Typical healthier narcissistic personality disorders can develop significant skills and talents, but the autonomy of these functions remains dependent on the ability to elicit confirming response from an external object. Their self-esteem is more vulnerable to humiliating shame experienced in response to failures in their pursuit of illusions of perfection for their self-representation.

THE OEDIPAL STAGE AND LATENCY

Erikson's third stage of psychosocial development, "initiative versus guilt," corresponds to the oedipal stage of psychosexual development. Of initiative Erikson states: "Initiative adds to autonomy the quality of undertaking planning and attacking. . . . It suggests pleasure in attack and conquest" (1950, p. 255). This character trait is built on the subject's experience of his primary object's comfort and pleasure in their infant's or toddler's emerging focused aggression and "love affair with the world." Oedipal competition adds the requirement that parents be able to tolerate and encourage their children's competitiveness with them, without excessive envy, anxiety, or rage. Such oedipal-stage parental responsiveness facilitates, in a phase-appropriate manner, the child's developing assertiveness. During this stage of development, the child must integrate the narcissistic injury of oedipal defeat in a way that fosters processes of identification and internalization and that mitigates against a sense of humiliating disappointment. The child may not be perfect but the parents are, and there is the hope of regaining that lost perfection via processes of identification.

The oedipal and latency stages of development

require empathically available parents as viable repositories of the child's lost narcissistic perfection. In this regard, the narcissistic component of the negative oedipal constellation deserves emphasis. To negotiate the loss of the positive oedipal object, the child and the positive oedipal object both have to admire the negative oedipal object. An idealizable negative oedipal object contributes to the development of a well-integrated superego and ego ideal. In the absence of an idealizable negative oedipal object, the repression of positive oedipal longings is interfered with. Often, these longings are intensified by the seductiveness of the positive oedipal object. In such a situation, the denigrated negative oedipal object may be enraged (consciously or unconsciously), and this intensifies the child's castration anxiety. Such family constellations are common in the histories of narcissistic personality disorders.

As a result of the absence of an idealizable negative oedipal object, a subject's life cycle may be characterized by repetitive attempts to restore a sense of narcissistic perfection to the self-representation. This quest is motivated by an attempt to recapture the pleasures of the seductive overvaluation of the positive oedipal object and to defend against the sense of the retaliating castrating presence of the negative oedipal introject. Such subject's lives are often also characterized by efforts to find other objects who might serve a reparative, idealizable negative oedipal function and empathically set limits for them so that they might resolve their oedipal situations.

The industry of the latency child (Erikson's fourth stage is "industry versus inferiority") reflects more complex ego development in relationship to the schema of societal demands and available identificatory opportunities. Traumatic disappointments in one's self-representation (the experience of a serious learning disability), or in one's object representations (when a parent becomes seriously ill) may prematurely and traumatically confront the child with an overwhelming sense of vulnerability and disappointment.

The latency child with a birth defect or a learning disability experiences the limit of his self-representation as a narcissistic injury. The child's experience interacts with the narcissistic injuries of his parents' life cycles. For example, a middle-aged father who is struggling to integrate the limits of his vocational success may find it particularly difficult to relate optimally to a child, experienced as defective, who cannot serve as a reparative repository for the father's narcissistic investments.

In the absence of an idealizable supportive adult milieu, traumatic disruption of ongoing structuralizations may herald regressive attempts to restore illusions of narcissistic perfection to the self-representation.

ADOLESCENCE AND YOUNG ADULTHOOD

Erikson's fifth stage of development, "identity versus role confusion," deals with adolescence and has received wide attention. I will not attempt to deal in depth with the vicissitudes of pursuits of narcissistic perfection in adolescence. Blos (1962) has accurately referred to adolescence as a "mourning" period. The mourning consists, in part, of a decathexis of the adolescent's narcissistic investments in the representations of his parents—a process that contributes to further autonomy. In pursuit of this goal the adolescent becomes more self-involved, often reflecting a renewed and intensified attempt to restore illusions of narcissistic perfection to his self-representation. Simultaneously or alternatingly, the adolescent discovers new objects and causes to invest narcissistically. These cathectic shifts lend a normative quality of transience to the adolescent's object relations in general and to the therapeutic alliance in particular (A. Freud, 1959, p. 115).

Kenniston (1973), working with a very talented university population, described "youth" as an additional stage of psychosocial development to be interposed between Erikson's fifth and sixth stages. For Erikson adolescence merges into early adulthood. For the adult the task is to achieve "intimacy" or to suffer in "isolation." Kenniston notes that for highly educated, ambitious young people this stage is often normatively delayed as they pursue the training that allows for adaptation to highly specialized societal niches. The fantasies and goals of such youths are often associated with illusions of restoring a sense of narcissistic perfection to their self-representations.

To achieve intimacy a young adult must have "the capacity to commit himself to concrete affiliations . . . even though they may call for significant sacrifices and compromises" (Erikson, 1950, p. 263). The young, typical narcissistic personality disorder is inhibited from such affiliations because they threaten to limit his pursuit of narcissistic perfection for his self-representation. Only infrequently do such young adults seek help from mental health professionals. When they do, it is most often in quest of succor in the face of narcissistic injury or in response to the pain of an impasse to their pursuit of narcissistic perfection for their self-representation. Their need lends an incomplete "adolescent" quality to their treatment alliances and formal involvements. It is often not until such individuals approach midlife that they become aware of the intimacy they are missing. At this time, these patients may be most available for a more thorough analytic experience. The accomplishment of a degree of real professional success may have diminished their anxiety and their often rigidly maintained narcissistically invested pursuits, enabling them to seek help. The analysis of their defensively motivated pursuits then facilitates these subject's pleasure in commitment and intimacy.

John Fowles has created a number of fictional characters, who are unable to successfully negotiate young adulthood because the traumatic quality of their childhoods did not prepare them to accept and enjoy the inevitably limited pleasures of a committed existence. Most of Fowles' major characters have experienced significant disappointments in their primal objects. In addition, many have experienced real object losses. Fowles' literary portrayal of these characters accentuates the frequently encountered clinical phenomena of real object loss in the history of narcissistic personality disorders, and his emphasis on real object loss in the history of his characters underlines the sensitivity of narcissistic personality disorders to disappointments in their parents. These are experienced as losses of idealized objects — objects, the representations of which are needed to sustain them through the cathectic shifts of adolescence and early adulthood.

The ability to tolerate "significant sacrifices and compromises" (Erikson, 1950, p. 263) in young adulthood leads to perhaps the most gratifying of life's pleasures, heterosexual intimacy. Caliban, in *The Collector*, the sickest of Fowles' fictional subjects, experiences profound disappointment in, and then the real loss of, his parents at the height of his separation-individuation processes. This loss, reinforced by the quality of his surrogate objects, makes heterosexual intimacy an impossibility for Caliban. When Caliban is two years old, his father, a heavy drinker, dies violently in an auto accident. His mother, a prostitute, abandons him for an adult man. For Caliban the death of his father and abandonment by his mother are real events.

Such content (patricidal death and guilt and maternal infidelity and abandonment) is not uncommon as unconscious fantasy in healthier narcissistic personality disorders, but for Caliban, these actual events provide the foundations for a suppliant personality disorder with schizoid integration. He is extremely mistrustful of others. His sense of initiative and his industry are limited to his interest in collecting and categorizing butterflies. His uncle covertly supports these activities, giving Caliban a five-pound note for winning a prize in a competition and telling him to keep the knowledge of the gift from his aunt. His uncle's anxiety-ridden caution reinforces Caliban's frightened mistrustful view of women, and his support provides a paternal type of mirroring, reinforcing his sense of initiative and his industry in regard to these activities. It is characteristic of Caliban, as of many sicker narcissistic and suppliant personality disorders, that he is able to maintain islands of intact and highly productive ego functioning in pursuit of illusions of perfection. These ego functions can be described as narcissistically invested.

Caliban remains isolated through latency and adolescence, although his collections of butterflies, his narcissistically invested activity, win prizes. While he experiences awe at the beauty of these creatures, he also expresses rage at them, as displaced, idealized symbols of the maternal object, by killing them. Caliban gains a sense of control over his fear of object loss by capturing the elusive butterfly and collecting it as a "perfect" prisoner. During adolescence and early adulthood, Caliban idealizes a girl, Miranda, whom he views with awe from afar. He is shy and quite pessimistic about any possibility of attracting her attention and admiration. As a young adult, his fears continue to contribute to his isolation and to his sense of the hopelessness of any intimacy with her. When he wins a lottery, this serendipitous event results in a regression, awakening a long-buried, narcissistically invested self-representation whose integration was organized on a psychotic level. The psychotic regression is associated with the loss of his sublimated involvement with butterflies. He kidnaps Miranda. By collecting idealized women rather than perfect butterflies, he shifts from suppliant personality disorder with a schizoid integration to narcissistic personality disorder with a paranoid schizophrenic integration; he shifts from passive awe to direct expression of sadism and murder. Active narcissistic investment is sought for his self-representation in the cold, calculated pursuit of women, who are perceived as contaminated by their sexuality.

Caliban's aversion for overt heterosexual activity, as contrasted with his passionate awe of the idealized object, is more than the expression of an incest taboo. Miranda's sexuality reawakens memories of his mother's *total* abandonment of him for another man. It is not atypical of the history of the male narcissistic personality disorder that the boy is mother's favorite, narcissistically invested object, at the same time the father is subtly, or not so subtly, denigrated. These boys find themselves temporarily abandoned by their mother's pursuit of adult sexual gratification. This limited oedipal defeat is linked to these boys' humiliating perception of the limits of their bodies. Some narcissistic personality disorders maintain a life-long, almost delusional belief, that their penis is smaller than that of other men. Their mothers' temporary desertion of them for their fathers, or for other adult males, is associatively linked to preoedipal experiences of her unavailability and of the subject's inability to maintain and control her attention and participation in his grandeur. The narcissistic injuries of the oedipal era are always associatively linked to the primal narcissistic injuries of the separation-individuation phase of development.

In Caliban's case, these intensified associations are linked to his belief that his malevolent, omnipotent mother drove his weak father to drink and suicide. Such a view of women as more powerful than men is usually unconscious, but it is typical of male narcissistic personality disorders. Complementing this view is the male narcissistic personality disorder's feeling that he needs a woman's attention and participation to survive.

Nicholas Urfe is a young man of twenty-six when we meet him at the beginning of Fowles' first novel, *The Magus*.[1] Nicholas is a typical narcissistic personality disorder who encounters conflicts of intimacy in young adulthood. His family history is representative of one that any typical narcissistic personality disorder, seen by a practicing analyst, might relate. He, like Caliban, is an only child, but with less disappointing parents. "There were things, a certain emotional gentleness in my mother, an occasional euphoric jolliness in my father, I could have borne more of; but always I liked in them the things they didn't want to be liked for" (1977b, p. 16). With denigrating sarcasm Nicholas relates his percep-

[1] In the introduction to his revised version of *The Magus* (1977b), Fowles states that, although *The Collector* (1963) was his first published novel. *The Magus*, first published in 1965, was the first novel he wrote.

tions of his parents:

> I had long before made the discovery that I lacked
> the parents and ancestors I needed. My father was,
> through being the right age at the right time rather
> than through any great professional talent, a briga-
> dier; and my mother was the very model of a would-
> be major general's wife. That is, she never argued
> with him and always behaved as if he were listening
> in the next room, even when he was thousands of
> miles away. I saw very little of my father during the
> war, and in his long absences I used to build up a
> more or less immaculate conception of him, which he
> generally—a bad but appropriate pun—shattered
> within the first forty-eight hours of his leave.
>
> Like all men not really up to their jobs, he was a
> stickler for externals and petty quotidian things; and
> in lieu of an intellect he had accumulated an armory
> of capitalized key words like Discipline and Tradi-
> tion and Responsibility. If I ever dared—I seldom did
> —to argue with him he would produce one of these
> totem words and cosh me with it, as no doubt in
> similar circumstances he coshed his subalterns. If
> one still refused to lie down and die, he lost, or
> loosed, his temper. His temper was like a violent red
> dog, and he always had it close at hand.
>
> The wishful tradition is that our family came
> over from France after the Revocation of the Edict of
> Nantes—noble Huguenots remotely allied to Honoré
> d'Urfé, author of the seventeenth-century bestseller
> L'Astrée. Certainly—if one excludes another equally
> unsubstantiated link with Tom Durfey, Charles II's
> scribbling friend—no other of my ancestors showed
> any artistic leanings whatever; generation after
> generation of captains, clergymen, sailors, squire-

lings, with only a uniform lack of distinction and a marked penchant for gambling, and losing, to characterize them. My grandfather had four sons, two of whom died in the First World War; the third took an unsavory way of paying off his atavism (gambling debts) and disappeared to America. He was never referred to as still existing by my father, a youngest brother who had all the characteristics that eldest are supposed to possess [1977b, pp. 15–16].

In addition to being a disappointed only child, Nicholas had been left alone for long periods of time with his mother during his father's long absences. Although his mother was superficially respectful of her husband, she was chronically disappointed in his achievements. She wished to be the wife of a major general rather than of a brigadier. Mrs. Urfe was seductively overinvolved in her narcissistically invested son. He was to fulfill the family myth and become a creative writer like his French ancestor Honoré d'Urfé who wrote the novel, *L'Astrée*.

His mediocre father was mostly pitiful pomp, prone to violent outbursts and corporal punishments that contributed to Nicholas' defiance.

One day I was outrageously bitter among some friends about the Army; back in my own rooms later it suddenly struck me that just because I said with impunity things that would have apoplexed my dead father, I was still no less under his influence. The truth was that I was not a cynic by nature; only by revolt. I had got away from what I hated, but I hadn't found where I loved, and so I pretended there was nowhere to love [1977b, p. 17].

The inability of General Urfe to sustain a delegation of Nicholas's narcissistic perfection, his penchant for violent outbursts of rage, and his preference for corporal limit setting contributed to the externalization of his son's superego function. Mrs. Urfe's seductive overvaluation and narcissistic investment in Nicholas contributed to his entitled sense of specialness, gratifying him and leaving him feeling a relative oedipal victor. Simultaneously he feels resentful and afraid of women, whom he views as extractive. His disappointment in his father contributes to his potential to experience an idealizing transference.

As a young adult, Nicholas finds himself in a relationship with a woman, Alison, that is of a type commonly experienced by narcissistic personality disorders who cannot establish the intimacy that Erikson considered the hallmark of adulthood. He is subtly mistrustful of women but addicted to the physical pleasures they offer. Women are chosen who can be physically seduced and subtly degraded. This gratifies his conscious longing for physical closeness and simultaneously expresses his rage at women while establishing his phallic prowess through their conquest and possession. As Nicholas perceives her, Alison is a perfect candidate.

> When she went out she used to wear a lot of eye shadow, which married with the sulky way she sometimes held her mouth to give her a characteristic bruised look; a look that subtly made one want to bruise her more. Men were always aware of her, in the street, in restaurants, in pubs; and she knew it. I used to watch them sliding their eyes at her as she passed [1977b, pp. 31–32].

Against his will Nicholas finds himself falling in love with her.

> Alison was leaning slightly against me, holding my hand, looking in her childish sweet-sucking way at a Renoir. I suddenly had a feeling that we were one body, one person, even there; that if she had disappeared it would have been as if I had lost half of myself. A terrible deathlike feeling, which anyone less cerebral and self-absorbed than I was would have realized was simply love. I thought it was desire. I drove her straight home and tore her clothes off [1977b, p. 35].

The terrifying closeness of the in-love state motivates Nicholas to "fuck" Alison—to get sex over, experience orgasm, and thereby aggressively reestablish body-ego boundaries. Nicholas's view of Alison as subtly degraded helps protect him from making a terrifying commitment to her: "Allison said very little, but I was embarrassed by her, by her accent, by the difference between her and one or two debs who were sitting near us" (1977b, p. 36).

In a manner quite common to patients of this character organization, Nicholas flees Alison to pursue his quest to restore illusions of narcissistic perfection to his self-representation. He goes to Greece, which he conceives as a perfect maternal ambience. Nurtured by this environment, he fantasizes developing his talent as a writer. When he fails in this quest he becomes depressed. At this point he is vulnerable to an in-love state with an idealized woman. This type of narcissistic regression is frequently experienced by men after they fail in an attempt to restore a sense of narcissistic perfection to their self-representations through their work (see chapter 8). If they cannot be perfect, they can find perfection in a narcissistically invested woman they lure from another man. This is regressive because it reflects a shift from interest and industry in activities that are socially adaptive (representing psychosocial development to latency and beyond) to involvement in self-destructive oedipal repetition.

Nicholas finds himself in-love with Lily, whose unavailability by virtue of her involvement with another man makes her all the more attractive. Nicholas fails in his quests—both with his writing and with Lily. Nicholas and patients like him can only shift from an in-love to a love state, with its associated intimacy, if they can significantly relinquish their pursuit of perfection for their self-representation and/or their addiction to idealized objects. This process can be facilitated by the experience of disappointment in and rage at their parents and themselves.

Charles of Fowles' third novel, *The French Lieutenant's Woman*, offers another opportunity to examine conflicts experienced by young adult male narcissistic personality disorders in making commitments to women and vocations.

Charles is the first-born son of wealthy parents, heir to their money, as well as prospective heir to the title and wealth of his childless uncle, the lord of Winsyatt. In Charles, we can see a character whose early life experience has concretely dubbed him, "His Majesty the Baby." His parents, particularly his mother, could view him as their creation—a creature who, by virtue of birth, would not experience the limits that lineage had imposed upon his father. Charles's first year of life was characterized by just such overvaluing adulation, but this nirvana was shattered by his mother's death in childbirth when he was a year old. Charles's father compounded this formative disappointment by deserting him in pursuits of "pleasures" that helped him defend against mourning the loss of his wife. He died, in Charles's adolescence, as a result of these excesses. Charles's upbringing was left to a series of surrogates.

The prospect of his titled inheritance is the integrating factor of his character organization. It allows him to expect to recapture the formative gleam in his mother's eye. Her death and his disappointing relationship with his debauching father have contributed to the untempered nature of his ambitions. If he can not be the greatest he will make no vocational commitment.

> But how could one write history with Macaulay so close behind? Fiction or poetry, in the midst of the greatest galaxy of talent in the history of English literature? How could one be a creative scientist, with Lyell and Darwin still alive? Be a statesman, with Disraeli and Gladstone polarizing all the available space? [1969, p. 16].

As Charles enters his early thirties, social pressures motivate him to marry. Just prior to his betrothal, Charles has a chance encounter with Sarah, the French lieutenant's woman. Sarah is a person who has defiantly expressed her rage at her own disappointing parents by openly flaunting social and sexual mores. It is this self-destructive, but overt, expression of rage that accounts for Charles's attraction.

If Charles were not intensely ambivalent toward his parents, he could easily satisfy his bachelor uncle and become the next lord of Winsyatt. Instead he pricks his uncle's narcissistic investment in the title by choosing for a marriage partner a subtly denigrated woman,

Ernestina, an untitled only child of a wealthy businessman. His uncle, the present lord of Winsyatt, does not
have children to whom he can delegate his original narcissistic perfection. He does have a title and Charles's
choice threatens to taint it.

As the day of his marriage approaches, Charles
bridles at the limits of his betrothed:

> He began to feel sorry for himself. . . a brilliant man
> trapped. . . and his mind wandered back to Sarah. . .
> some possibility she symbolized. His future had
> always seemed of vast potential; and now suddenly it
> was a fixed voyage to a known place. She reminded
> him of that [1969, p. 130].

It is not uncommon for men such as Charles to
marry with the fantasy that nothing is forever; they can
always divorce. In this case the intoxication of
Charles's inheritance is gratifying enough to his grandiose fantasies to compensate for the limits of a life
with Ernestina.

> Charles felt himself truly entering upon his inheri-
> tance. It seemed to him to explain all his previous idl-
> ing through life, his dallying with religion, with
> science, with travel; he had been waiting for this
> moment. . . his call to the throne, so to speak. The ab-
> surd adventure in the Undercliff [with Sarah] was
> forgotten. Immense duties, the preservation of this
> peace and order, lay ahead, as they had lain ahead of
> so many young men of his family in the past.
> Duty—that was his real wife, his Ernestina and his
> Sarah, and he sprang out of the chaise to welcome
> her as joyously as a boy not half his real age [1969,
> p. 197].

The issue of the unconsciously motivated self-destructiveness of patients such as Charles was raised in chapter 3. It is clear that Charles does not enjoy actively working to please his uncle. He resents his uncle and his uncle's interests, and it is clear that marrying Ernestina, a commoner, and thus tainting the Winsyatt lineage, is a choice layered upon a lifetime of inability to lovingly accept his uncle as a paternal surrogate. Charles's self-destructiveness derives, in part, from his rage at his parents for dying and disappointing him by virtue of who they were and of the nature of their narcissistic investment in him. His entitled attitude has been developed and perpetuated, in part, as a defense against the integration of these formative events. It is worth considering what part the repetition compulsion, deriving from activity as a defense against passivity, contributes to his fate. His early development consisted, in part, of his passively being dubbed "his Majesty" by this mother, and her death was experienced as a traumatic loss of that overvaluing investment. His ambivalence about concretely becoming lord of the manor derives from his expectation that gratification will inevitably be linked to traumatic loss. Consciously he pursues his title; unconsciously he flirts with and courts its loss. And his throne is lost.

Charles's uncle decides to marry and have children. Charles will never be "His Majesty." In the fantasy of being lord of Winsyatt, he had felt he would be "ascending to perfection" (1969, p. 206), a perfection that will recapture those moments of adultation when his mother treated him as "His Majesty." His life is overwhelmed by limits he experiences as imposed by an anthropomorphized fate. These are associatively linked to the loss of his mother. These concrete events represent a universal dynamic; the limits of adult life recapitulate the primal limits of the separation-individuation processes. Limits are always narcissistic injuries. Charles, like many young adult narcissistic personality disorders, experiences them as traumatically threatening.

His passivity in the face of his humiliating insult heralds a deeper depression. Charles, like Vronsky, cannot face his narcissistic injury. He cannot mourn his loss or find other adaptive activities to narcissistically invest. This lack of flexibility on the part of his ego limits his adaptive potential, and he turns his back on an opportunity offered through Ernestina to become a prince of commerce: an opportunity he experiences only as further humiliation.

> But there was one noble element in his rejection: a sense that the pursuit of money was an insufficient purpose in life. He would never be a Darwin or a Dickens, a great artist or scientist; he would at worst be a dilettante, a drone, a what-you-will that lets others work and contributes nothing. But he gained a queer sort of momentary self-respect in his nothingness, a sense that choosing to be nothing—to have nothing but prickles—was the last saving grace of a gentleman; his last freedom, almost. It came to him very clearly; if I ever set foot in that place I am done for [1969, p. 294].

If he cannot be what he has felt entitled to be, lord of the manor (unconsciously associated with a representation of union with the overvaluing maternal object), he will at least be in charge of his own destruction. If he cannot be his mother's prince he will not be anyone else's. He wants it his way. Active self-destructive defiance of a frustrating society is his only outlet.

He breaks his engagement to Ernestina and pursues an even more degraded object—Sarah whose terror of commitment contributes to their inability to establish a lasting relationship. Her definitive rejection of him leaves Charles feeling helpless.

> He did not know where to go. It was as if he found himself reborn, though with all his adult faculties and memories. But with the baby's helplessness—all to be recommenced, all to be learned again [1969, p. 465].

The absence of an object to narcissistically invest reawakens a sense of helplessness associatively linked to similar experiences of his first year of life. It is against the emergence of such feelings that narcissistic investments protect.

MIDDLE AGE

For all but exceptionally successful narcissistic personality disorders, life is characterized by the progressive difficulty of maintaining the hope of recapturing a sense of narcissistic perfection for the self-representations in the vocational arena. The illusion of starting again with another mate is a common reparative fantasy. With such a person, they feel they can be different, they can achieve the greatness that has eluded them. They look outside themselves in quest of a solution rather than introspectively consider their inner lives as the source of their difficulties. To shift this orientation is a major goal of analytic work with these patients. It cannot usually be achieved until the analysand is convinced that he cannot solve his problems his way: by altering external reality.

Erikson considered that the psychosocial tasks of

midlife deal with the pleasures of "generativity" versus the sense of "stagnation." Erikson described generativity as "concern in guiding and establishing the next generation" (1950, p. 267). In part these activities are motivated by the ubiquitous narcissistic investments Freud (1914) described:

> The child shall have a better time than his parents....Illness, death, renunciation of enjoyment, restriction on his own will, shall not touch him. ...At the most touchy point on the narcissistic system, the immortality of the ego, which is so hard pressed by reality, security is achieved by taking refuge in the child [p. 91].

The contemporary cultural milieu makes is progressively harder for midlife adults to take such refuge in their children. Many women, at this point, find themselves facing a sense of stagnation, depression, and void associated with their children's growing up. Such women face the rewarding but difficult task of defining a new identity. Some are inhibited because they cannot imagine themselves becoming anything worthwhile—a feeling often derived from a sense that if a pursuit cannot restore illusions of narcissistic perfection to their self-representations, as their children had, then it is not a worthwhile pursuit.

Some people find themselves having achieved significant success at midlife, only to feel the depression that derives from the perception that realistic success is always relative. Such feeling states motivate midlife adults to seek the restoration of illusions of narcissistic perfection for their self-representation in nonvocational, frequently regressive, activities. Vronsky typifies a male narcissistic personality disorder facing the limits of his career. He seeks the conquest of another man's woman. Obtaining the unavailable woman, a victory of the bedroom to mitigate against the defeat of the boardroom, assuages his depressing perception of the limits of his adult life.

Family commitments frustrate the wish to be "one and only," and this kind of narcissistic injury is more intensely felt at midlife. It is not uncommon for a family system to remain intact in young-adult life while the father pursues illusions of perfection in his vocation and the mother nurtures her investments in the nursery. These systems are often threatened as midlife confronts parents with the loss of the possibility of actualizing their fantasies in these pursuits. Such midlife adults may strive to recapture in an affair a sense of specialness and a sense of adulation that they resist mourning in their more complicated realistic involvements. The affair or the second marriage is not infrequently associated with the fantasy of starting life anew: of being reborn.

The life cycle, by virtue of its breadth, is prone to generalizations, but it is worth noting that for an individual, specific stages of life may have uniquely individual meanings. The analytic situation offers an optimal setting for assimilating the effects of such meaning. I have worked with three men whose lives were profoundly influenced by the exact age their fathers died. These men, with oedipal constellations of the type described in chapter 3, had fathers who died in middle age. The internalized presence of a denigrated, disappointing, and prematurely dead paternal introject profoundly influenced the vicissitudes of their narcissistic investments throughout their lives. The fact that their fathers had all died in their forties lent particular meaning to their experience of middle age. As these men approached the age at which their fathers died, they became increasingly anxious. Analysis revealed that they anticipated their fathers would not let them live longer than they had lived. This provoked castration anxiety more akin to what Annie Reich (1960) referred to as "catastrophic feelings of annihilation" (p. 224). This anxiety motivated these subjects to vigorously pursue the restoration of illusions of narcissistic perfection for their self-representations.

Midlife increasingly confronts the subject with the limits and ultimate finiteness of his body. Parents and contemporaries get sick and die. Recently there has been an increasing interest in physical exercise. While the realistic benefits of such activity cannot be doubted, the more extreme preoccupation with it observed in some acquires the characteristics of a narcissistic addiction. The marathon runner, like the weightlifter, strives for perfection in concrete aspects of his body and in the increasingly improving times of his races. These pursuits attempt to restore in concrete form and associated fantasy the illusion of transcending the limits perceived all around them. To run a marathon at midlife is to be young again, to live forever, to fly.

David Williams in *The Ebony Tower* is a married father of two children, a narcissistic personality with a neurotic ego organization who has achieved a modicum of success as a critic, teacher, and painter. He is sent to France to write an introduction for the recent works of one of the art world's "immortals." He is provoked by the success of Henry Breasley, a painter in old age who is struggling now with awareness of his transience, his success having allowed him to negotiate midlife without a meaningful confrontation with the limits of his self-representation.

David Williams had been nurtured in the kind of environment more likely to facilitate the development of an ego organization on the healthier, neurotic to normal end of the spectrum.

> It was not quite a case of a young unknown visiting an old master, David Williams' parents were both architects, a still practicing husband-and-wife team of some reknown. Their son had shown natural aptitude very young, an acute color sense, and he was born into the kind of environment where he received nothing but encouragement. In the course of time he went to art college, and settled finally for painting. He was a star student in his third year, already producing salable work. He was not only rara avis in that; unlike the majority of his fellow students, he was highly articulate as well. Brought up in a household where contemporary art and all its questions were followed and discussed constantly and coherently, he could both talk and write well [1974, p. 14].

In contrast to Henry's family, David's parents are happy with their lives and with each other. They (particularly his mother) had been less intensely adulating of him and more consistently, empathically available to him. Henry's father was a wealthy dilettante who did not work and dabbled in art collecting. His self-involvement and his death made him a less viable repository for Henry's idealizing investment. As Vronsky's defiance assuages a longing for paternal "attention and participation" and defends against parenticidal rage, so does Henry Breasley's. The more empathic consistency of Mr. and Mrs. Williams has left David feeling more satisfied and less enraged, attracted to pursuits of perfection for his self-representation but, by virtue of his more structured, abstract, and depersonified superego and ego ideal, less free and less driven to pursue them. His parents served as models for processes of internalization that have resulted in a relatively intact superego and ego ideal. David feels comfortable and compelled to be like his parents. While Breasley lives to defy repression, David's life is characterized by repression, reaction formation, and a quieter, less creative sublimatory potential that contributes to his creative products and his creative experience being more like work: "Always rather fond of being liked, he developed a manner carefully blended of honesty and tact" (1974, p. 14). In contrast to Breasley: "David was a young man who was above all tolerant, fair minded" (1974, p. 17).

Despite David's more normal character integration, he is nevertheless quite ambitious.

If he disliked pretention, he was not on the other hand devoid of ambition. He still earned more by his painting than his writing, and that meant a very great deal to him; as did what one might call the state of his status among his own generation of painters. He would have despised the notion of a race, yet he kept a sharp eye on rivals and the public mention they received. He was not unaware of this; in the public mention constituted by his own reviewing, he knew he erred on the generous side with those he feared most [1974, p. 16].

His character organization seems to have fated him to be a "good boy" rather than a "bad boy" like Breasley. As such he is destined to be a fine student in someone else's school rather than the defiant creator of his own.

He finds himself painfully envious of Breasley's success.

> To someone like David, always inclined to see his own life (like his painting) in terms of logical process, its future advances dependent on intelligent present choices, it seemed not quite fair. Of course one knew that the way to the peak was never by the book, that hazard and all the rest must play its part, just as action and aleatory painting formed an at least theoretically important sector in the modern art spectrum. But some such mountaineering image drifted through his mind. One had acquired the best equipment one could afford—and one looked up. There on the summit stood a smirking old satyr in carpet slippers, delightedly damning all common sense and calculation [1974, p. 53].

The narcissistic injury of recognizing he will never be a great artist makes David's middle age particularly difficult. He may be a leading critic or even a professor at the Royal Academy but his work will probably never be more than decorative accessories in posh London apartments. His perception causes the limits of his monogamous family status to be more intensely felt, and he falls in-love with Breasley's favorite woman, "the Mouse."

If he can not beat Henry in more direct competition then perhaps he can beat him in the bedroom. The narcissistic injury caused by perceiving the limits of his creative ability provokes David to dabble with the possibility of an acting-up affair. Patients with neurotic character organizations may act-up in defensive response to narcissistic injuries. The more typical narcissistic personality disorder acts-up chronically in defensive character response to the narcissistic injuries of his childhood. Like all comparisons, this is relative. A "Henry" with less talent would certainly also be tempted to act-up in response to the perception of his mediocrity.

Impelled by the pain of the perception of the limits of his life, David fantasizes an affair with the Mouse.

> They talked banally enough; and once again the ghost of infidelity stalked through David's mind—not any consideration of its actuality, but if he hadn't been married, if Beth... that is to say, if Beth didn't sometimes have certain faults, an occasional brisk lack of understanding of him, an overmundane practicality, which this attractively cool and honest young mistress of a situation would be too intelligent (for he saw in her something that he aimed at in his own painting, a detachment and at the same time a matter-of-factness) to show or at any rate to abuse. It wasn't that one didn't still find Beth desirable, that the idea of a spell together in France without the kids after Coët (hovering in it Beth's tacit reacceptance of motherhood, a third child, the son they both wanted) ...just that one was tempted. One might, if one wasn't what one was; and if it were offered—that is, it was a safe impossibility and a very remote probability away [1974, pp. 60–61].

The Mouse might be everything Beth is not; he might be reborn. This ubiquitous fantasy of starting again and thereby of avoiding the limits that derive from one's life and choices confronts David's well-structured superego. He kisses the Mouse but cannot freely pursue an affair with her. Instead he encourages her not to sacrifice her life for Henry and to find someone like him.

> "What do you think I should do?"
> He hesitated, then smiled. "Find someone like me? Who isn't married? If that doesn't sound too impossibly vain."

She tied the final bow in the tags of black ribbon. "And Henry?"

"Not even a Rembrandt has the right to ruin someone else's life" [1974, p. 94].

Everyone would like to have everything. Henry has tried to obtain the gratifications of total oedipal victory, to avoid the narcissistic injuries arising from the limits of his childhood in activities that symbolically represent such gratifications. Simultaneously he has sought, in the action of self-imposed exile from his motherland, the gratification of assuaging his superego. David is more neurotic, his superego more intact and less prone to defensive externalization; therefore he is more inhibited. This being so, he pursues his gratification in fantasy rather than in action. He attempts to seduce the Mouse into leaving Henry for someone like him. He wishes to defeat Henry and by avoiding intercourse with the Mouse protect himself from his superego's disdainful glances.

The Mouse does not gratify David. She does not take his bait. It seems that she might be willing to leave with him but not because of his words alone. Impelled by the perception of this insult, David thinks, "If one only had two existences" (1974, p. 97). If that were the case he would not have to deal with his superego, for the thought of defying his conscience fills him with *terror*.

And he thought of Beth, probably in bed by now in Blackheath, in another world, asleep; of his absolute certainty that there could not be another man beside her. His real fear was of losing that certainty. Childish: if he was unfaithful, then she could be. No logic. They didn't deny themselves the sole enjoyment of any other pleasure: a good meal, buying clothes, a visit to an exhibition. They were not even against sexual liberation in other people, in some of their friends; if they were against anything, it was having a general opinion on such matters, judging them morally. Fidelity was a matter of taste and theirs happened simply to conform to it; like certain habits over eating or shared views on curtain fabrics. What one happened to like to live on and with. So why make an exception of this? Why deny experience, his artistic soul's sake, why ignore the burden of the old man's entire life? Take what you can. And so little: a warmth, a clinging, a brief entry into another body. One small releasing act. And the terror of it, the enormity of destroying what one had so carefully built [1974, pp. 97–98].

David's superego and ego ideal are the internalized presence of parents who offered love and the illusion of a guaranteed safety if he lived up to their standards. The thought of violating those tenets have left David a helpless little boy, Cain expelled from Eden, forever vulnerable, alone, and subject to the malevolent disapproval of archaically invested parental object representations. He cannot have two lives and he cannot defy his conscience. He is faced with the definitive limit of losing the Mouse and the fantasied rebirth as a creative artist that he has associated with their imagined union. Together they would have been what he was incapable of being alone.

David is limited by who he is: by the physical and emotional limits of his body and his character organization. The narcissistic personality disorder, whatever the integration of his quest for narcissistic perfection for his self-representation, struggles with murderous rage when he is definitively frustrated in that quest.

His mind slid away to imaginary scenarios. Beth's plane would crash. He had never married. He had, but Diana [the Mouse] had been Beth. She married Henry, who promptly died. She appeared in London, she could not live without him, he left Beth. In all these fantasies, they ended in Coët, in total harmony of work and love and moonlit orchard [1974, p. 107].

Instead David rationalizes his inhibition:

Underlying all this there stood the knowledge he would not change; he would go on painting as before, he would forget this day, he would find reasons to interpret everything differently, as a transient losing his head, a self-indulgent folly [1974, p. 112].

David is left rationalizing his longing and, to some extent, mourning his disappointment.

OLD AGE

Erikson's final stage of psychosocial development deals with old age. If one feels one has lived one's life well, one achieves a sense of "ego integrity." This implies an acceptance of and pleasure in one's life style with an emphasis on its relationship to past and future. The antithesis of "ego integrity" is "despair." Erikson's points are well taken, but their relativity must be stressed. The acceptance of one's finiteness and death is never easy and it is questionable whether it is ever complete. Experiencing oneself in a humanistic continuum may make the insult of dying easier to tolerate, but even this attempted integration hinges, to some degree, on belief in the immortality of one's values, civilization, and species, and one must face the ultimate narcissistic injury posed by Darwin's *On the*

Origin of Species: that *species*, like individuals, *die*.

Old age is a confrontation with the concrete limits of one's body and with the more abstract idea that life is finite. Human beings struggle to maintain an interminable split in the self-representation that is challenged by these perceptions. The body is treated like an offending other person. The body is referred to as "my" rather than "I." The self-as-agent, the "I," struggles to maintain its immortality by saying, "I won't accept the limits of 'my' body."

Daniel Martin, in the novel of the same name, is a Hollywood scriptwriter, successful by the public's standards. He is the only child of an Episcopal minister (not unlike Nicholas's father); his mother died when he was four years old. He is the middle-aged, divorced father of a daughter entering early adulthood. His work is not great and he knows it. Liaisons with beautiful young actresses do not assuage his depressing awareness of the limits of who he is. He has the fantasy of writing a novel. He meets Jane, an old love, and fantasizes starting again. They would reciprocally enable each other to accomplish more than either believes he or she can achieve alone. He encourages her:

> "Perhaps you should stand for Parliament."
> She smiled. "La Pasionaria of the detergent counter?"
> "Seriously. Local government, anyway,"
> "I have thought about it." She added, "As schoolgirls dream of winning Wimbledon or dancing with Nureyev."
> "You can project. That's half the battle."
> "Could project."
> "It would come back" [1977a, p. 387].

She encourages him:

"I couldn't just write a novel about a script-writer. That would be absurd. A novelist who wasn't a scriptwriter might do it. But I'm a scriptwriter who isn't a novelist."

"Until you try" [1977a, p. 391].

Jane and Dan reciprocally facilitate each other's new "self-as-possible" fantasies. These interactions associatively recapture experiences that are based on formative experiences of empathic support for tentative exploration of new and frightening activities. As the fledgling toddler struggles to stand erect, his parents say, "You can do that." As he does, they applaud and smile with glee.

Daniel Martin realizes he does not have the talent to write a great novel. As he does, he grudgingly accepts an important limit to his self-representation. This mourning process facilitates his attempt to make a commitment to working on a more realistic, shared life with Jane. He will not achieve immortality. He may experience heterosexual intimacy. At least he will not have to face the narcissistic injuries of old age alone.

Henry Breasley has achieved fame. Throughout his life he has been admired and envied. His ability to elicit the public's attention and participation in his activities has assuaged painful formative memories. However, fame cannot soothe his depressing awareness that he is in the twilight of his life. His ability to win as his wife a younger woman, the Mouse, transiently facilitates his denial that his life will soon be over. Through her presence and her smile, he can momentarily feel he is a young man. His intact sense of reality, however, ensures the ultimate failure of these defensive efforts. Nighttime and sleep, from which he may never awaken, are associated with an anxiety that can only be soothed

by inebriation. Sleep is not always gratifying narcissistic regression, for many narcissistic personality
disorders, falling asleep recaptures memories of a
primal separation that was experienced as a narcissistic injury. For others it is an opportunity to attempt to assimilate painfully, in the dream life, the
distorted perceptions of other events. For Henry, it is
also a reminder of his finitude.

In *Daniel Martin*, Fowles describes the inability of
even the greatness achieved by Rembrandt to assuage
the artist's perception of his finiteness. Daniel stands
before the famous late self-portrait:

> The sad, proud old man stared eternally out of his
> canvas, out of the entire knowledge of his own genius
> and of the inadequacy of genius before human reali-
> ty.... The supreme nobility of such art, the plebeian
> simplicity of such sadness; an immortal, a morose
> old Dutchman [1977a, p. 628].

Rembrandt's art is immortal, but his life was depress-
ingly limited. Mourning one's finiteness is probably an
interminable process. The commitment to that process
and the associated diminution in the degree and rigidity of one's narcissistically invested pursuits renders
one more able to enjoy generativity.

References

Andreas-Salome, L. (1921), The dual orientation of narcissism. *Psychoanal. Quart.*, 31:1–30, 1962.

Arlow, J. A. (1980), The revenge motive in the primal scene. *J. Amer. Psychoanal. Assn.*, 28:518–541.

———— Brenner, C. (1964), *Psychoanalytic Concepts and the Structural Theory*. New York: International Universities Press.

Bach, S. (1977), On the narcissistic state of consciousness. *Internat. J. Psycho-Anal.*, 58:209–233.

Bergler, E. (1961), *Curable and Incurable Neurotics*. New York: Liveright.

Berliner, B. (1958), The role of object relations in moral masochism. *Psychoanal. Quart.*, 27:28–56.

Blos, P. (1962), *On Adolescence*. New York: The Free Press.

Blum, H. P. (1974), The borderline childhood of the Wolf Man. *J. Amer. Psychoanal. Assn.*, 22:721–742.

———— (1976), Masochism, the ego ideal and the psychology of women. *J. Amer. Psychoanal. Assn.*, 24(5):157–191.

Brenner, C. (1974), Depression, anxiety and affect theory. *Internat. J. Psycho-Anal.*, 55:25–36.

Cooper, A. (1977), The narcissistic-masochistic character. Paper presented to the Association for Psychoanalytic Medicine, May 24, 1977.

Easser, B. R. (1974), Empathic inhibition and psychoanalytic technique. *Psychoanal. Quart.*, 43:557–580.

Eidelberg, L. (1959), Humiliation and masochism. *J. Amer. Psychoanal. Assn.*, 7:274–283.

Eisnitz, A. (1974), On the metapsychology of narcissistic pathology. *J. Amer. Psychoanal. Assn.*, 22:279–291.

Eissler, K. (1953), The effect of the structure of the ego on psychoanalytic technique. *J. Amer. Psychoanal. Assn.*, 1:104–143.

Erikson, E. (1950), *Childhood and Society*. New York: Norton.

———— (1954), The dream specimen in psychoanalysis. *J. Amer. Psychoanal. Assn.*, 2:5–55.

Fowles, J. (1963), *The Collector*. Boston: Little, Brown.

———— (1969), *The French Lieutenant's Woman*. Boston: Little, Brown.

———— (1974), *The Ebony Tower*. Boston: Little, Brown.

315

—— (1977a), *Daniel Martin*. Boston: Little, Brown.

—— (1977b), *The Magus*, Rev. Ed. Boston: Little, Brown.

Freud, A. (1936), *The Ego and the Mechanisms of Defense*, Rev. Ed. New York: International Universities Press.

—— (1958), Adolescence. *The Psychoanalytic Study of the Child*, 13:255–278. New York: International Universities Press.

—— (1959), Clinical studies in psychoanalysis. *The Psychoanalytic Study of the Child*, 14:122–131. New York: International Universities Press.

—— (1968), Acting out. *Internat. J. Psycho-Anal.*, 49:165–170

Freud, S. (1895), Project for a scientific psychology. *Standard Edition*, 1:295–387. London: Hogarth Press, 1966.

—— (1900), The interpretation of dreams. *Standard Edition*, 4 & 5. London: Hogarth Press, 1953.

—— (1905), Three essays on the theory of sexuality. *Standard Edition*, 7:135–243. London: Hogarth Press, 1953.

—— (1911a), Psycho-analytic notes on an autobiographical account of a case of paranoia. *Standard Edition*, 12:9–82. London: Hogarth Press, 1958.

—— (1911b), Formulations on the two principles of mental functioning. *Standard Edition*, 12:213–226. London: Hogarth Press, 1958.

—— (1913), The disposition to obsessional neurosis. *Standard Edition*, 12:311–326. London: Hogarth Press, 1958.

—— (1914), On narcissism: An introduction. *Standard Edition*, 14:69–102. London: Hogarth Press, 1957.

—— (1915a), Instincts and their vicissitudes. *Standard Edition*, 14:117–140. London: Hogarth Press, 1957.

—— (1915b), Mourning and melancholia. *Standard Edition*, 14:243–259. London: Hogarth Press, 1957.

—— (1916), Some character-types met with in psycho-analytic work. *Standard Edition*, 14:311–335. Hogarth Press, 1957.

—— (1917) On transformations of instinct as exemplified in anal erotism. *Standard Edition*, 17:125–133. London: Hogarth Press, 1955.

—— (1918), From the history of an infantile neurosis. *Standard Edition*, 17:7–122. London: Hogarth Press, 1955.

—— (1920a), Beyond the pleasure principle. *Standard Edition*, 18:7–64. London: Hogarth Press, 1955.

—— (1920b), Group psychology and the analysis of the ego. *Standard Edition*, 18:69–143. London: Hogarth Press, 1955.

—— (1923), The ego and the id. *Standard Edition*, 19:12–66. London: Hogarth Press, 1961.

—— (1924a), The economic problem of masochism. *Standard Edition*, 19:159–170. London: Hogarth Press, 1961.

—— (1924b), The loss of reality in neurosis and psychosis. *Standard Edition*, 19:183–187. London: Hogarth Press, 1961.

—— (1926), Inhibitions, symptoms and anxiety. *Standard Edition*, 20:87–174. London: Hogarth Press, 1959.

——— (1933), New introductory lectures on psychoanalysis. *Standard Edition*, 22:7–128. London: Hogarth Press,

——— (1937), Analysis terminable and interminable. *Standard Edition*, 23:216–253. London: Hogarth Press, 1964.

——— (1940), An outline of psycho-analysis. *Standard Edition*, 23:141–207. London: Hogarth Press, 1964.

Frosch, J. (1970), Psychoanalytic considerations of the psychotic personality. *J. Amer. Psychoanal. Assn.*, 18:24–50.

Gedo, J. E. (1975), Forms of idealization in the analytic transference. *J. Amer. Psychoanal. Assn.*, 23:485–505.

——— (1979), *Beyond Interpretation*. New York: International Universities Press.

——— (1981), *Advances in Psychoanalysis*. New York: International Universities Press.

——— Goldberg, A. (1973), *Models of the Mind*. Chicago: University of Chicago Press.

Hartmann, H. (1939a), Psychoanalysis and the concept of health. In: *Essays on Ego Psychology*. New York: International Universities Press, 1964, pp. 3–18.

——— (1939b), *Ego Psychology and the Problem of Adaptation*. New York: International Universities Press, 1958.

——— (1950a), Psychoanalysis and developmental psychology. *The Psychoanalytic Study of the Child*, 5:7–17. New York: International Universities Press.

——— (1950b), Comments on the psychoanalytic theory of the ego. *The Psychoanalytic Study of the Child*, 5:74–96. New York: International Universities Press.

Jacobson, E. (1954), The self and the object world. *The Psychoanalytic Study of the Child*, 9:75–126. New York: International Universities Press.

Jacobson, E. (1954), The self and the object world. *The Psychoanalytic Study of the Child*, 9:75–126. New York: International Universities Press.

Kahn, M. M. R. (1963), The concept of cumulative trauma. *The Psychoanalytic Study of the Child*, 18:286–306. New York: International Universities Press.

Kenniston, K. (1973), Developmental aspects of psychological disturbances. *J. Amer. Acad. Psychoanal.*, 1:22–38.

Kernberg, O. (1967), Borderline personality organization. *J. Amer. Psychoanal. Assn.*, 15:641–685.

——— (1970a), Factors in the psychoanalytic treatment of narcissistic personalities. *J. Amer. Psychoanal. Assn.*, 18:51–85.

——— (1970b), A psychoanalytic classification of character pathology. *J. Amer. Psychoanal. Assn.*, 18:800–822.

——— (1971), The course of the analysis of a narcissistic personality with hysterical and compulsive features. *J. Amer. Psychoanal. Assn.*, 19:451–471.

———— (1974), Further consideration to the treatment of narcissistic personalities. *Internat. J. Psycho-Anal.*, 55:215–240.

———— (1975), *Borderline Conditions and Pathological Narcissism*. New York: Jason Aronson.

Kohut, H. (1960), Discussion of "A note on beating fantasies" by Niederland, W. B. In: *The Search for the Self*, ed. P. Ornstein. New York: International Universities Press, 1978, pp. 263–266.

———— (1966), Forms and transformations of narcissism. *J. Amer. Psychoanal. Assn.*, 14:243–272.

———— (1968), The psychoanalytic treatment of narcissistic personality disorders. *The Psychoanalytic Study of the Child*, 23:86–113. New York: International Universities Press.

———— (1971), *The Analysis of the Self*. New York: International Universities Press.

———— (1972), Thoughts on narcissism and narcissistic rage. *The Psychoanalytic Study of the Child*, 27:360–400. New York: Quadrangle.

———— (1977), *The Restoration of the Self*. New York: International Universities Press.

———— Wolf, E. (1978), The disorders of the self and their treatment: an outline. *Internat. J. Psycho-Anal.*, 59:413–425.

Kris, E. (1956), The recovery of childhood memories in psychoanalysis. *The Psychoanalytic Study of the Child*, 11:54–88. New York: International Universities Press.

Levin, S. (1970), On the psychoanalysis of attitudes of entitlement. *Bull. Phila. Psychoanal. Assn.*, 20:1–10.

Loewald, H. (1960), On the therapeutic action of psychoanalysis. *Internat. J. Psycho-Anal.*, 41:16–33.

———— (1973), Review of *The Analysis of the Self* by Heinz Kohut. *Psychoanal. Quart.*, 42:444–451.

Loewenstein, R. M. (1957), A contribution to the psychoanalytic theory of masochism. *J. Amer. Psychoanal. Assn.*, 5:197–234.

Mahler, M. S. (1971), A study of the separation-individuation process and its possible application to borderline phenomena. *The Psychoanalytic Study of the Child*, 26:403–424. New York: Quadrangle.

———— (1972), On the three subphases of the separation-individuation process. *Internat. J. Psycho-Anal.*, 53:333–338.

———— Pine, F., & Bergman, A. (1975), *The Psychological Birth of the Human Infant*. New York: Basic Books.

McDougall, J. (1980), *Plea for a Measure of Abnormality*. New York: International Universities Press.

Mehlman, R. D. (1976), Transference mobilization, transference resolution and the narcissistic alliance. Paper presented to the Boston Psychoanalytic Society and Institute, February 25, 1976.

Meissner, W. (1981), *Internalization in Psychoanalysis*. New York: International Universities Press.

Menaker, E. (1953), Masochism: a defense reaction of the ego. *Psychoanal. Quart.*, 22: 205–220.

Michels, R. (1973), Is anatomy destiny? Paper presented to the Association for Psychoanalytic Medicine, October 30, 1973.

Modell, A. H. (1976), "The holding environment" and the therapeutic action of the psychoanalysis. *J. Amer. Psychoanal. Assn.*, 24:285–307.

Moore, B. (1975), Toward a clarification of the concept of narcissism. *The Psychoanalytic Study of the Child*, 30:243–276. New Haven: Yale University Press.

Murphy, W. F. (1961), A note on trauma and loss. *Psychoanal. Quart.*, 49: 423–455.

Murray, J. M. (1964), Narcissism and the ego ideal. *J. Amer. Psychoanal. Assn.*, 12:477–511.

Olinick, S. (1964), The negative therapeutic reaction. *Internat. J. Psycho-Anal.*, 45:540–548.

Pulver, S. (1970), Narcissism: The term and the concept. *J. Amer. Psychoanal. Assn.*, 18:319–341.

Reich, A. (1953), Narcissistic object choice in women. *J. Amer. Psychoanal. Assn.*, 1:22–44.

———— (1960), Pathologic forms of self-esteem regulation. *The Psychoanalytic Study of the Child*, 15:215–231. New York: International Universities Press.

Reich, W. (1933), *Character Analysis*. New York: Noonday.

Rothstein, A. (1980), Toward a critique of the psychology of the self. *Psychoanal. Quart.*, 49:429–455.

———— (1981), The ego: an evolving construct. *Internat. J. Psycho-Anal.*, 62:435–445.

———— (1983), *The Structural Hypothesis: An Evolutionary Perspective*. New York: International Universities Press.

Sander, L. (1964), Adaptive relationships in early mother-child interaction. *J. Amer. Acad. Child Psychiat.*, 3:231–264.

———— (1976), Issues in early mother-child interaction. In: *Infant Psychiatry: A New Synthesis*, eds. E. N. Rexford, L. Sander & T. Shapiro. New Haven: Yale University Press, pp. 127–247.

Sandler, J. (1960), On the concept of superego. *The Psychoanalytic Study of the Child*, 15:128–162. New York: International Universities Press.

———— Joffe, W. G. (1967), Some conceptional problems involved in the considerations of disorders of narcissism. *J. Child Psychother.*, 2:56–66.

———— Rosenblatt, B. (1962), The concept of the representational world. *The Psychoanalytic Study of the Child*, 17:128–145. New York: International Universities Press.

Schafer, R. (1960), The loving and beloved superego in Freud's structural theory. *The Psychoanalytic Study of the Child*, 15:163–168. New York: International Universities Press.

———— (1968), *Aspects of Internalization*. New York: International Universities Press.

———— (1976), *A New Language for Psychoanalysis*. New Haven: Yale University Press.

———— (1978), The role of appreciation in the analytic attitude: Technical and theoretical implications. Paper presented to the Association for Psychoanalytic Medicine, Jan. 3, 1978.

Searles, H. (1963), Transference psychosis in the psychotherapy of schizophrenia. In: *Collected Papers on Schizophrenia and Related Subjects*. New York: International Universities Press, 1965, pp. 654–716.

Segal, N. (1969), Repetition compulsion, acting-out, and identification with the doer. *J. Amer. Psychoanal. Assn.*, 17:474–488.

Stern, D. (1974), Mother and infant at play: the dyadic interaction involving facial, vocal and gaze behaviors. In: *Effect of the Infant on Its Caregiver*, eds. M. Lewis & L. Rosenblum. New York: Wiley, pp. 187–214.

Stolorow, R. D. (1975a), Toward a functional definition of narcissism. *Internat. J. Psycho-Anal.*, 56:179–186.

———— (1975b), The narcissistic function of masochism (and sadism). *Internat. J. Psycho-Anal.*, 56:441–448.

Stone, L. (1954), The widening scope of psychoanalysis. *J. Amer. Psychoanal. Assn.*, 2:567–594.

Strachey, J. (1934), The nature of the therapeutic action of psycho-analysis. *Internat. J. Psycho-Anal.*, 15:127–159.

Tolstoy, L. (1878), *Anna Karenina*. New York: Random House, 1965.

Waelder, R. (1936), The principle of multiple function: Observations on overdetermination. *Psychoanal. Quart.*, 5:45–62.

———— (1960), *Basic Theory of Psychoanalysis*. New York: International Universities Press.

Weil, A. P. (1970), The basic core. *The Psychoanalytic Study of the Child*, 25:442–460. New York: International Universities Press.

———— (1978), Maturational variations and genetic-dynamic issues. *J. Amer. Psychoanal. Assn.*, 26:461–491.

Wolfenstein, M. (1966), How is mourning possible? *The Psychoanalytic Study of the Child*, 21:93–123. New York: International Universities Press.

———— (1969), Loss, rage, repetition. *The Psychoanalytic Study of the Child*, 24:432–446. New York: International Universities Press.

INDEX